AT THE BORDERS OF THE HUMAN

At the Borders of the Human

Beasts, Bodies and Natural Philosophy in the Early Modern Period

Edited by

Erica Fudge

Ruth Gilbert

Susan Wiseman

First published in hardcover 1999

First published in paperback 2002 by
PALGRAVE
Houndmills, Basingstoke, Hampshire RG21 6XS and
175 Fifth Avenue, New York, N. Y. 10010
Companies and representatives throughout the world

PALGRAVE is the new global academic imprint of
St. Martin's Press LLC Scholarly and Reference Division and
Palgrave Publishers Ltd (formerly Macmillan Press Ltd).

ISBN 0–333–72186–1 hardback (*outside North America*)
ISBN 0–312–22038–3 hardback (*in North America*)
ISBN 0–333–97384–4 paperback (*worldwide*)

This book is printed on paper suitable for recycling and made from fully managed and sustained forest sources.

A catalogue record for this book is available from the British Library.

The Library of Congress has cataloged the hardcover edition as follows:
At the borders of the human : beasts, bodies and natural philosophy in the early modern period / edited by Erica Fudge, Ruth Gilbert and Susan Wiseman.
p. cm.
Based on papers from an informal colloquium held at the University of London in 1995.
Includes bibliographical references and index.
ISBN 0–312–22038–3 (cloth)
1. Philosophical anthropology—History.   2. Human beings—Animal nature—History.   I. Fudge, Erica.   II. Gilbert, Ruth.   III. Wiseman, S. J.
BD450.A8   1999
128′.09′03—dc21   98–55365
                                                                     CIP

10   9   8   7   6   5   4   3   2   1
11   10   09   08   07   06   05   04   03   02

Printed and bound in Great Britain by
Antony Rowe Ltd, Chippenham, Wiltshire

For Isaac

Contents

Acknowledgements

This collection arises out of an informal colloquium held in Senate House, University of London in 1995. We would like to thank all those who were involved in that meeting, particularly Catherina Albano, Kate Chedgzoy, Lucy Hartley, Tom Healy and Peter Smith. Other people who have helped substantially at earlier and later stages include: Tim Armstrong, Amanda Boulter and Nicola Bown who also participated in the original meeting, Anita Guerrini, Helen Hackett, Michael Hawkins, James Knowles, Jonathan Sawday, and members of the London Renaissance Seminar. We would also like to thank the staff of the British Library, the Hartley Library at the University of Southampton, University of Sussex Library, and University of Warwick Library. Special thanks must go to Charmian Hearne at Macmillan – now Palgrave –, who met with us often, offered incisive advice and helped us to shape the collection.

List of Illustrations

Notes on the Contributors

Brian Cummings (University of Sussex) is a lecturer in English in the School of European Studies. He is the author of *Grammar and Grace: the Literary Culture of the Reformation*.

Jess Edwards (University of North London) is currently working on the aesthetics of enclosure.

Erica Fudge (Middlesex University) is lecturer in the School of Humanities and Cultural Studies. She is the author of *Perceiving Animals: Humans and Beasts in Early Modern English Culture* (Palgrave, 2000) and editor of *Renaissance Beasts* (forthcoming).

Ruth Gilbert (University of Southampton) is lecturer in English. She is the author of *Early Modern Hermaphrodites: Sex and Other Stories* (Palgrave, 2002).

Margaret Healy (University of Sussex) is a lecturer in English. She is the author of *Fictions of Disease: Bodies, Plagues and Politics* (Palgrave, 2001).

Michael Newton is the author of *Savage Girls and Wild Boys* (forthcoming). He is currently editing Edmund Gosse's *Father and Son* and is co-editing *Science and Polite Culture*.

Mary Peace (Sheffield Hallam University) is the co-editor with Vincent Quinn of a *Textual Practice* special edition entitled 'Luxurious Sexualities and the Body Politic in Eighteenth-Century Britain'.

Julie Sanders (Keele University) is Reader in English. She is the author of *Ben Jonson's Theatrical Republics*, *Caroline Drama*, *Novel Shakespeares* (2001) and co-editor of *Refashioning Ben Jonson* (1998).

Jonathan Sawday (University of Strathclyde) is Professor of English Studies. He is co-editor of *Literature and the English Civil War* and author of *The Body Emblazoned: Dissection and the Human Body in Renaissance Culture*.

Stephen Speed (Buckinghamshire Chilterns University College) is author of *To Map a Body: Essays on Anatomy, Cartography and History.*

Alan Stewart is Reader in Renaissance Studies at Birkbeck College, University of London. His publications include *Close Readers: Humanism and Sodomy in Early Modern England, Hostage to Fortune: The Troubled Life of Francis Bacon,* co-authored with Lisa Jardine and *Philip Sidney: A Double Life.* He is currently editing Bacon's Correspondence for the new Oxford Francis Bacon.

Susan Wiseman (Birkbeck College, University of London) lectures in the School of English and Humanities.

Introduction: the Dislocation of the Human

Erica Fudge, Ruth Gilbert, Susan Wiseman

I THE HUMAN? THEN AND NOW

What is, what was, the 'human'? This was the question we began with. At stake in such a question is what the history of the human can mean at a moment when, arguably, the active status of the category 'human' has lapsed under analysis from philosophy and the history of science, and been challenged by practices such as modifications of the body using prosthetics, robotics and artificial intelligence. The project of this book is to examine the categories and dynamics constituting the fragile category of the 'human' in the Renaissance to Enlightenment period, and to do so bearing in mind some of the critical reconsiderations of the term 'human' and its analogues – humanism, humanity, humane – made in the mid- to late twentieth century.

The essays in this volume investigate what Donna Haraway has called the 'leaky distinction[s]' between such states as human and animal, human and machine.[1] An awareness of the human as a problematic, violent, category is sometimes understood as characteristic of modernity, and cultural theory, offering a critique of liberal humanism, repeatedly gestures towards the origins of the term in 'humanism'. However, while writings questioning the status of the human (including the writings of Haraway and Jean-François Lyotard of the 'inhuman') in themselves represent an increasing awareness of the unstable place of humanity, the category of the 'human' has never been stable or consensual.[2] The late twentieth century may eventually be recalled as a period of the anti-cogito, the movement away from the accepted status of the human, but this emphasis tends to obscure other narratives within which the 'human' has been seen as problematic.

Late-twentieth-century thinking on the posthuman and the inhuman arguably has its own partially effaced genealogy in the grand narratives it rejects, not only in the writings of Marx and Darwin, but in the ways in which the early modern and

1

Enlightenment texts discussed in this collection struggled to constitute the human. However, it is also the case that contemporary theorists of the human, in analysing the category's functions, and
sometimes arguing for its obsolescence or abolition, have also provided critical resources with which to trace the instability of the
human in its relations with its others. In her 'Cyborg Manifesto' of
1985 Haraway proposed the present as the moment of the cyborg,
'by the late twentieth century, our time, we are all chimeras, theo-
rized and fabricated hybrids of machine and organism; in short we
are cyborgs.'[3] She also outlined three boundary divisions between
the human and its others, arguing that these have become eroded
in this increasingly posthuman age: the border between the human
and the animal; between the animal-human organism and the
machine; and between the physical and the non-physical.[4] These
three categories – the animal, the machine, the non-physical – are
illuminating when we contrast their twentieth-century significance
with the roles they played in the early modern period, when they
were both important, and problematic. Questions about hybridity,
about the 'transgressed boundaries, potent fusions, and dangerous
possibilities' that Haraway cites as essential to her utopian cyborg
vision were also, though differently, central to the early modern
period. One significant difference is that, though apparent precur-
sors of Haraway's cyborg vision in their concentration on hybrid
categories, many early modern texts attempt to discipline and
define, seeing danger and disorder where she sees the potential for
social transformation. As the following essays suggest, the boundaries between the categories of the human and its others were not,
in the European Renaissance and Enlightenment, experienced as
anything like secure.

The experienced fragility of the separation of the human and its
others is illuminated by the history of the category of the human
itself. This category, as Diana Fuss indicates, has a history of being
used to produce and taxonomise a variety of non-humans, themselves constituted to be violently expunged from the terrain of the
human.[5] Theories of the human relentlessly produce animals, people,
conditions as not human. Yet this production of the non-human,
although often violent, is never a simple choice in which x is human
and y is not, but a continual and repeated process determined by circumstances. A central category in the early modern period, the
'human' nevertheless has no sharp or evident frontier and is for its
existence in constant need of contrasting border-figures, partly

human – or, rather, intermittently human and inhuman according to their context.

The complexity of the debate on the human in the early modern period is illuminated by the conundrum of the human in Descartes's thinking. The Cartesian subject is based in part on an accepted differentiation of the human from the animal, defined by the possession of a soul. The site of the soul, which was only to be traced in the human, and which signified both rationality and immortality (and from this humanity), was the pineal gland. How did Descartes know this? He knew this because he had a soul, and therefore had the rationality to recognise its existence. He had no proof. The (solely human) soul exists during life in the pineal gland, and on death leaves the body to rise to the afterlife. To discover, to see the soul is out of the question, because it would entail opening up, vivisecting the human – a moral impossibility. A human can only be dissected when dead, by which time the soul has left the body, so the soul remains unseen. Instead, the animal is vivisected – there are no moral strictures against this because the animal has no soul – so, of course, an examination of the pineal gland would only reveal a void, the place where the soul would be if the creature were human. We never see the soul. Descartes's differentiation of the species is unproveable – the soul is always beyond us – and yet it is undisproveable, because we can never say it is not. The difference between the human and the beast remains intact, and yet also remains elusive.

The humanness of the human body itself was also problematic: theology taught that human form was no guarantee of humanity when angels or devils might take that shape; when, under certain circumstances – as in the case of children, the mad, the colonised other – creatures that appeared to be human might also be understood to be closely associated with the animal. Similarly, the wearing of clothes – which seems to differentiate the human from the non-human – was sometimes interpreted as threatening or destroying that identity. Under certain circumstances, as in the theatre, the clothing of the body was seen to signify a deterioration or deviation from full humanity. Not only was actorly display a temptation to bestial lust in all its forms, but the use of clothing could, perhaps, alter the body within.

Possession of a human shape did not ensure full access to the privileges of humanity, and deviation from that category was figured in terms of monstrosity. If the scientific discourse of

Descartes might be said to speak to a relatively small number of the cognoscenti, then the theatre had as its stock in trade the making pleasurable of concerns central to the culture. Moreover, where Descartes's 'Second Meditation' concludes that only the self can be known and others can exist only as clothed automata, dramatic discourse articulated the question of the 'human' in relational terms. For example, in *The Tempest* – a play arguably motivated by a discussion of the human and its monstrous or supernatural others – Ariel and Prospero briefly discuss the term in relation to the fate of those from the ship:

> *Ariel*:
> ... Your charm so strongly works 'em,
> That if you now beheld them, your affections
> Would become tender.
> *Pros*:   Does thou think so, spirit?
> *Ariel*: Mine would, sir, were I human.
> *Pros*:   And mine shall.
> Hast thou, which art but air, a touch, a feeling
> Of their afflictions, and shall not myself,
> One of their kind, that relish all as sharply
> Passion as they, be kindlier mov'd than thou art?
> (V.i.16–24)[6]

Sometimes read as revealing Prospero's humanity, or as the turning point at which his compassion prompts him to abandon his arts in favour of both forgiveness and a more equal relation with the humans he has manipulated, the speech stands for a revelation of the Renaissance concept of the human. Frank Kermode's gloss on 'kindlier' as 'Not only "more sympathetically" but also "more in accordance with my kind, which is human"' compounds 'kindly' qualities understood as central to the human – compassion (affection, tenderness, clemency) – with Prospero's apparent linking of himself with the other, struggling humans.[7] What could also be remarked on, though, is that this exchange takes place between two figures neither of whom articulate themselves as human in the present. Ariel will never be human ('were I human') and Prospero's reply is ambiguous: is he moved now, or would he be moved in the future, when he will be (by an act of art in the abandoning of his art) human? The distinguishing quality of the humans discussed is their suffering and, noticeably, neither of the speakers claim to actually *experience* compassion – they imagine circumstances in which they would. This passage articulates the desired qualities associated with the human, but in their absence: full humanity is highly artificial, potentially unattainable for some, and significantly absent from the world of political influence. The human, even in a speech apparently extolling it, is deferred and in a vexed relation to the speakers.

Thus, the story of human separation from its others which can be traced in the narrative of the Cartesian soul is repeated in other writings in this period. The border between self and other, human and animal, human and machine, would seem to offer proof of difference. Yet the borders of the human turn out to change according to context and point of view. The tension between the clarity and the confusion implied by borders is central to this collection. The borders examined include the physical borders of the human as an individual corporeal body, and the borders of the 'species' itself. We do not find, in the texts examined here, what Lyotard finds in *humanist* texts – the assumption that 'man' is 'a certain value which need not be interrogated'.[8] In different ways, the essays see the borders of the human as dangerously flexible, and uncontrollable. Sometimes the borders appear strong, well guarded, at other times fragile and porous. Sometimes one thing is human, whereas at other times in other places that same thing is not. The issue of what it is to be human is revealed as both problematic in itself, and made problematic by its others.

II   ROUTES THROUGH THE COLLECTION

A reader who follows the broadly chronological arrangement of the essays will chart shifts in the implications of the 'human' as the early modern period gives way to the Enlightenment. The volume begins with Alan Stewart's exploration of how an underlying rivalry, even carnality, implicit in early sixteenth-century humanism troubles the claims of humanism, and ends with Mary Peace's study of the construction of female sexuality – and through this, civilisation itself – in eighteenth-century medical discourse.

The reader who wishes to read thematically might take other routes. A number of essays chart the manufacture of the 'human' through processes of division. These studies tend to show how partial and inadequate strategies which attempted to taxonomise the human by isolating it from its others were. Through explorations of humanism and Baconian science Alan Stewart and Erica Fudge discuss the theoretical systems which could not hold the excesses which were implicit within them. For Stewart, humanism is constantly prey to the desires and material investments it disavows. Fudge analyses the way in which Bacon found it hard to produce a category of the human fully distinct from the animal – and the particular problems in this caused by the ambiguous figure of the child.

Jess Edwards and Stephen Speed both investigate the early modern rhetoric of mapping, examining the operation of of physical boundaries: the colonisation of America and the Harveian anatomised body. These essays suggest how even the imposition of material divisions defied closure. The first part of Edwards's title, 'The Doubtful Traveller', quoted from William Wood's 1634 colonial text, signals the uncertainty of the colonial venture that the essay will trace. Similarly, for Speed, the Harveian anatomised body presents a site of incomplete limits and only temporary 'Cartographic Arrest'.

Where the problem of the border of the human is in some early modern texts figured as division, the excesses which troubled the establishment of borders or the rigid imposition of the 'new' scientific discourses emerge in other texts in figures of excess and doubling. Such border creatures appear in Ruth Gilbert's analysis of how hermaphrodites were represented in seventeenth-century scientific and pornographic images in Michael Newton's exploration of the body-soul divide in early eighteenth-century representations of Peter the Wild Boy; and in Susan Wiseman's discussion of Edward Tyson's representation of the chimpanzee, or 'pygmie'. Each of these creatures is represented as a kind of hybrid, a double creature that is neither fully animal or human. These essays focus in particular on how these hybrid creatures were examined, scrutinised and displayed as objects which were alien, strange, and other. Such hybrid creatures give evidence of the overlapping of and competition between different ways of thinking about the human. Thus, Gilbert's essay shows how the languages of science and pornography could not be clearly separated in discussions of early modern hermaphrodites. Wiseman's essay also highlights the inextricable connections between seemingly contradictory discourses: anatomy is bound together with myth in a way which undercuts current readings of seventeenth-century science.

Women, too, are found at the border of the human and its others. Julie Sanders's essay looks at the relationship between midwifery and the New Science in the seventeenth century. She shows how women were represented as both present and absent in discourses of childbirth. They were seen as both powerful agents in the processes of birth whilst they were marginalised from the masculinised authority of the New Science. Mary Peace also draws on the relationship of women to medical science in her exploration of the representation of the female disease known as the *furor uterinis*. She shows that the pathologisation of female sexuality has implications for notions of science, and for eighteenth-century notions of civilisation.

While some essays concentrate on texts which have a drive to establish the border between human and animal, human and machine, human and material, others focus specifically on the point where the human appears to fade in and out of view as a dissolving presence. Brian Cummings's study of early modern discourses of the passions shows how the distinction between humans and beasts was often represented as an unstable, eroded divide. The passions, he argues, occupied an uneasy borderland divided between the mental and the bodily, the rational and the physiological, the intellectual and the appetitive. His essay suggests that early modern interpretations of the act of blushing highlight key areas of cultural interpretations of difference in ethnic, sexual and animal terms. In this exploration of the rhetoric of embarrassment and shame Cummings suggests the fragile self-consciousness of early modern constructions of the human. Similarly Margaret Healy's essay focuses on the human body as porous and vulnerable to disturbance and invasion. She reads Elizabethan and Jacobean domestic tragedies against contemporary discourses of plague contagion to argue that this was a period 'in which imagination and trepidation – alone – could appear to some to act like a magnet attracting physical or psychic contagion across fragile body borders surrounded by hostile forces'.

Jonathan Sawday's essay engages specifically with Haraway's cyborg manifesto. For Sawday the cyborg stands for fluidity, a decoupling of dualistic, post-Cartesian modes of thought. He argues that the cyborg is the ultimate dissolver of boundaries, that it 'above all teaches us how to undo that familiar construction of the European Renaissance, "Man"'. Sawday returns to the early modern construction of the human body as a machine (a cyborg fusion of technology and the body) in order to reach a point where such distinctions can be dissolved.

The material covered in this book ranges from the scientific and the medical, to the pornographic and the dramatic; from the zoological and the humanist, to the geographical and the colonial. In telling stories about the human – through science, literature, anatomy – the writers from the early modern period studied here all, ultimately, probe the possibility of the *absence* of an innate human. From their anxieties of absence perhaps we can begin to rethink contemporary debates about human status. Perhaps we can look back to the early modern period, a period when the modern self – self-determining, individual, self-knowing – was apparently being created and see instead – or as well – the beginnings of human dislocation.

Notes

1. Donna Haraway, 'A Manifesto for Cyborgs: Science, Technology, and Socialist Feminism in the 1980s' (1985) in *Feminism/Postmodernism*, ed. Linda J. Nicholson (London: Routledge, 1990), pp. 190–233, p. 193.
2. Jean-François Lyotard, *The Inhuman* (1988) translated Geoffrey Bennington and Rachel Bowlby (Cambridge: Polity Press, 1991).
3. Haraway, 'Manifesto', p. 191.
4. Haraway, 'Manifesto', pp. 193–5.
5. Diana Fuss, 'Introduction: Human All Too Human', in *Human All Too Human*, ed. Diana Fuss (London: Routledge, 1996), p. 2.
6. William Shakespeare, *The Tempest*, ed. Frank Kermode (1954) (Reprinted, London: Methuen, 1961).
7. Kermode, *The Tempest*, p. 113.
8. Lyotard, *The Inhuman*, p. 1.

1

Humanity at a Price: Erasmus, Budé, and the Poverty of Philology

Alan Stewart

The borders of the human are never marked solely by the threat of the non-human beyond them. Much of what we accept as 'human' is defined in distinction to that which is not fully 'human', that which does not correspond to a notion of a 'humane' humanity. To be human means not only to be not a beast, but also to subscribe to a specific code of humanity. In various periods and in various locations this notion of humanity has been used both to support and to subvert dominant ideologies built along lines of difference in gender, ethnicity and class. More subtly, humanity has been linked to ineffable concepts such as 'taste' and 'sensibility'.

This essay argues that our understanding of what constitutes humanity is bound up with and reproduces itself through the educational process which we call 'the humanities'. This academic discipline is usually traced to the movement now recognised as 'Renaissance humanism', dating perhaps from trecento Italy.[1] Unlike many other academic pursuits it does not draw its ultimate legitimacy from religious doctrine or political dogma; instead, although the focus of humanist scholarship may be spiritual and its motivation political, it defines itself in a peculiarly secular, non-partisan manner – free not only of doctrinal and religious bias, but also of material and bodily considerations. In this essay I argue that key humanist texts contain faultlines that reveal the material basis for their existence: the academic programme which boasts of its humanity as being beyond bodily human concerns is revealed as being essentially carnal in its orientation.

I

The early modern programme which we now recognise as 'humanist' drew self-consciously on a confusion which can be dated at least to the second century AD, when Aulus Gellius wrote in his *Noctes Atticae*:

Those who have spoken Latin and have used the language correctly do not give the word *humanitas* the meaning which it is commonly thought to have, namely, what the Greeks call *philanthropia*, signifying a friendly spirit and good-feeling towards men without distinction; but they gave to *humanitas* about the force of the Greek *paideia*: that is, what we call *eruditionem institutionemque in bonos artes*, or 'education and training in the liberal arts'. Those who earnestly desire and seek after these are most highly humanised [*maxime humanissimi*]. For the pursuit of this kind of knowledge, and the training given by it, have been granted to man above all the animals, and for that reason it is termed *humanitas*, or 'humanity'.[2]

Gellius makes explicit the notion that *humanitas* places man 'above all the animals'; clearly, however, not all of mankind pursue this kind of knowledge, which implies that not all of mankind achieve 'humanity'.

The rise and eventual success of a 'humanist' programme is often portrayed as the inevitable outcome of a series of events occurring throughout Europe in the Renaissance: the rediscovery of various classical texts, the Reformation and Counter Reformation, and the rise of the new print culture. Although there are many problems with the identification of the humanists as a distinct community, a range of recent work has demonstrated that there were clear attempts by groups of men in the Northern Renaissance (men we would now identify as humanist) to distinguish themselves from other intellectual groups,[3] and through an inspired manipulation of the new and burgeoning print culture, to present themselves as a coherent pan-European intellectual élite. This latter project was heavily reliant on what Lisa Jardine has called the 'confected correspondence' between key humanist figures, in which promotion of friends and peers was masked by the familiar letter. The practical power of this form lay both in the extended circulation and instant permanence afforded by print culture, and in the affective power of the letter form itself.[4]

Erika Rummel has traced the ways in which a (retrospectively identified) 'humanist' movement distinguished itself from a 'scholastic' movement. Some of the humanist rhetoric sought to identify the scholastic theologians as sub-human: Willem Nesen wrote in 1519, 'If men of letters know what's good for them, they'll sharpen their pens and overwhelm [the theologians] with a myriad of books. They don't deserve mercy. They are beasts, not human beings'. Johann Reuchlin similarly described the theologians as 'more inhuman than brute beasts ... rather like pigs or sows delighting in their own filth and treading on the pearls of others'.[5]

But the definition of humanism through its intellectual impetus was by no means the most prominent. In his study of *The Civilising Process*, Norbert Elias describes how a representative and influential humanist text, Erasmus's treatise *De civilitate morum puerillium*, was written 'at a time of social regrouping', in the transitional period between medieval and modern social hierarchies. 'This situation', writes Elias, 'gave, among others, the representatives of a small, secular-bourgeois intellectual class, the humanists, and thus Erasmus, not only an opportunity to rise in social station, to gain renown and authority, but also a possibility of candour and detachment that was not present to the same degree either before or afterward'. This distancing allowed men such as Erasmus 'to identify totally and unconditionally with none of the social groups of their world'. It is what Elias calls 'the humanistic intellectual class' which claims to give even the nobility their true nobility: as Erasmus writes, 'Let others paint lions, eagles, and other creatures on their coats of arms. More true nobility is possessed by those who can inscribe on their shields all that they have achieved through the cultivation of the arts and sciences.'[6]

The inexorable rise of the humanists was, and still is, figured as a pitched battle between the emergent middling classes fitted with relevant textual skills and a feudal nobility who clung to the bearing of arms and the leisure pursuits of hunting and hawking, contemptuously rejecting the new learning. This tells us little or nothing about the social realities of the period; it tells us a great deal about the humanist portrayal of their own positions (and the enduring success of that portrayal). The image, not surprisingly, can be traced to a number of early writings which succeed in portraying chivalry (incorrectly) as coterminous with feudalism. The social reality, and the previous literary representation, of the learned chivalric knight was suppressed in favour of an artificially polar distinction of the nobleman and the humanist scholar. At the same time, the 'gentleman' supplanted the knight as a social ideal, absorbing those aspects of the knight that were still valued; the humanist portrayal of the nobleman was as a ridiculous, drunken, philistine.[7]

A typical example is found in Thomas Starkey's *Dialogue between Pole and Lupset*: the 'educatyon of the nobylyte' who are 'custumably brought up in huntyng & hauking dysyng & cardyng etyng & drynkyng & in conclusyon in al vayn plesure pastyme & vanyte'; they should rather be brought up in 'featys perteynyng to nobylyte no les then lernyng & letturys, as in al featys of chyvalry'.[8] Alexander Barclay complains in 1519 that 'at this tyme [the understandyng of latyn] is almost contemned of gentylmen.'[9] For Juan Luis Vives too, the nobility's inadequate education – here figured as illiteracy – is a comic butt: when the noble Manricus cries, 'I don't know how it is inborn in me [Nescioque pacto naturale est mihi] to plough out my letters so distortedly, so unequally and confusedly,' Mendoza retorts sardonically, 'You have this tendency from your noble birth [Hoc habes nobilitatis].'[10]

Perhaps the most famous account of chivalric feudal ignorance as portrayed and purveyed by the humanist polemicists is Richard Pace's drunken nobleman, presented in a prefatory letter to *De fructu qui ex doctrina percipitur* (1517). At a dinner, Pace encounters a nobleman, of the kind 'who always carry horns hanging down their backs as though they were going to hunt while they ate'. The nobleman lambasts a humanist education: 'By God, I'd rather my son were hanged than he should study letters. Sons of the nobility ought to blow the horn properly, hunt like experts, and train and carry a hawk gracefully. Studies should really be left to country boys.' Pace responds to the drunken onslaught by objecting angrily but still courteously: 'I don't think you're right, my good man. For if some foreigner came to the king, a royal ambassador, for example, and he had to be given an answer, your son, brought up as you suggest, would only blow on his horn, and the learned country boys would be called on to answer him. They would obviously be preferred to your son, the hunter or hawker, and using the freedom that learning gives, they would say to your face, "We would rather be learned [docti], and thanks to learning, no fools, than to be proud of our stupid nobility".'[11]

In these ways, the humanists attempted to define themselves in opposition to the alleged negative qualities of an ignorant nobility and an intellectually hostile scholasticism (which answered these slurs in kind).[12] More subtly, however, they developed a way of talking positively about their own intellectual activity, led by Desiderius Erasmus. As part of the campaign to establish his reputation, Erasmus had in some way to valorise his own independence from the institutional structures that supported competitive scholarship – either church- or university-sponsored. While these institutions came with their own traditions of pious and intellectual respectability, the path trodden by Erasmus was effectively dependent on personal pecuniary patronage. To circumvent this potential slur, it became necessary, therefore, to portray humanism in a manner which suppressed the financial necessities on which it was based.

The personal liaisons of this group of men were presented as an important cut above the common herd, their intercourse founded on intellectual concerns rather than material considerations. 'Friends of the commonplace and homespun sort, my open-hearted Pieter', wrote Erasmus, dedicating his *Parabolae* to Pieter Gilles, 'have their idea of relationship, like their whole lives, attached to material things; and if they ever have to face a separation, they favour a frequent exchange of rings, knives, caps and other tokens of the kind, for fear that their affection may cool ... or actually die away through the interposition of long tracts of time and space. But you and I, whose idea of friendship rests wholly in a meeting of minds and the enjoyment of studies in common, might well greet one another from time to time with presents for the mind and keepsakes of a literary description ... Minds can develop an even closer link, the greater the space that comes between them.'[13]

These ideas remained common currency in the thought and works of later scholars who saw themselves in an Erasmian tradition. For example, when the Strasbourg humanist Jean Sturm was confecting a correspondence with his English counterpart Roger Ascham, whom he never met, he included a lengthy consideration of the factors that distanced the kind of work they did from the kind of work done by other men:

Indeed the nature of our studies demands a busy leisure and a leisurely business, for to the common folk we seem to be leisurely in our work and to work in our leisure. When other men are hunting or fishing or building, they are considered to be working. When educated men read, write, or prepare commentaries, they

are considered idlers, when as a matter of fact their minds while
at work stir up anxieties and cares, not because of fear or danger
or the hardships of their toil, but because they undertake to think
about matters of great, eternal significance. Since you have the
best kind of leisure, it will yield the ripest and most delightful of
fruit for me.[14]

Sturm divides the world into two groups: 'we' and 'other men'
(cæteri homines) – and their difference seen through the eyes of
'the common folk' (vulgus). Here humankind is divided into two
discrete groups, with distinct notions of what constitutes humanity,
but the work of division is carried out by only one of the groups;
and it is this group to which the writer, the recipient and of course
the reader all belong. The reader is thus coerced into membership of
and belief in a superior, properly educated group. Not only is 'our'
occupation the only really valuable occupation, but 'our' viewpoint
is the definitive viewpoint. The value of 'our' work is and can only
be visible to 'us'.

These vague 'other men' were not the only section of the population in opposition to which humanist scholars defined themselves.
In their bid to pursue pure intellectual activity, they often claimed
to eschew the ordinary claims of marital life. Francis Bacon put it
succinctly in his essay 'Of marriage and single life': 'He that hath
wife and children hath given hostages to fortune; for they are
impediments to great enterprises, either of virtue or mischief.
Certainly the best works, and of greatest merit for the public, have
proceeded from the unmarried or childless men; which both in
affection and means have married and endowed the public.'[15]
Childless himself, Bacon was often to revive the figure of leaving
works to posterity rather than goods to his children.[16]

Clearly what we are dealing with here is figurative. Bacon could
write of a wife being a hostage to fortune while being married
himself. Ascham's correspondence with Sturm emerged strategi-
cally just as Ascham was embarking on an embassy mission to
Germany. Erasmus could claim that Pieter Gilles's friendship was
on a purely intellectual level, but Gilles also arranged the printing
and sale of Erasmus's books, a friend who was indeed attached to
the material considerations of Erasmus's life. But the version of
events which we can trace in Erasmus's writings has retained a
hugely persuasive emotional power – in Lisa Jardine's terms, the
picture that we still possess of Erasmus is of Erasmus's own

drawing, in which he was 'so entirely and consummately successful'. Jardine continues:

> The care with which Erasmus composed his version of himself as
> symbol of enduring success in the domain of 'letters' (or *bonae lit-
> terae*), out of available cultural models of timeless, universal schol-
> arly and spiritual achievement, has shaped our own version
> almost entirely. It has so permeated our understanding of the
> effectiveness and impact of learning that for centuries since,
> academics in the humanities have taken it for granted that
> our professional practice – the professional practice of reading,
> commenting, and editing – is a source of, and means of access to,
> limitless power and influence in a world which values our under-
> takings. Learning elevates individual thought into universal
> significance, it knows no national boundaries, it can influence
> world events, it can shape and make political outcomes.[17]

According to Erasmus and Sturm, the value system of humanism
lay in its own perceptions of the world. What the common folk see
is not relevant. However, although this may be the message, the
letters themselves contain faultlines which point to the dependence
of these men on other value systems which they threaten, and
which threaten them. Although they may attempt to define the
human in terms of their own intellectual prowess, these writers are
irresistibly drawn to images of marriage, patronage, and monetary
transactions. In the remainder of this essay, I shall examine a correspondence which Erasmus exploited at length in his published
oeuvre and show how, in its repeated and persistent figures of
speech, this correspondence brings into question Erasmus's preferred self-image as a lone scholar driven solely by a pious love of
learning.

II

The correspondence between Erasmus and the great French
humanist Guillaume Budé (Budæus) runs to some fifty extant
letters which, in the words of editor James McConica, 'tell us a great
deal about the style and mentality of a humanist friendship.'[18] The
earliest surviving letter, from Budé to Erasmus, is dated 1 May
[1516] and claims to be a response to a previous letter from

Erasmus. Half in Greek and half in Latin, the letter ostentatiously displays the classical learning of both men, and opens by staging their mutual admiration:

'My dear Budé', you say, 'I cannot tell you how much I wish to see you famous, and admire your learning'. That second phrase – do you really mean it? 'Yes, really', you say. And you expect me to believe it? 'Of course'. For my part I would gladly do as you say.

It is in the closing lines of this first letter that Budé introduces an issue which was to recur insistently in the Budé-Erasmus correspondence (and beyond), and was, I shall argue, to cause Erasmus no small distress. Budé concludes by complaining of the limited time he can devote to his scholarship. This spare time, he writes, is 'devoted to domestic business [oeconomico] rather than philosophy. How can it be otherwise when I have six sons to educate, brothers of my one small daughter, and am as devoted as anyone to my relations? So neglectful have I always been hitherto of the skills needful for a man with many children'.[19]

The remark is clearly intended as a compliment to Erasmus: Erasmus is the true scholar because his scholarly work is not compromised by the distractions of marital, paternal and domestic responsibilities. In contrast, Budé's intellectual activity is necessarily curtailed by his household commitments and therefore cannot compare with Erasmus's. Unfortunately, the remark could be taken the other way: Budé's literary output had been signally impressive, including his *Annotationes in xxiv Pandectarum libros* (1508) and his study of Roman money *De asse* (1515) (Erasmus pointed out that 'your books are sufficient evidence that you are not wholly without leisure'). By showing how this impressive record had been attained alongside his domestic commitments, Budé threatened to put into the shade the prowess of Erasmus, who ostentatiously lacked competing domestic commitments. So, in his reply, dated 19 June 1516, Erasmus invents a domestic demand of his own: 'Then against your children, your wife, and your other household cares I set my one sole wife, that accursed Poverty, whom I still cannot shake off my shoulders, such is her love for him that hates her.'[20]

Erasmus's financial concerns were real. Despite the international success of his books, Erasmus's only regular source of income was a £20 per annum pension from the English Archbishop of

Canterbury Warham (which Erasmus accepted in place of a proffered cure).[21] However, by utilising the figure of Poverty, a female,
uxorial, monetary figure, Erasmus inserts himself dangerously in
two difficult positions: first, as the 'compromised scholar' with
Budean commitments (albeit figuratively); second, by highlighting
the figure, casting himself in opposition as the 'pure scholar' whose
only commitments are figurative. However, this second model begs
the question: what sort of man has no such commitments?
    Budé was particularly struck by the figure of Poverty, and con-
tinued to utilise her in further letters. He was not, however, about
to allow Erasmus to claim Poverty as his own. What Erasmus had
written, he suggested, made it appear that he (Budé) was free of
Poverty: in his next letter (7 July), Budé upbraids Erasmus for
expressing regret for his own situation only:

> For bachelor as you are, you complain that you have a wife called
> Lady Poverty, who not merely sits at home but travels around
> with you, whom you cannot be quit of, range widely as you may,
> such is the devotion of your tedious spouse; and you set off the
> tedium and disgust she causes you against all my household
> cares [oeconomici curis] as a husband and a father, just as though
> in place of your Poverty I had a pretty boy called Riches [Plutum
> pusionem iucundum] in whom I could take pleasure to my
> heart's content.

Budé here opposes Erasmus's 'wife' to his own 'pretty boy', setting
in place an opposition between the man with marital responsibilities, and the man who can indulge his money because he lacks
those responsibilities. This indulgence is figured as sodomitical. The
figurative opposition between sodomy and marital relations is a familiar Renaissance trope: as Guido Ruggiero writes in his study of
sex crime in early modern Venice, 'sodomy threatened to under-
mine the basic organisational units of society – family, male-female
bonding, reproduction – which struck at the heart of social male
perceptions.'[22] Jonathan Goldberg goes further and argues that, by
definition, 'sodomy is, as a sexual act, anything that threatens alliance – any sexual act, that is, that does not promote the aim of
married procreative sex ... these acts – or accusations of their performance – emerge into visibility only when those who are said to
have done them also can be called traitors, heretics, or the like, at
the very least, disturbers of the social order that alliance – marriage

arrangements – maintained'. When this 'alliance' is not threatened, he continues, it is unlikely 'that those sexual acts called sodomy, when performed, would be recognised as sodomy.'[23] Once again, the well-intentioned figure of speech threatens Erasmus. By introducing the possibility of sodomy in this context, even though Budé associates it with himself, it is inevitably the bachelor who becomes vulnerable to accusation. Humanist scholars living outside church and university institutions were particularly prone to such accusations: often unmarried, and living with no visible means of support, it was easy for their intimacy with their male patrons to become the cause of scurrilous gossip. By introducing the 'pretty boy Riches', Budé plays comically on these anxieties: but he is safely married, while Erasmus precariously lacks any such alibi.[24]

In fact, however, Budé has not been indulging himself with a pretty boy. On the contrary, he objects, 'she whom you call your wife has been pretty much my bedfellow [contubernio] ever since I fell victim to this crazy love of learning.' The only difference between the two men, he continues, 'is that you call her cursed Poverty in jest, and I in all seriousness the poverty that never leaves one's side; so true is it that all serious scholars (few enough!) are haunted by this rival to Philology [aemula philologiae], who sticks closer almost than a shadow.' In this formulation Poverty becomes both an *aemula* [rival] and an undesirably close adjunct to Philology, the physical expression and indulgence (the bedfellow) of the beloved Philology.

Budé goes on to claim that this situation is a timeless state of affairs:

> This results from the habits of our age and of earlier ages too; to this the love of learning tends by its very nature: those who have once become its enthusiastic followers must forgo worldly goods and credit in the eyes of ignorant men, while those who have begun or intend to be rich must forthwith cast away or lay aside the love of the humanities [amorem ilico disciplinarum], as I fear we shall find true of you, if ever (as you hope) you are gilded o'er. As far as I am concerned, I accept and virtually comprehend my fate, to such a degree that neither love of literature nor its companion will ever leave me. This I endure with ease, but come to terms with Fortune I cannot. I have long been indignant with her because, besides that Poverty of yours, she has inflicted on

me my habitual bad health ... Both these troubles, indifferent health and loss of worldly goods, my friends and kinsfolk turn to my discredit, and lay the blame on Philology, simply because when I was a child I was lucky enough to be acquainted with neither of this precious pair. As for bidding farewell to literature – which my relatives, my friends, my doctors recommend, threatening me with dire penalties if I do not obey – I cannot bring myself to do it, not if Chance in person were to offer me, as the comic poet [Aristophanes] puts it, 'Plutus himself, and Battus' wealth of spice'.

In the next breath, however, Budé details how he is now 'building two country houses on two of my estates some distance apart, real seats in the Lucullan style, and I have to keep running back and forth between them, or pay the penalty of my neglect by heavy losses. How easy this is for a man who is a literary type [studioso] to begin with, with no experience of such things, and above all, modestly supplied with coin, you can imagine.'[25] Erasmus does not let this slip: 'remember that some people may find a lack of consistency in what you say in your letter – that you have Poverty on your hands, when at the same time you are building two country houses fit for Lucullus, as you say yourself.'[26] Later, answering Erasmus's charge, Budé argues that 'this shows how that runaway character Riches has deserted me (confound him!) and how that Poverty of yours has quickly slipped into my home in his place (a murrain on her!) ... In my building programme I have unintentionally issued an invitation to Poverty, and when she leaves your house, I fear she will cling to me as her special victim tighter than any ivy.'[27]

When Erasmus wrote to Budé from Brussels on 28 October, he took umbrage that Budé had criticised his shoddy penmanship, a result of his extensive paperwork which would take at least five servants to accomplish. It was another chance to introduce his newfound spouse. 'Yet that wife of mine, at whose expense you wax so merry, barely allows me to keep a single one; such is the henpecked life I lead from an imperious mistress rather than a wife' [domina verius quam vxor].[28] The wife here evolves suddenly into a woman to whom Erasmus is in a socially subservient position. He then comically picks up on Budé's claims on Poverty: 'But in heaven's name, what is this I hear? My wife has been 'pretty much your bedfellow'? How lucky I am not to be jealous! I only wish she had cleared off somewhere long ago, not to live with you ... but with the Franciscan brethren who have such a passion for her, or anyone else who may love her even more than they do'. The attempt to banish Poverty to the monastic life which Erasmus had himself escaped marks the beginning of an attempt to dissociate his own academic endeavours from Poverty, an attempt that will become more emphatic as the correspondence progresses.

This distancing effect is then reinforced as Erasmus goes on to make it clear that this is all in jest and that he is in fact quite comfortably off: 'Though (to be done with fooling) my modest fortune does not altogether distress me', citing the patronage of Archbishop of Canterbury Warham and his failure to acquire possessions as proof of his financial security ('If it did, I might long ago have increased my possessions, had I not always been convinced that money in the hand is better than substantial assets'). 'What severely plagues me, my dear Budé, is to have Poverty at my side, but not Philology; I have the shadow always with me, not the substance. How happy should I be if I might have both to share my home! ... Furthermore, when you say in your humorous way that there is some risk of my one day losing my love for the humanities, once I have had the good fortune to be hung with gold, as far as that goes at any rate I can assure you there is no need to lose a night's sleep.'[29]

The joke did not remain a private joke between Erasmus and Budé. With Erasmus's encouragement, Budé entered into a correspondence with the English diplomat and churchman Cuthbert Tunstall. Writing to Tunstall in May 1517, Budé explicitly laid out Philosophy's 'own scale of values', which meant nothing in 'the market-place and the lawcourt', because Philosophy

> sets a price equivalent to the minimum upon transitory objects which are bound to perish with the lapse of time, and a price equivalent to the maximum upon those that are eternal (not to go beyond the language of legal draftsmen). From time to time Philology, my second wife, assures me that the benefits of this kind of valuation will at length inure me as part of her dowry; whom I love not as other men do in this country of ours but – so my friends and kindred tell me with some irritation – with an absorbing passion. Ever since I brought her into my house, or so they say, I have never been thought to devote proper attention to my own prospects or my health. Let this, rightly or wrongly, be held against me as the father of six sons and one small daughter, by men who consider that they have proved their own worth if

they know how to run a banking business and build up a patrimony on the most ample scale. Never mind: not my wife's embraces and the endearment of my children, not the persistent demands of my financial affairs, no threat nor ultimatum from physicians, nor sickness with all its tedium and its torments has ever been able to persuade me or compel me to refrain from consorting with my Egeria day and night, at home or abroad, in city or country. [In Roman mythology, Egeria was a fountain-goddess whose grove was visited by King Numa for inspiration].[30] Even at that moment twelve years ago when I married a wife, the mother of my children, against the expectation of almost all devoted husbands I never wrote her a bill of divorcement. This was my chosen course of action: to have a lawful wife to bear me children, and by Philology to procreate books to win me an eternal name, if my modest gifts should prove equal to my industry, and to be immortal offspring.[31]

The figure has changed. Now, instead of Poverty (the shadow) as the wife, Philology (the substance) is a second wife. Budé acknowledges his wife Roberte Le Lieur[32] and his wife Philology as rivals for his attention, and as complementary ways of preserving his name to posterity, via children and books respectively. Budé admits that 'As it is, I have produced rather more children than I have books, indulging the body perhaps more than the mind. Hereafter I hope, as my body grows weaker, my mind will become keener and more active day by day. It is impossible for the two of them to be equally productive both at once, but as one's bodily powers begin to reach their retiring age, the powers of the mind will be mobilized for full activity.' He has kept hold of literature throughout frequent illness, he writes. 'Had not philosophy been in my horoscope, I should long ago have shown the door to my beloved Philology and confronted her, to use the traditional formula, with a dissolution of conjugal rights.'[33] Whereas before illness had been linked to Poverty, now it is both caused by, and helps to facilitate, the pursuit of Philology.

Despite the insistent disclaimers that the lovers of Philology occupy a different value-system from that inhabited by 'other men', the imagery used by Erasmus, Budé and Tunstall just as insistently proclaims its dependence on that value-system. The life that Erasmus leads – apparently free from the strictures of university tenure, religious institutionalisation and domestic (for which read marital) responsibilities – is, as Budé points out, a myth. They are all dependent on the financial support (and other support in kind) given by the patronage system. In Elias's account, although the humanist intellectuals distanced themselves from all social groups, nonetheless, 'they always stood closer to one of them, that of the princes and of the courts, than to the others'.[34] The image of a carefree life is conjured in the figure of a pretty boy named Riches – the desirable commodity (riches) available only in the form of the dangerously immoral and illegal (the pretty boy).

III

But, as we have seen, the 'shadow' Poverty, disappears from the 'substance' Philology in 1517. The explanation for this may, I believe, be found in Richard Pace's anecdote of the drunken nobleman, to which I referred earlier. The exchange neatly highlights the new requirements expected in the king's service, the textual and oratorical skills of international diplomacy rather than hunting etiquette. But almost without exception, commentators tell this story without including the nobleman's full speech, which reads:

> What nonsense are you talking, friend? To hell with your stupid studies. Learned men are all beggars; even the most learned of them all (so I hear), Erasmus, is a pauper. In one of his letters he calls *ten kataraton penian*, that is, cursed poverty, his wife, and complains bitterly that he's not able to get her off his back and throw her in the ocean, *bathykêtea ponton*. By God, I'd rather my son were hanged than he should study letters ...[35]

Pace is clearly referring to Erasmus's letter to Budé. But Erasmus was not pleased with Pace's work. To Thomas More on 22 February 1517/18, he writes, 'In the Muses' name, has he not bethought him that it is a serious matter to broadcast a friend's name to the world and to posterity? ... What was all the point of putting in that nonsense about ... my complaints of poverty? Does he suppose that what any noisy fellow anywhere drivels over his cups deserves to be set forth for the world to read?'[36] Throughout March the complaints were reiterated in letters to Beatus Rhenanus and Paolo Bombace,[37] and to his 'longest-standing Maecenas', William Blount, Lord Mountjoy, he protests that 'Richard Pace has caricatured me in his little book as a poor starveling, though anyone might almost take me for a Midas'; while joking uneasily that 'If this is my reputation, some of it is to be laid at your door', he claims that he has patrons galore to whom he can turn.[38] Writing to Pace himself on the same day, however, Erasmus employs a very different tone: after complaining of his characterisation in *De fructu*, he enlists Pace's help in prodding various benefactors, claiming 'What I need is ready money' [opus est praesente pecunia].[39] So while admonishing Pace for portraying him as impoverished, Erasmus is happy to recruit him in a personal cash-raising drive.

As Tony Davies astutely notes in his recent survey of humanism, print culture provided humanism with a central contradiction. At precisely the same time as humanist texts met with an unprecedentedly 'public' commodification, the texts thus commodified disclosed 'quite unprecedented depths and ardours of privacy, of intimate colloquy and self-communing inwardness'. In other words, 'The complex web of relations between writers, readers and characters, so potently charged with subjective warmth and fantasy, is wholly contingent upon an economy of cold commercial exchange.'[40] In this exchange of letters, with their confessions of poverty, Erasmus and Budé do indeed produce an illusion of 'intimate colloquy and self-communing inwardness', while simultaneously selling that inwardness in bulk, in 'cold commercial exchange'.

Difficulties arise when the 'opposition', in the form of the drunken nobleman, utters the truth about Erasmus's poverty in Pace's preface. It is on the question of commercial exchange that the inwardness founders: Erasmus is in future forced to repudiate the edgy 'in-jokes' about poverty that were so much a feature of their continuing banter. In order for the humanist friendship to function, it must hide its basis in commercial transactions: in order for humanism to be humane in its own terms, it must police its own borders of the human.

Notes

1. See Anthony Grafton and Lisa Jardine, *From Humanism to the Humanities: Education and the Liberal Arts in Fifteenth- and Sixteenth-Century Europe* (London: Duckworth, 1986).
2. Aulus Gellius, *Noctes Atticae*, translated by J. C. Rolfe (Cambridge, Mass.: Loeb Classical Library, 1967), pp.457–8, cited in Tony Davies, *Humanism* (London: Routledge, 1997), p.126.

3. Erika Rummel, *The Humanist-Scholastic Debate in the Renaissance &
    Reformation* (Cambridge, Mass.: Harvard University Press, 1995).
4. Lisa Jardine, *Erasmus Man of Letters: the Construction of Charisma in
    Print* (Princeton, NJ: Princeton University Press, 1993).
5. Willem Nesen, *Epistola de magistris nostris* in H. de Vocht (ed), *History
    of the Foundation and the Rise of the Collegium Trilingue Lovaniense*
    (Louvain, 1951–2), 4 vols., vol.1, p.595; Johann Reuchlin, *Defensio
    contra calumniatores suos Colonienses* (Tübingen, 1513), sig.C.i.[r]; both
    cited in Rummel, *Humanist-Scholastic Debate*, p.5.
6. Norbert Elias, *The Civilizing Process: The History of Manners*, translated
    by Edmund Jephcott (Oxford: Basil Blackwell, 1978), pp.73–4, citing
    Erasmus, *De civilitate morum puerilium*.
7. Robert P. Adams, 'Bold Bawdry and Open Manslaughter: the English
    New Humanist Attack on Medieval Romance', *Huntington Library
    Quarterly*, 23 (1959–60), 33–48; Arthur B. Ferguson, *The Chivalric
    Tradition in Renaissance England* (Washington DC: Folger Shakespeare
    Library, 1986). For a study which takes seriously Elizabethan chivalry
    literature as an ideological resource, see Richard C. McCoy, *The Rites
    of Knighthood: the Literature and Politics of Elizabethan Culture* (Berkeley
    CA: University of California Press, 1989).
8. Thomas Starkey, *A Dialogue between Pole and Lupset*, ed. T. F. Mayer
    (London: Royal Historical Society [Camden 4th ser., vol.37], 1989),
    pp.86, 124.
9. Alexander Barclay, *Here begynneth the famous croncycle of the warre,
    which romayns had agaynst Jugurth usurper of the kyngdome of Numidy*
    (London: Richard Pynson, 1525), sig.a.iiij.[v].
10. Juan Luis Vives, *Linguae latinae exercitatio* (Basel: Robert Winter, 1541),
    sig.d5[v]; translated by Foster Watson as *Tudor School-Boy Life* (London:
    J. M. Dent, 1908), p.68.
11. Richard Pace, *De fructu qui ex doctrina percipitur* (Basel: Johann Froben,
    1517), sig.b4[r – v]; translated by Frank Manley and Richard S. Sylester
    as *The Benefit of a Liberal Education* (New York: Renaissance Society of
    America, 1967), pp.23–5.
12. Rummel, *Humanist–Scholastic Debate*, pp.5–6.
13. Erasmus to Pieter Gillis, 15 October [1514], Basel. Ep.312. *Opus episto-
    larum Des. Erasmi Roterodami*, ed. P. S. Allen, 12 vols (Oxford:
    Clarendon Press, 1906–1958) [hereafter Allen]; translated in *Collected
    Works of Erasmus* (Toronto: University of Toronto Press, 1976 –) [here-
    after CWE] 3:43–4.
14. Jean Sturm to Roger Ascham, 9 September 1550, Strasburg. 'Rogeri
    Aschami et Ioannis Sturmij Epistolæj duæj, de nobilitate Anglicana'
    in Conrad Heresbach, *De laudibus Græjcarum literarum oratio*
    (Strasbourg: Wendelin Rihel, 1550), sig.Fiij[r]; *Letters of Roger Ascham*,
    trans. Maurice Hatch and Alvin Vos, ed. Alvin Vos (New York: Peter
    Lang, 1989), p.170.
15. Francis Bacon, *The Essayes or Counsels, Civill and Morall*, ed. Michael
    Kiernan (Oxford: Clarendon Press, 1985), pp.24–5.
16. See Lisa Jardine and Alan Stewart, *Hostage to Fortune: the Troubled Life
    of Francis Bacon 1561–1626* (London: Gollancz, 1998), ch.18.

17. Jardine, *Erasmus Man of Letters*, p.30.
18. McConica, CWE 3:273. The standard critical work is Marie-Madeleine de la Garanderie, *La correspondance d'Erasme et de Guillaume Budé* (Paris: J. Vrin, 1967).
19. Guillaume Budé to Erasmus, 1 May [1516], Paris, Ep.403. Allen 2:283; CWE 3:280.
20. Erasmus to Budé, c.19 June [1516], [Antwerp]. Ep.421. Allen 2:255; CWE 3:308.
21. Garanderie, *Correspondance*, p.63, n.33.
22. Guido Ruggiero, *The Boundaries of Eros* (Oxford: Oxford University Press, 1985), pp.109–10.
23. Jonathan Goldberg, *Sodometries: Renaissance Texts, Modern Sexualities* (Stanford CA: Stanford University Press, 1992), p.19.
24. This theme is explored in Alan Stewart, *Close Readers: Humanism and Sodomy in Early Modern England* (Princeton NJ: Princeton University Press, 1997).
25. Budé to Erasmus, 7 July [1516], Paris. Ep.425. Allen 2:275–6; CWE 3:332–3.
26. Erasmus to Budé, 28 October 1516, Brussels. Ep.480. Allen 2:363; CWE 4:103.
27. Budé to Erasmus, [26 November 1516], Paris. Ep.493. Allen 2:401; CWE 4:150.
28. Ep.480. Allen 2:363; CWE 4:103.
29. Ep.480. Allen 2:366; CWE 4:107.
30. McConica adds that Egeria was 'used as a courtesy title for female companions where the relationship is entirely or principally intellectual, and the woman perhaps of higher standing than the man'. CWE 4:354, n.113.
31. Budé to Cuthbert Tunstall, 19 May [1517], Paris. Ep.583. Allen 2:562–4; CWE 4:354–5.
32. It is only through this letter that scholars are able to date the marriage to his real 'first wife', Roberte Le Lieur.
33. Ep.583. Allen 2:563–4; CWE 4:355.
34. Elias, *The Civilizing Process*, p.73.
35. Pace, *De fructu*, sig.b4ʳ; Manley and Sylvester, p.25 [translation modified].
36. Erasmus to Thomas More, 22 February 1517/18, Antwerp. Ep.776. Allen 3:219; CWE 5:301.
37. Erasmus to Beatus Rhenanus, 13 March 1517/18, Louvain. Ep.796. Allen 3:251; CWE 5:344. Erasmus to Paolo Bombace, 14 March 1517/18, Louvain. Ep.800. Allen 3:354–5; CWE 5:349.
38. Erasmus to William Blount, c.5 March 1517/18, Louvain. Ep.783. Allen 3:235–6; CWE 5:322.
39. Erasmus to Pace, 5 March 1517/18, Louvain. Ep.787. Allen 3:242; CWE 5:331.
40. Davies, *Humanism*, p.80.

2

Animal Passions and Human Sciences: Shame, Blushing and Nakedness in Early Modern Europe and the New World

Brian Cummings

'What is it to be human?' This most Aristotelian of questions divided the Aristotelian sciences. Early modern discourses of the passions (what might now be called the emotions) occupied an uneasy borderland between the mental and the bodily, the rational and the physiological, the intellectual and the appetitive. Neither one thing nor the other, the passions moved ambiguously in a state of constant liminality. 'These passions then be certaine internall actes or operations of the soule bordering vpon reason and sense ... causing therewithall some alterations in the body.'[1] Thomas Wright's *The Passions of the Minde* of 1601, the longest treatment in English of the period, struggles even to locate its subject: are the passions properly of the body (since they are expressed in physical movements of, say, the blood in the face or the heart) or of the mind (since they appear to be caused nonetheless by some mental motivation)? The association with psychological activity raises the passions above mere instinct or mechanism, and yet in the process drags the mind down into an indecorous connection with organic pathology. For the passions are uncertainly rational, and intrinsically unruly, threatening to spread their disease to the highest faculties: 'the inordinate motions of the Passions, their preuenting of reason, their rebellion to virtue are thornie briars sprung from the infected roote of original sinne.'[2]

Worst of all, the passions reduce the mind to the level of the beasts. For it was obvious to Wright that animals were prone to the same array of emotions as humans: fear, desire, anger, hatred, sorrow.[3] Animals, moreover, registered these emotions through similar alterations of the body, including often intimate expressions of face and voice. Unendowed with language, nevertheless their bodies talked. Philosophical enquiry into the passions in humans therefore required methods of distinguishing emotional from rational activity, by sometimes desperate measures. Such measures had a distinguished and complicated history. Plato had invented a third psychological category especially for the emotions, so as to avoid identifying them completely with either reason or appetite.[4] He acknowledged the susceptibility of even the most superior intellect to unregimented desires, but held superiority to reside in the capacity in time to discipline these emotions. The Stoics, on the other hand, asserted that the wise man was entirely immune to passions. Augustine later recounted with sarcastic relish the story of a famous Stoic momentarily succumbing to terror during a storm at sea. In extenuation, the Stoic had argued that he had not fallen prey to emotion at all but rather to 'fantasy'. Augustine dismissed the argument as sophistry, but was not above using some himself in describing the Christian as prone to emotions but gradually learning to feel only the right ones.[5]

The classical discussions of passion were full of equivocation. Aristotle's most extensive treatment was hidden away in the *Rhetoric*, as an aid to successful oratorical excitation.[6] As if in embarrassment at having to discuss them at all, he devotes considerable energy to attempting to get rid of emotions altogether. Typical in its ambivalence is the Aristotelian account of shame. Shame is something that a good man will never feel since he will not commit a shameful act in the first place. Shame is therefore normally confined to old men, to adolescents and, naturally, to women, who are capable of anything and have unlimited need to reproach themselves. Concealed in Aristotle's discussion there is nonetheless a psychology of considerable complexity. He is baffled into attributing to shame a subtle and tenacious power. The person who is ashamed is both sensitive and self-conscious. She cares what other people think of her and most of all those people whom she loves and respects. She feels shame not only when caught in the act but in her imagination, in anticipating a stranger's reaction to what she has done or even in imagining the consequences of an act she has not done at all.

In unconscious recuperation, Aristotle thus makes this most embarrassing of emotions an index for characteristically human intelligence and reflectiveness. For an animal can be thought neither to experience nor to recognise shame; indeed Aristotle goes so far as to say that a human will never feel shame in front of an animal, since an animal is incapable of understanding it. Aristotle thus creates a turn in his own argument: for the very emotion which aligns a person with the beasts also sets her apart.

II

In 1872, in *The Expression of the Emotions in Man and Animals*, Darwin opened his chapter on blushing with the striking remark:

> Blushing is the most peculiar and the most human of expressions. Monkeys redden from passion, but it would require an overwhelming amount of evidence to make us believe that any animal could blush.[7]

Darwin's reasoning depends on the inference of mental processing implicit in the apprehension of the blush: 'It is the mind which must be affected', he says.[8] Yet there is something contradictory about this reasoning, since it is based on an observation of the comprehensive involuntariness of blushing: 'We can cause laughing by tickling, weeping or frowning by a blow... but we cannot cause a blush ... by any physical means – that is by any action on the body.'[9] Darwin attempts to persuade the reader of the mental basis of blushing, paradoxically, by revealing its opacity to a voluntarist form of interpretation. The sudden efflux of blood into the capillaries at the surface of the skin, he notes, is not caused by any movement of the heart, but is entirely local, the result of a muscular relaxation at the limits of the body's performance. But while this process is only peripherally related to the heart there is no immediate physiological evidence to link it to the brain. The body seems to know what it is doing but the mind does not: indeed, Darwin confirms, the blusher often does not know he is blushing, and when he realises, by trying to stop only increases his suffering. The effect is visible and palpable but also deeply mysterious, casting retrospective doubt on the initial assertion that a monkey can flush but certainly cannot blush; for, in the circumstances, probably only a monkey would know.

A physiological explanation of emotions within the medical vocabulary of sixteenth-century Europe encountered a distinctly different set of inhibitions. In one sense a bridge between the mental and the physical was ready-made, since Galenic theory proposed an axiomatic relationship of psychological 'humours' to the physical 'temperature' of the body. An association between mental traits and physical appearance was thus presumed, so that even anatomical text-books could happily delineate a theory of 'complexions' to correspond to the 'simple members' of bones, nerves and so on. In practice, this theory was thoroughly metaphorical in both directions. Thomas Vicary's *The Anatomie of the Bodie of Man* (1548), for instance, distinguishes 'bloud nutrimentall' (the veins) from 'bloud spirituall or vitall' (the arteries), and thus finds no difficulty in attributing spiritual motivation to the passage of blood from one part of the body to another.[10] Nowhere is this more apparent than in the cheeks, which are 'the cheefe beautie in man', and which unveil the secrets of his soul as they change tincture through the motions of the blood in the apprehension of fear, desire or shame:

> the Cheekes doe not only shew the diuersities of complexions, but also the affection and will of the heart: for by the affection of the heart, by sodaine ioye or dread, he waxeth either pale or red.[11]

Some forms of emotional expression prove easily accommodable to the prescribed pattern of humours. Anger, in particular, in addition to its semantic connotation with the 'choleric', is characterised by physical symptoms which have a natural corollary in the ruddy complexion of the hot and dry humour:

> countenaunce, colour, grymme visage, cruell and fierye eyes, puffinge & wrynkled nosethrilles, byting lippes, enraged mouth, trembling and shakinge lymmes, vnsteadye gate, stammerynge and fearfull voyce.[12]

Other emotions, however, signify at cross purposes with humour theory. Shame resists humoristic classification, and remains a puzzle in its precise physiognomic formation. Wright, who is unusual in taking the problem face on, as it were, improvises a convoluted theory of the causation of blushing in compensation. He multiplies the canonical types of passion from Aquinas's eleven to include eleven or any number more (including Mercie, Shamefastnesse, Excandescencie, Anxietie, Zelotypie), while maintaining a strict adherence to the principle that all the passions can be observed in bodily 'alterations' of one kind or another. Of all these locations of bodily signification the primary is the face. Yet Wright acknowledges a residual opacity of the body even as he asserts its transparency. The heart, he comments ruefully, is 'inscrutable, and onely open vnto God'; only by 'coniectures' can the meaning in one person be determined by another, and then 'rather a shadowe, then a face'. Wright approves to his readers his methodology of 'externall phisiognomie and operations', and yet admits that it offers not 'a perfite and resolute knowledge', but only 'an image of that affection that doth raigne in the minde'.[13] This is a remarkable reservation, projecting the body as a site of mimesis and signification rather than of quantifiable physical states. He takes away the power of anatomising the body and offers instead to read it. Like any signs, the signs of physiognomy are interpretive and irresolute.

Such diffidence disappears, however, as in practice it appears that Wright can read anyone, and especially women, like a book:

> And this point especially may be obserued in women, whose passions may easely be discouered; for as harlots by the light & wanton motions of their eyes and gestures may quickely be marked, so honest matrons, by their graue and chaste lookes, may soone be discerned.[14]

Most conspicuous of all is the propensity of women to blushing. Like Aristotle before him and Darwin later ('Women blush much more than men'), Wright finds the female blush a flagrant signal, and like them he is drawn by it into undeniable but unaccountable ambiguity. The blush announces at once a scandalous confession and yet also a balancing re-assertion of modesty, a self-defeating openness to fault which nonetheless triumphs by gaining simultaneous credit for moral honesty.

In this analysis, Wright's attempt at discovering the precise causatory trigger for the physical mechanism of blushing seems a transparent failure:

> they blush, because nature, being afrayde, lest in the face the fault should be discouered, sendeth the purest blood to be a defence and succour, the which effect, commonly, is iudged to proceede from a good and vertuous nature, because no man can be allowe, that it is good to be ashamed of a fault.[15]

The moral explanation plays havoc with the physiological, as the compensatory qualification ('it is good to be ashamed of a fault') retrospectively denies the need for the initial mechanism of defence ('lest in the face the fault should be discouered'). The blush blanches itself in moral self-negation, as if to embarrass itself out of existence. Confessing his perplexity, Wright notes that the face is not after all 'the roote and kore' of the problem but only 'the rhinde and leaues': he now proposes to seek out the core of the matter in the heart. Yet it could be said that it is the superficial explanation which most precisely eludes him.

At the other end of the scale from Wright's problematically physiological account of blushing lies Juan Huarte's *Examen de Ingenios* (translated into English in 1594). This takes an unremittingly philosophical and even metaphysical approach to shame, but once again contains the now familiar return of the body. What is it, he asks, which causes the reflex of shame which convulses every human being at the sight or even mention of the human genitals?[16] Hardly able to cover his own bashfulness, Huarte deploys a variety of euphemisms in further demonstration of the obscenity of his topic. Mindful of the natural modesty of his readers, he promises to 'fetch certain, not ill pleasing biasses of speech' – such as calling a spade a 'cod', for instance – but the device threatens only to embarrass his argument altogether. Huarte's discussion cannot choose whether to hold itself in or to let it all hang out.

Aristotle had argued that sexual shame was due to the sexual act not being a strict necessity, thus striking the human agent as an embarrassing superfluity. Huarte replies, conversely, by noticing that genital modesty extends to the act of excreting, which is overwhelmingly necessary, but which a man will go to any lengths to do in private, and if forced to do in public, will find himself unable to perform:

> Yea, we find men so shamefast, as though they haue a great will to make water, yet cannot do it if any looke vpon them, whereas if we leave them alone, straight-waies the vrine taketh his issue.[17]

Necessity, too, then, brings its burden of prudishness. Huarte seeks instead a more complex moral explanation. Shame, he says, originates in self-consciousness. He recalls that Adam, the first man, was not ashamed in his first creation, but only when 'he saw himselfe'.[18]

In the recognition of his naked body as being naked, he immediately looked to cover himself.

Huarte is presumably influenced here by the Vulgate version of Genesis 2:25, *erant autem uterque nudi Adam scilicet et uxor eius et non erubescebant* (literally, 'for they were both naked Adam and his wife and were not blushing'). The first blush of creation comes *cumque cognovissent esse se nudos* (Genesis, 3:7, 'when they knew themselves to be naked'). The Latin of Jerome's text locates both the moment of shame and the moment before it within a pattern of physiological observation – of blushing, and of the sensation of another's eyes upon one (*aperti sunt oculi amborum*, 3:7). It is this which leads to Huarte's location of shame within the self-apprehension of the human body of itself as a body. This is an access of emotion unknown to animals, which do not know themselves as animals. At the same time, it reveals to the human condition its own ambiguous position:

> for that it partaketh of the same generall nature with the Angels, it shameth to behold it selfe placed in a body which hath fellowship with brute beasts.[19]

The recall of the body to itself is a recognition of mortality and corruptibility. To know one's own parts is to know that they are organic and subject to chemical decomposition, and to recognise in them the function of reproduction is to realise that in time one's own body will give way to another in its place. The origin of shame is the origin of consciousness in a special sense, as a self-recognition of animal nature in oneself.

III

Science collides with culture throughout these pseudo-medical analyses of the passions. The interpretation of physiological process gives way to a preforming narrative of moral valuation. At every point, the study of physiognomy is in danger of being overlooked in psychological and social speculation. A cultural model of shame anticipates any incipient science of the blush. The passions lie between science and culture as they do between the mind and the body.

The demands of science and culture, on the other hand, seem themselves to be enveloped in a deeper bafflement between the mind and the body, and between literal and metaphorical modes of description. At some level, the body appears (in Wright's word), 'inscrutable' to the inquiring mind. To interpret the body is immediately to invade it with categories already saturated with mentalist forms of meaning. Here, the blush appears the most frustrating of bodily signifiers. For what bodily response is more seemingly calculated to invite explication, and yet what bodily response is stranger and more recalcitrant in its physical form to the assumption of calculation? Nothing is more impossible than the calculated blush, as it were the crocodile blush. Blushing is an intense form of self-attention but the blusher may not even be aware of blushing and certainly cannot control it. The blush in this way reveals the structural meaning of the 'passions' as contained in the Greek root πάθος: emotions are things we suffer from (παθεῖν), not do.

The emotional category of shame thus acts as a vital intersection in the human sciences. The status of the human as animal is brought into focus in a peculiar way. In this process, the word 'animal' itself in early modern discussion divides in connotation: the animal on the one hand is a creature inhabited by *anima*, by a 'soul' or living principle; on the other, the animal is a physical compound of organic, corruptible and mortal flesh. In the conflict between these meanings the cultural definition of the human animal is as divisive as the medical. The scientific discourse of the body, and the cultural discourse, are both mutually dependent and mutually disruptive.

The passions as it were corrupt the categorical definition of the body as a scientific object, but at the same time call into question the cultural definition of the human subject. The epistemology of the blush incorporates duplicitous forms of knowledge, in ways which are significant not only for the human science of biology, but for that other hybrid discipline, anthropology. I will now consider alongside the contest between human and animal faculties which takes place within the psychological categories of medical writing, a similar contest in the developing ethnographic language of colonial writing. At the centre of this contest can be found a problem over the identification of the passions in native populations; and once again, no passion proves more problematic than the significatory paradox of bodily shame.

The early colonists were transfixed by the lack of shame exhibited by the colonial native subject. Thus Jean de Léry, encountering the Tupinamba in coastal Brazil in the 1550s, is captivated not only by their nudity but by their lack of awareness of it:

non seulement sans cachers aucunes parties de leur corps, mais aussi sans en auoir nulle honte ni vergogne, demeurent & vont coustumierement aussi nuds qu'ils sortent du ventre de leur mere.[20]

This reaction assumes the status of a cliché: 'All of them goe naked as well men as women and haue no kind of apparell, and are nothing ashamed' (from a Portuguese treatise of Brazil).[21] In Puerto Rico, Dr Layfield found the women as flagrant as usual, but gratefully perceived 'some sparkes of modestie' in their habit of covering themselves up in the presence of clothed colonists.[22] Robert Harcourt in Guiana, on the other hand, while welcoming the use of linen briefs among the superior class of men, declared that he never saw any woman clothed either above or below the waist, but all 'starke belly naked'.[23]

The absence of exterior signs of modesty cries out for interpretation. Doing what is natural to them, the natives disturb the normative natural standards of the colonists, which assume that genital shame is endemic to the human condition. Huarte had believed that 'this natural shame' could be explained by some 'naturall reason',[24] and had invented a moral psychology to account for it. Léry, conversely, sought an ethnological explanation for the native lack, 'nulle honte ni vergogne'. Here he created a conundrum for himself. On the one hand, nakedness could be seen as the sign of an absence of culture. The Tupinamba in this sense are presented as primitive, that is, pre-cultural. They live like beasts, 'aussi nuds qu'ils sortent du ventre de leur mere'. Yet such an apprehension is contradicted by other physical observations. The Tupinamba paint their skin using a variety of colours and patterns, they wear jewellery, and on ceremonial occasions they don the plumage of exotic birds as head-dresses. With his dry Calvinist humour, Léry comments that one of the chiefs was dolled up almost as finely as the Pope. Although the women neither paint their skin nor wear plumage, they show care over their appearance: they wear their hair long and wash it frequently, adopting a style which Léry calls 'descheuelees' and obviously finds attractive.[25]

The women's hairstyle signifies in complex ways, since it is evidently a 'style', yet it is a style in imitation of nature. It is a natural look which is also chosen. This reflects back in ambiguous fashion on native nakedness. For the alternative explanation is that far from being pre-cultural, this nakedness is evidence of their own independent culture. Indeed the natives appear to choose to be naked in the same way as they choose to paint their skins. As if to enhance their nakedness, the male Tupinamba remove all their body hair; and the women all but the hair of their heads.[26] In this way, their nakedness is not like the beasts at all, because no animal wears make-up or shaves.

In Léry's analysis of nudity are seen the first stirrings of anthropology. Appropriately, given the history of that discipline, such stirrings show uneasy signs of self-reflection, of the gaze of the other entailing a further gaze back on the self. For the sign of nudity contradicts the whole system of signs within a European cultural context. It is taken not only as axiomatic, but axiomatically natural, that human beings wear clothes to hide their nakedness. No human culture previously reported in the West, however outlandish, chose to go naked. Nudity was a clear indication of monstrousness or of bestiality.

The woodcuts accompanying Léry's text manifest a similar doubleness of meaning. In one example from the second edition (Fig. 2.1), illustrating the practice of warfare, the foreground shows a group of savages firing arrows, naked but festooned with feathers and decorative anklets. In the background is a domestic scene, telling in its detail. A woman, naked, caresses her infant while her husband dozes in a hammock behind, shaded by a palm tree. Such signs of pastoral innocence are vitiated, however, by the presence of two armed warriors passing by, and by the family hearth to the left, on which can clearly be seen a barbecue of human limbs. The savages are cannibals, and to reinforce the point that they are less than human, to the wife's left, as if part of the family, with his face to the viewer, sits a monkey. Nakedness signifies in parallel with cannibalism as a connection with the beasts.

A second example is very different (Fig. 2.2). In this, Léry presents in exemplary pose a native nuclear family which is described in loving detail in the text. A man and wife, erect and tall, stand facing the viewer, filling the whole frame of the woodcut. The woman carries her baby in a delicate cotton pouch, while the baby fondles her neck and glances curiously towards the side. The woman's hair is long and flowing, she is entirely naked and without any physical adornments. With a look of steadfast frankness she meets the gaze of the viewer head on, unashamed. The engraver, on the other hand, compensates for her uninhibition by modestly withdrawing her private parts behind the figure of the

36

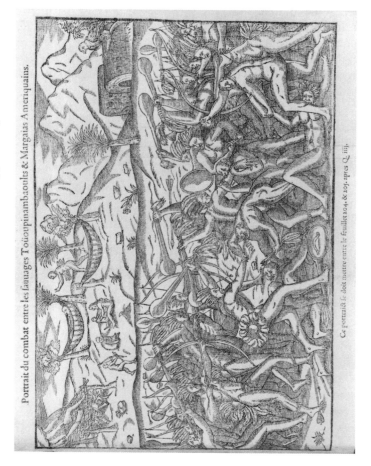

2.1 The Tupinamba at War, from Jean de Léry, *Histoire d'vn voyage faict en la terre du Bresil*, second edition (La Rochelle: Antoine Chuppin, 1580).

male. Her husband, who is in the foreground of the group, is more openly naked. His hair is shaved into an elegant tonsure, and he wears a simple necklace. In his hands he bears his arrows and longbow, and behind them he has positioned the family hammock, of neat and simple construction. Otherwise, the eye is drawn to the centrepiece of the whole picture, a naked male body, 'bien formé & proportionné de ses membres',[27] supple and muscular, with just a hint of enhanced pectorals. On the ground, discreet but meaningful in their way, there lies by the woman's foot a bowl with a pair of ripened calabash fruit, and by the man's, a pineapple in the full vigour of its maturity. The native couple cannot but put the reader in mind of Adam and Eve, the primal narrative which lies behind Léry's contorted response both to nudity and to sexual shame. At the end of his chapter on the culture of the Brazilian body, Léry makes a direct comparison with Genesis in a fashion which encapsulates the contortions of his argument:

> Ce n'est pas cependant que contre ce qu'enseigne la saincte Escriture d'Adam & Eve, lesquels apres le peché recognoissans qu'ils estoyent nuds furent honteux, ie vueille en facon que ce soit approuuer ceste nudité: plustost detestay ie les heretiques qui contre la loy de nature (la quelle toutes fois quant a ce point n'est nullement obseruee entre nos pauures Ameriquains) I'ont voulu autresfois introduire.[28]

Léry goes this way and that, both inviting and denying the analogy with the primitive couple. Like Adam and Eve, the Brazilians wear no clothes and feel no shame, and seem to share in their prelapsarian innocence. For a moment, the natives seem to offer an image of Edenic perfection, a moral world which does not need shame because it is free from original guilt. Léry acknowledges how close he has come to 'approuuer ceste nudité', but he immediately banishes the thought, and evicts the native couple from their pastoral Eden. He pictures a philosophy of nudism but rejects it as heretical, something 'contre la loy de nature'. The nudity of the Tupinamba is, after all, after the Fall, and beyond the pale. Unlike Adam and Eve in their nakedness, the Americans already have original sin, but unlike their European counterparts, they have no concept of natural law. Far from idyllic, their life of nudity condemns them doubly.

2.2   The Naked Tupinamba Family, from Jean de Léry, *Histoire d'vn voyage faict en la terre du Bresil* (La Rochelle: Antoine Chuppin, 1578).

And yet Léry implies a further moral turn. If the natives must be condemned for living uncovered 'sans nulle vergogne', Europe exceeds in the other extremity, in its predilection for 'baubances, superfluitez & exces en habits'.[29] Indeed, he declares that the nakedness of the savage women is less alluring to concupiscence than such fineries, and is less not more indecent. The natural simplicity of the native appearance reveals the immodesty of European dress, its extravagance, its dissemblance, it inutility. It seems as if Léry cannot respond to the alternative culture of the Tupinamba without reflecting in turn on his own. He cannot see their nudity in isolation: when he looks at their uncovering, he discovers his own clothedness. He knows that he is not naked and yet he feels ashamed.

Léry is troubled as much by the lack of shame as by the lack of clothing. On the one hand he is attracted to it, and makes a sympathetic defence, one which as he admits comes close to contradicting the theological and philosophical basis of his project. But he is forced finally to reject it as a false index of innocence. Other reactions were less circumspect. 'How can he be trusted', ran the conquistador cliché, 'who knows not how to blush?' A lack of shame in this sense signifies merely shamelessness. Spanish proverbial literature was rich in such associations: 'Do no hay vergüenza, no hay virtud.' Cervantes cited a similar expression: 'más vale vergüenza en cara que mancilla en corazón.'[30] Such phrases had classical origins, as in the often repeated expression, 'blushing is the colour of virtue.'[31]

However, the conquistador phrase has an extra edge, as it implies that the pigmentation in the native skin makes it incapable of blushing. The native is thus made out to be stereotypically shameless in physiology as if to match the bestiality of his behaviour. There were deep roots to this stereotype in psychological theory. The Aristotelian account of the passions was inimical to the sensation of shame, but it was equally hostile to its opposite, shamelessness. Shamelessness was a sign of apathy – in its literal sense the incapacity to feel passions at all. The desirable condition according to Aristotle lay not in an absence of passion but in a mean between the passionate and the indifferent. A state of passionlessness was a clear sign of a lower nature, and was indicated by physical torpor, listlessness, and lack of mental energy.

Alexander von Humboldt, revisiting the colonial scene of the conquistadors in 1799, reinscribed precisely this economy of prejudice.

The Indians, he noted, were slow to show emotion, and dull in response. This corresponded to the unvarying habits of their lives: influenced only by physical needs, and untouched by strong desire, their existence drags on in dull monotony. As a result, the physiological expressiveness of their bodily features is similarly undeveloped. Civilisation, by contrast, brings with it both sensibility and emotional expressiveness. Impassively, Humboldt finds proof of his speculative theory in the distinctive European physiology of the blush, and cites dispassionately the old conquistador slur:

> If the variety and mobility of the features embellish the domain of animated nature, we must admit also, that both increase by civilization, without being solely produced by it. In the great family of nations, no other race unites these advantages in so high a degree as the Caucasian or European. It is only in white men that the instantaneous penetration of the dermoidal system by the blood can produce that slight change of the colour of the skin which adds so powerful an expression to the emotions of the soul. 'How can those be trusted who know not how to blush?', says the European, in his dislike of the Negro and the Indian.[32]

Here we have the ultimate recuperation of the blush, as the index of civilisation.

Native passivity was one of the first ethnographical observations made by Columbus in 1492, and is connected with a lack of advanced technological civilisation. The natives have no iron or steel weapons, and are in any case incapable of handling them because of their extraordinary timorousness: *muy temerosos á maravilla*.[33] Even when colonial discourse chose for other reasons to present native populations as fierce and martial, brave to the point of reckless risk of death, the signals of a general mental and emotional torpor might be retained. Pero de Magalhães, in his *Histories of Brazil* of 1576, commended the lusty stature of the natives and their martial daring, but went on in the next sentence to associate this with a low standard of emotional life:

> They are very ungrateful, inhuman and cruel, inclined to fight and extremely vindictive. They live at their ease, without any preoccupation save eating, drinking and killing people; and so they grow very fat, but with any vexation they immediately grow thin again.[34]

Physical courage is a sign not of nobility but of bestiality, in line with an inhuman cruelty and an emotional development which has not progressed beyond instinct. All of this is confirmed by a torpid indolence and a fickle and insensitive nature, which, lacking the variety of emotional life available to the European, leads inevitably to indifferent, immobile obesity.

The colonial native is caught between two contradictory discourses of the passions which nonetheless conjoin to subject him. On the one hand he is prey to uncontrollable passions, lacking the rational capacity to govern them. On this basis, the Spanish jurist Juan de Matienzo argued that the Indians of Peru were neither fully human nor exactly animal; they inhabited a liminal psychological state:

> participants in reason so as to sense it, but not to possess it or follow it. In this they are no different from the animals (although animals do not even sense reason) for they are ruled by the passions.[35]

As in Magalhães's account of the Brazilians, Matienzo's Peruvians have no sense of tomorrow, but live for the moment, driven only by appetite. Irredeemably subject to their passions, these passions are nonetheless under-developed. Each of these indicators is proof of inferiority. They are at once overly passionate and not passionate enough, sensual and insensitive, prone to animal ferocity and yet also to animal indolence.

Each of these stereotypes is derived from different parts of Aristotelian psychology, and both were used to confirm with remorseless logic Aristotle's doctrine of natural slavery.[36] Aristotle's natural slave was human in that he could apprehend reason, unlike the lower animals; but human only in a diminished sense, since he could not use this rationality to control his passions.[37] At the same time the slave's docility made him accept the mastery of his superior since he was incapable of superior emotions. Like a domestic animal, he accepts the rule of his master because it is good for him. In fact, Aristotle avers, the natural slave and the tame animal are very similar in the uses to which they are put.[38] At the root of this is their similar nature, which is to live more or less randomly, at the whim of instinct, without higher sensibility.[39]

In the complex debates surrounding the argument of natural slavery among Spanish theologians and jurists in the sixteenth century, the passions played a characteristically ambivalent role in determining the boundaries of human subjectivity. Spanish sovereignty over the Indians was justified on the basis of the latter's dubious human status. The Indian was not a human proper but a *homunculus*, bereft of civility and culture:

> as inferior to the Spaniards as children are to adults, women are to men, the savage and ferocious to the gentle, the grossly intemperate to the continent and temperate and finally, almost as monkeys are to men.[40]

The insidious logic follows the distinctive pattern of Aristotelian psychology. Sepúlveda's aggressive dichotomies, leading to a seemingly inexorable divide between the human and the animal, are constructed around the prior psychological division between the mental and the bodily, the intellectual and the emotional. Temperance is the ability of the self to discriminate these areas, and thus to remain in control of the passions. The child does not know how to govern its desires until educated to do so. Women remain ever at the mercy of their emotions. Self-control is therefore the mark of the adult, rational male, who alone is capable of reaching true justice. The Indians, in their intemperance, demonstrate their incapacity for distinctively human reason. They are subjects to passion. Like pigs, their eyes are always on the ground.[41]

Anthony Pagden has described how the theory of natural slavery was applied with ruthless ingenuity in juridical arguments justifying Spanish sovereignty over the Amerindians. The familiar tropes of cannibalism and human sacrifice played a crucial role in the determination of this semi-bestial character. However, the cultural interpretation of the under-developed human condition of the native populations was more complex and varied than such obvious indicators of the monstrous. Violence and libidinousness were signified in subtler ways, too, through the diverse everyday cultural rituals of social behaviour, diet, sexual mores and so on. Savagery was read into native practice in terms of the indiscriminate choice of food (rats, snakes, insects or worms) or the predilection for the raw over the cooked. It was found in the indiscriminate choice of sexual partner, in the common reports of sodomy or bestiality. Underlying such narratives was an insidious psychology of the passions, which gave a seemingly scientific explanation for the native lack of *ingenium* or *ratio*. Savage customs were attributed to natures which had been formed *insensati*, incapable of higher sympathies or sensitivities. Nakedness in these terms was a complex signal not only of primitiveness, or of incivility, but of an inferiority of nature, an incapacity for the superior human sentiments of modesty. The Mexican Chichimeca, it was said, defecated in public, and, like beasts, performed carnal acts in front of each other.[42]

Such arguments encountered vigorous opposition in the work of Bartolomé de Las Casas. His reasoning represented an appeal for the claims of culture against the claims of nature. Sepúlveda's crude ethnology had made a rigid natural distinction between the civilised Spaniard and the barbarian other. Las Casas delivered the riposte in his *Argumentum apologiae* that the term 'barbarian' is a function of accumulated culture rather than inherited nature. Scrupulously, he derived this approach from unreproachably Aristotelian sources, notably Aquinas's commentary on the *Politics*. There are several kinds of barbarian, according to Aquinas, not one undifferentiated mass of incivility. According to one such definition, a barbarian is anyone who has, even momentarily, given way to his passions. Civilised societies, too, Las Casas concludes, may include those who are *ciegos de pasión*. Witness, indeed, the *ferocitas* of the Spaniards themselves, who in their savage treatment of the Indians have outdone all the brutality of the 'barbarians'.

With this ironic flourish, Las Casas completes a subtle deconstruction of the terms of civility and barbarism. In the process, he reorders the meaning of passions. He allows the passions ambiguous passage between different states of nature, capable of infiltrating either side rather than, as in Sepúlveda, conforming to rigid poles of psychological condition. Only at the other extreme, in his third definition of the barbarian, does Las Casas allow for a kind of emotional apathy which sets a people apart which

> either because of their evil and wicked character or the barrenness of the region in which they live, are cruel, savage, sottish, stupid, and strangers to reason.[43]

Such a category Las Casas confirms as Aristotle's natural slave. But, countering the stereotype, Las Casas refuses to number the Indians among such a group. This is a condition which he finds to be a freak of nature, something 'rarely found in any part of the world and ... few in number.'[44] To consider otherwise, to consign the Indian nations to this irredeemable state, is to conclude that God's design of the world has been ineffective, which is unthinkable for any Christian.[45]

Las Casas's more general definition of barbarism is one that is inalienably restored to the realm of culture. Such a people may have an inferior level of language, script, and other cultural perform-ances, but is nonetheless distinctively human and retains its legal rights to its own lands and to govern itself independently. It is only within such a definition that the Amerindians may be said to be bar-barians. Barbarians in this sense are not condemned to primitive life by nature, but may imbibe civilisation in time. Even the British, Las Casas remarks (quoting Gerson via Aquinas, in a tradition which goes back to Gregory the Great) have gradually acquired a civilised language. In this way, Las Casas asserts the contingency of culture.

Within this argument Las Casas carefully includes the psycholo-gical dispositions. Only by a freak of nature is a man predetermined by a particular appetite. Here, too, he asserts his Aristotelian cre-dentials, for Aristotle had stated that out-and-out brutishness was as rare as the 'god-like' man.[46] In his voluminous defences of the Amerindian peoples, Las Casas everywhere described the Indian character as emotionally fluid, capable of change. In this way, he reclaimed their capacity for education, and crucially, their aptitude to receive in time the Christian religion. The Indians were therefore not so much docile as docible.

In direct contrast to Aristotle's depiction of the natural slave as a physical brute built for manual labour, Las Casas pictures the Indians as 'most delicate and tender, enjoying such a feeble consti-tution of body as does not permit them to endure labour.'[47] They are marked by emotional sensitivity as well as by a natural kind-ness. And yet in this sympathetic portrait, so imaginatively resistant to the prevailing stereotypes, Las Casas finds his own obstacle in the inhibiting form of the theory of shame. He cannot quite bring himself to understand the native lack of bashfulness at their own nakedness. It remains an affront not only to the 'undecencies of nature' but to his own attempts at anthropological understanding. What is it that makes the Indians so resistant to shamefastness?

Although Las Casas can attribute the passions in general to the influence of culture, shame proves a step too far. Shame, it seems, must be retained as a natural category. Perhaps here Las Casas is once again remembering his Aristotelian training. For shame appeared to Aristotle as equivalent to a bodily state – rather like fear – for it produced a bodily reaction. The disgraced person blushes red, just as a person who is frightened to death turns ashen white.[48] Blushing, as a bodily reaction, cannot finally be attributed to a newly conceived emotional system of acculturation. Blushing comes naturally, it cannot be willed; by analogy, it cannot either be learned. Shame therefore has something of the status of the modern biological taboo of the inherited acquired characteristic.[49] Shame is the emotional expression the colonial writers find it hardest to believe or to disbelieve in the natives. Its absence and its presence are equally disturbing. Pagden has located in Las Casas and in Joseph de Acosta's *Historia Natural y Moral de las Indias* 'the origins of comparative ethnology'. Certainly, the writings of both men offer striking examples of anthropological apologetics in the Spanish literature of the period. Yet, as Pagden shows, Acosta is nonetheless torn between asserting the essential sameness of human beings and asserting a historical explanation for all cultural differences. For Acosta, too, shame is a powerful ethnographic taboo, and it is natural for him when he comes to attempt to account for Mexican sexual ethics to find a culture of *grande confusion y verguença*.[50] Less sympathetically, but equally dividedly, Magalhães dismisses the Brazilian tribes as viciously sensual, copulating at random, and yet observes in their sexual congress certain inevitable signs of *alguna vergonha*.[51]

Shame has played an illicit part in the development of the sciences of the human. Located at the borders of the human body, in a physiological reaction so marginal as to be almost outside the body altogether, blushing has produced shamefaced responses in medical science and in anthropology alike. At once too bodily and too mental for comfort, the blush embarrasses knowledge. Most of all, it discomforts the relation between observer and observed. In the act of observation, the observer is all too likely to become implicated and even overwhelmed, for blushing is also contagious. With decency and delicacy, even Darwin at times is rendered almost incapable by the indelicacy and indecency of his topic, as when he reports the observations of his friend Dr Paget as to whether his female patients ever blush below the neck.

The history of anthropology has turned on such moments of acute reflexiveness. The writing and the unwriting of shame has created classical sites of difficulty: witness such diverse examples as Margaret Mead, who proscribed it from the adolescent experience of the girls of Western Samoa; or Clifford Geertz, who expends several careful pages emptying the Balinese term *lek* of any stigma of Western 'shame' or 'guilt'.[52] However, the inference of emotional absence may be as much a condition of prior cultural categories as its presence. It is therefore disconcerting yet in its way fitting to find that one of the very first responses to the American other should be completely overcome by the perplexing topic of shame and its lack. Pedro Álvarez Cabral's expedition, following on from Vasco da Gama's voyage of 1499, landed on the shore of Brazil in 1500. Reporting to the King of Portugal in a private memorandum, Pedro Vaz de Caminha recorded his immediate observations of the native body of the Tupinamba:

> in appearance they are dark, somewhat reddish, with good faces and good noses, well shaped. They go naked, without any covering; neither do they pay more attention to concealing or exposing their shame than they do to showing their faces, and in this respect they are very innocent.[53]

His difficulty is revealed by the fact that his very word for the private parts is the Portuguese word for shame, *vergonha*, which he has excluded from the native experience. It is an exemplary instance of how even the most alien aspects of the encounter with the American are already inscribed in the culture and the language of the European.

Almost immediately, however, European culture and language turn back on themselves in the meeting of the gaze between coloniser and colonised:

> There were among them three or four girls, very young and very pretty, with very dark hair, long over the shoulders, and their privy parts so high, so closed, and so free from hair that we felt no shame in looking at them very well.[54]

Who is looking at whom? The gaze of the Portuguese sailor looks as it were straight through the Brazilian girls, and in this blankness reflects back only on himself. The feelings of the girls have become a cipher, to be replaced by the feelings of the observer who (apparently) 'felt no shame in looking at them very well.' And yet is this curious expression an indication of a lack of shamefastness or of open shamelessness? Has the opportunity of uninhibited observation merely reinscribed a habitual prurience, or has it after all disturbed the ethical categories of the observer, forcing him into reflections on new modes of sexual seeing, what might be called incipient bashlessness?

The writer seems himself perplexed, recalling himself into his own culture before, in a sudden and remarkable shift in perspective, interrupting his observations of the beguiling charms of the genipap body-paint so as to uncover the sources of his own European culture of shame:

> one of the girls was all painted from head to foot with that paint, and she was so well built and so rounded and her lack of shame was so charming, that many women of our land seeing such attractions, would be ashamed that theirs were not like hers.[55]

The meaning of shamelessness is subtly translating itself within his account, and interposing itself with the terms of conventional modesty. Self-attention is so catching that when he turns from the women to describe the sexual mores of the men, the nudity of the Indian male prompts him to offer some physical observations on his own genitals, which are, he informs the King (like the Indians') uncircumcised.[56]

The narrative culminates in a strange cross-cultural ritual as the Portuguese celebrate mass in front of the Indians. Embarrassed at the nakedness of their guests, the Portuguese offer a cloth to the one woman who is present.[57] She does not know what to do with it, so they put it around her; but it is to no avail: as she sits down she makes no effort to keep herself covered. The report of the Portuguese sailor attempts to cover over his embarrassment at her lack of self-consciousness, and with the standard reference, he compares her to Eve before the Fall. Nonetheless, he awaits her conversion. He does not say whether this will include a conversion to sexual embarrassment, to the culture of shame. Nor does he say whether in this conversion she will become more or less innocent. He attests to their common human subjectivity but he is entirely embarrassed by their inalienable cultural and sexual differences.

Notes

1.   T[homas] W[right], *The Passions of the Minde* (London: V. S., 1601), p. 14.
2.   Wright, *Passions of the Minde*, pp. 2–3.
3.   Wright, *Passions of the Minde*, p. 12.

4. Plato, *Republic*, IV, 441a. In the *Phaedo* there is no intermediate category.
5. Augustine, *De civitate Dei*, IX, 4.
6. Aristotle, *Rhetoric*, II, 1278a–1288b.
7. Charles Darwin, *The Expression of the Emotions in Man and Animals* (Chicago: Chicago University Press, 1965), p. 309.
8. Darwin, *Expression of the Emotions*, p. 310.
9. Darwin, *Expression of the Emotions*, pp. 309–10
10. Thomas Vicary, *The Englishemans Treasure: with the true Anatomie of Mans bodie* (London: George Robinson, 1587), p. 9.
11. Vicary, *Englishemans Treasure*, p. 23.
12. Levinus Lemnius, *The Touchstone of Complexions*, translated by Thomas Newton (London: Thomas Marsh, 1576), p. 59.
13. Wright, *Passions of the Minde*, pp. 50 and 51.
14. Wright, *Passions of the Minde*, pp. 53–4.
15. Wright, *Passions of the Minde*, p. 55.
16. Juan Huarte, *Examen de Ingenios. The Examination of mens Wits* (London: Adam Islip, 1594), p. 264. The English version is translated from Spanish via Italian.
17. Huarte, *Examen de Ingenios*, p. 265.
18. Huarte, *Examen de Ingenios*, p. 266.
19. Huarte, *Examen de Ingenios*, p. 266.
20. Jean de Léry, *Histoire d'vn voyage fait en la terre dv Bresil* (La Rochelle: Antoine Chuppin, 1578), p. 110: 'not only without concealing any parts of their bodies, but also having no shame or embarrassment, they live and go about their business as naked as when they came out of the mother's womb' (my translation).
21. Excerpted and translated in *Purchas his Pilgrimes*, 5 vols (London: William Stansby, 1625), IV, 1291.
22. *Purchas his Pilgrimes*, IV, 1158.
23. *Purchas his Pilgrimes*, IV, 1268.
24. Huarte, *Examen de Ingenios*, p. 264.
25. Léry, *Histoire d'vn voyage*, pp. 122 and 123–4.
26. Léry, *Histoire d'vn voyage*, pp. 110 and 123.
27. Léry, *Histoire d'vn voyage*, p. 119.
28. Léry, *Histoire d'vn voyage*, p. 131. 'I do not mean, however, to contradict what the Holy Scripture says about Adam and Eve, who, after their sin, were ashamed when they recognised that they were naked, nor do I wish in any way that this nakedness be approved; indeed, I detest the heretics who have tried in the past to introduce it over here, against the law of nature (which on this particular point is by no means observed among our poor Americans)', *History of a Voyage to the Land of Brazil*, translated by Janet Whatley (Berkeley: University of California Press, 1990), p. 68.
29. Léry, *Histoire d'vn voyage*, p. 131.
30. 'Better a blush on the cheek than a spot in the heart'. Miguel de Cervantes, *Don Quixote*, Pt ii. ch. 44.
31. Diogenes Laertius, *Diogenes*, sec. 54.
32. Alexander von Humboldt, *Personal Narrative of Travels to the Equinoctial Regions of America*, 3 vols (London: Routledge, 1851), I, p. 305.

33. *Select Documents Illustrating the Four Voyages of Columbus*, translated and edited by Cecil Jane, 2 vols (London: Hakluyt Society, 1930), I, p. 6; discussed in Stephen Greenblatt, *Marvelous Possessions: The Wonder of the New World* (Oxford: Clarendon Press, 1991), p. 68.
34. Pero de Magalhães, *The Histories of Brazil*, facsimile edition and translation by John B. Stetson, 2 vols (New York: Cortes Society, 1922), II, p. 83.
35. Anthony Pagden, *The Fall of Natural Man: The American Indian and the Origins of Comparative Ethnology*, rev. ed. (Cambridge: Cambridge University Press, 1986), p. 42, citing Guillermo Lohmann Villena (ed.), *Gobierno del Perú* (Paris and Lima, 1967), p. 17.
36. On the use of this doctrine in relation to the American Indians, see Pagden, *Fall of Natural Man*, pp. 27–56.
37. Aristotle, *Politics*, I, 1254b.
38. Aristotle, *Politics*, I, 1254b.
39. Aristotle, *Metaphysics*, XII, 1075a.
40. 'ac humanitate tam longe superantur ab Hispanis, quam pueri a perfecta aetate, mulieres a uiris, saeui, et immanes a mitissimis, prodigiose intemperantes a contentibus, et temperatis'; Juan Ginés de Sepúlveda, *Democrates secundus*, ed. Angel Losada, 2nd edition (Madrid: Instituto Francisco de Vitoria, 1984), p. 33; translated in Pagden, *Fall of Natural Man*, p. 117. The final phrase (denique quam Simiae propre dixerim ad hominibus), Pagden notes (p. 233), is erased from the manuscript used in Losada's edition.
41. Pagden, *Fallen of Natural Man*, p. 117.
42. Dr Juan de Cárdenas in 1591, cited in Pagden, *Fall of Natural Man*, p. 88.
43. Bartolomé de Las Casas, *Argumentum apologiae*, translated by Stanford Poole in *In Defence of the Indians* (Dekalb: Northern Illinois University Press, 1974), p. 32.
44. Las Casas, *Argumentum apologiae*, pp. 33–4.
45. Las Casas, *Argumentum apologiae*, p. 36.
46. Aristotle, *Nicomachean Ethics*, VII, 1145a; see also Albertus Magnus's commentary, *Ethicorum*, VII; discussed by Pagden, *Fall of Natural Man*, p. 21.
47. Las Casas, *The Tears of the Indians*, translated by J[ohn] P[hilips] (London: Nathaniel Brook, 1656), p. 2.
48. Aristotle, *Nicomachean Ethics*, V, 1128b.
49. Darwin notes, but dismisses as absurd, the opinion of two nineteenth-century anthropologists that some Brazilians had been observed in the process of learning to blush: '"it was only after long intercourse with the whites, and after receiving some education, that we perceived in the Indians a change of colour expressive of the emotions of their minds"'; Darwin, *Expression of the Emotions*, p. 318.
50. Joseph de Acosta, *Historia Natural y Moral de las Indias* (Seville: Juan de Leon, 1590), p. 374.
51. Pero de Magalhães, 'Historia da prouincia Sancta Cruz', *Histories of Brazil*, I, p. 33.
52. Clifford Geertz, *The Interpretation of Cultures*, (reprinted London: Fontana Press, 1993), pp. 400–402.

53. Letter of Pedro Vaz de Caminha to King Manuel, 1 May 1500, W. B. Greenlee (ed.), *The Voyage of Pedro Álvares Cabral to Brazil and India* (London: Hakluyt Society, 1938), pp. 10–11.
54. Letter of Pedro Vaz de Caminha, p. 15.
55. Letter of Pedro Vaz de Caminha, p. 16.
56. Letter of Pedro Vaz de Caminha, p. 16.
57. Letter of Pedro Vaz de Caminha, p. 32. I would like to thank several friends for their help in the writing of this essay: Margaret Boden, Jeremy Lane, Noel Malcolm. All blushes are my own.

3

Bodily Regimen and Fear of the Beast: 'Plausibility' in Renaissance Domestic Tragedy

Margaret Healy

I

In this Chapter, is entreated of good and ill Angells which being entermingled with the humours and spirites cause sondry chaunges and mutations in mens minds.

Thomas Newton, physician, 1576[1]

Elizabethan and Jacobean tragedy is much preoccupied with 'the borders of the human', with depicting the type of behaviour deemed excessive, horrific, and 'in-humane', which aligned man with the beast and the tyrant, and woman with the antithesis of the nurturing mother – the murderous, unnatural monster. Figures like Husband in *A Yorkshire Tragedy*, and Ferdinand in *The Duchess of Malfi*, exemplify the male type, whilst Shakespeare's Lady Macbeth and Alice Arden in *Arden of Faversham* are archetypal female 'monsters'. The domestic tragedies are rendered particularly gripping through the co-mingling of the ordinary and the everyday with monstrous and demonic elements. In *Arden of Faversham* (1592), *A Yorkshire Tragedy* (1608), *A Woman Killed with Kindness* (1603), and *The Witch of Edmonton* (1621),[2] homely domestic settings, familiar rural gatherings and celebrations are thrown into chaos when a destructive influence enters the 'domus', wreaking havoc and perpetrating one 'unnatural' act after another. Theirs is a universe in which seeming harmony and normality give way to lust, adultery, spousal abuse, murder and even infanticide. The realistic domestic settings and the inclusion of some true details, in fact, serve to heighten the dramatic tension aroused by the spectacle of embodied evil unleashed in 'everyman's' backyard: 'Beware, this could happen to you!', these plays simultaneously warn, and relish.

There is something tangibly and beguilingly 'modern' about this dramatic cocktail of realism and sensationalism, sex and sin, and critics have been lavish in their praise of the journalistic flavour, 'rich circumstantiality', 'immediacy', 'truth to life', and 'new bourgeois realism' which they locate in the domestic tragedies.[3] The applause often abates, however, around issues of psychological plausibility and motivation: *A Woman Killed with Kindness* has attracted particular attention in this respect. Henry Hitch Adams lamented in 1943 that whilst Thomas Heywood's play 'possesses undoubted dramatic power':

> At several of the crucial stages in the action motivation is insufficiently presented. Sir Francis Acton's sudden infatuation with Susan, the fall from virtue of Miss Frankford, the decision of Wendoll to betray his patron – none of these incidents is made convincing.[4]

The majority of subsequent critics have found common ground with Adams, producing a chorus of dismay throughout the 1980s and 1990s about Anne Frankford's 'sudden and unmotivated adultery'; a chorus which has – strangely – become most audible at a time when scholarship is emphasising the difference of early modern culture and its categories.[5] It is as if a desire to see the recognisably modern emerging from this fascinating and sophisticated dramatic arena has led some scholars to elide the fact of the powerful occult influences obviously at work in these plays,[6] and most to overlook the cultural 'otherness' inherent in these character portrayals: twentieth-century notions of interiority, and beliefs about what constitutes the 'real', are projected back onto the late sixteenth and early seventeenth centuries and the effect is an uncomfortable disjunction which must somehow be accounted for.[7] Henry Hitch Adams argues, for example, that Heywood 'so emphasizes moral instruction that he neglects or distorts human motivation the better to make clear his point.'[8] The most frequent explanation of Anne Frankford's 'unmotivated' desire is, however, that Heywood has slipped up and failed to make his characters convincing (his dramaturgy is at fault), and that, in this respect, the play is flawed.

My point is a very simple one: explanations of 'plausibility' and 'motivation' are historically and culturally determined and early modern notions of the relation between body, mind and behaviour were markedly different from ours. Twentieth-century myths of the mind, and particularly our panoply of explanations to account for unpredictable, irrational and frightening behaviour bordering on the inhuman, are not appropriately projected back into past eras.[9] Psychoanalytic theories of the unconscious, like theories of faulty genes, brain chemical imbalance, aberrant parenting, and too much nasty-video-watching, provide little help in understanding early modern representations of behaviour deemed deviant and 'monstrous'.

This essay argues that in terms of early-seventeenth-century mind–body paradigms, phenomena like the sudden reversals of behaviour or 'sondry chaunges and mutations in mens minds' (see epigraph) we see in these plays are entirely plausible. Drawing extensively on popular medical books (or books of regimen) targeted at the educated lay person, it maps out sixteenth-century shifts in ideas about the mind–soul–body relation, and the interplay of the individual with his social and spiritual environment. Focusing particularly on the ideological underpinning of representations of the porous vulnerable body and its correct maintenance in late sixteenth- and early seventeenth-century England, this approach will illustrate how the combined pressures of Protestantism, Neoplatonism, and Paracelsianism, together with attempts to understand how plague contagion was transmitted, helped fashion a range of plausible medical myths about psychic functioning, rampant appetites, and 'in-humane' behaviour which inform the drama of the period.

II

Early modern medical regimens were humanist-inspired, pocket-size self-help guides to managing the body in health and sickness; as such they are rich repositories of information about how English Renaissance men (none were by women) construed their bodies and minds. Written in the vernacular to reach a wide audience, they were penned by physicians, clerics, lawyers, grammar-school teachers, statesmen and 'men of letters': professional categories which were much more fluid and hybrid than they are today and authors of regimens often worked, in true humanist fashion, across several of these fields. What these little volumes reveal is that representations of the body, and theories about its care, altered significantly through the course of the sixteenth century and appear to have been acutely responsive to changing intellectual, biological, and social currents. Of particular interest here are the anxious discussions and warnings about losing reason, succumbing to dangerous ungovernable passions and becoming beast-like, which emerge in the vernacular medical books from the second half of the sixteenth century. Such concerns are not evident in the two early sixteenth-century regimens which functioned as models for numerous later imitations: the first by the cleric-scholar-diplomat Thomas Paynell, and the second by the lawyer-civil servant Thomas Elyot. In terms of the sheer numbers of editions produced these medical books certainly seem to have been popular: Paynell's *Regimen Sanitatis Salerni* went through nine editions between 1528 and 1634, and Elyot's *The Castel of Helth*, through seventeen between 1534 and 1610. Both volumes are remarkably secular, pragmatic, and optimistic in tone compared to later regimens. Echoing the theories of the medical school in Salerno (derived from Hippocrates, Galen and Avicenna), Paynell foregrounds three essential rules 'if we desyre corporall helthe': first, 'to lyve joyfullye: for joye & myrthe cause man to be yonge & lustye'; secondly, to maintain 'tranquillitie of mynde'; and thirdly, to eat a 'moderate diete'.[10] Elyot's much lauded *Castel* (see William Bullein's comment below, for example) is entirely concerned with corporal health, and, as in the *Regimen Sanitatis*, staying happy is the key ('There is no thynge more ennemy to lyfe, then sorrowe … for it exhausteth bothe naturall heate and moysture of the body'): diseased morals and behaviour (apart from mention of the sickening effects of 'contynuall gourmandyse') do not come within its medical province.[11]

The Castel is, in fact, heavily indebted to Thomas Linacre's new Latin translation of Galen. Faithful to the classical text, it eschews religious and supernatural explanations of ill-health, providing the reader with a down-to-earth account of the body's composition – its 'elementes, complexions, humours, membres, powers, operations, spirits'[12] – and how to maintain these in an ideal balanced state. From among the lists of 'signs' of the various complexions – the sanguine, phlegmatic, choleric, and melancholic – the reader must first identify his own type. The signs are given in some detail: among those for the melancholic individual, for example, are that he is lean, has hard skin, plain thin dark hair, is watchful, has fearful dreams, is stiff in opinions, is timorous and fearful, is prone to anger, seldom laughs, has slow digestion, weak pulse and watery urine.[13] Having established his complexion, the reader must follow the programme of bodily care specific to his type. The regimen instructs the choleric man, for example, in what he should eat and drink, and when he should wash, sleep, engage in Venus (sexual intercourse), have his blood let and be purged, in order to maintain his bodily vessel in an optimum balance: according to humoral theory, only a body too full or too empty could succumb to infection from outside through 'corrupted' air ('miasma').

The Galenic model of the body was not, however, the only medically sanctioned one in the sixteenth century; it was, in fact, facing its gravest challenges to date at the time this regimen was written, both from Vesalian anatomy and from the Swiss-German medical-religious prophet, Theophrastus von Hohenheim. Paracelsus, as he was commonly known, established his medical reputation opportunistically through publishing two treatises on the fearful 'new' disease of the Renaissance, syphilis, and introducing the mercury treatment which proved so popular.[14] For this enigmatic and audacious physician, medical and religious reform were inseparable: both required radical renewal. He declared Aristotelian and Galenic scholastic medicine heathen and obsolete (like Roman Catholicism); its practitioners greedy (like Catholic priests); and its treatments ineffective (like Catholic absolution). Paracelsus's 'cure' was to formulate a rival myth of bodily functioning which was intensely spiritual and informed by the mystical approaches of both alchemy and Neoplatonism. A book written by one of Paracelsus's English disciples R. Bostocke, provocatively entitled *Auncient and Later Phisicke* (1585), reveals the strong Platonic underpinning of Paracelsus's theories: 'For all thinges good or bad, be derived and doe flowe from Anima ... into the body and to every parte of man'. According to this system there are (since the Fall) 'spirituall Seedes of al maner diseases, indowed with lively power'.[15] Consequently, although many diseases can be cured by the vegetable and mineral cures ('Arcana') so prized by Paracelsians, some can only be helped by 'supernaturall meanes': 'if the disease bee caused by influences of the heavens, neather of the other Arcana will serve, but they are to be cured by astronomy and influences. But those Diseases and griefes that come by supernaturall meanes, will not be holpen by any meanes aforesayde, but by supernaturall meanes'[16]. The essence of Paracelsus's 'religion' of medicine is a 'supernaturall' universe inhabited with spirits (and unified by spirit), in which stones, roots, plants and seeds, all have 'powers' accessible via the practice of chemistry, which can only be channelled into the service of medicine by the true (reformed) Christian. Paracelsus's chemical cures were widely adopted by English surgeons – indeed, Elizabeth I's surgeon, William Clowes, used them – and, although the Galenic body is never entirely superseded by the Paracelsian one in England, its influence, particularly its engagement with a moralised spiritual universe associated with health and disease, is apparent in late-sixteenth-century medical regimens.

It is undoubtedly significant that descriptions of disordered morality and behaviour begin to emerge in medical books written by committed Protestant Reformers, from the late 1550s. The authors of these regimens were not usually Paracelsian practitioners but were often former Marian refugees and frequently clerics who had trained as physicians during their time in Protestant enclaves in northern Europe. William Bullein was just such a figure and for him, the regeneration of the nation after Mary's disastrous reign required the expertise and methods both of Protestant spiritual physicians (reformed clerics), and of charitable medical practitioners of the true church who were prepared to make their physic available to the poor, as well as to the rich. A distinctive Protestant polemic thus emerges in Bullein's four medical regimens which shrewdly harness the authority of Elyot's *Castel*, acknowledging it as their distinguished forebear: 'I have builded this little Fort, callyng it my Bulwarke. Not beyng able to builde any bigger woorke of defence, against sickenes, or evill diate: as that manne of worthie memorie, Sir Thomas Eliot knight did, when he builded his Castle.'[17] A marked socio-moral-religious discourse is evident in Bullein's medical writings which are unequivocal about the focus of the nation's 'sickness':

> There are many idle people in citees, and in noble houses, dooe thinke the chief felicitee onely, to be from bedde to bellie … to bedde again: none ther lives thei wil use, then Cardes, Dice, or pratlying title tatle … slepyng, eatyng and laughyng.[18]

This manner of 'idle' living, the physician instructs his reader, quickly makes a noble person 'a deformed monstrous man' and reduces him to beggary. 'Laughyng' is closely associated with idleness here: by inference, the formerly health-giving emotions, 'joye & myrthe' (see Paynell's 'rules' above), are now highly suspect. Bullein's prodigal types bear a distinct resemblance to those found in Edwardian dramatic Interludes; for example, the anonymous play *Nice Wanton*,[19] in which Ismael's predilection for 'Carde, dyce, kysse, clippe, and so furth' (l.451), is the source of his degeneration, criminal behaviour and eventual death by hanging. Ismael's sister, Dalila, who is unable to control the passion for whoring instilled in her by corrupt Catholic types, meets an equally disturbing end: slow death through 'the pockes' (syphilis). This is didactic, cautionary drama preaching strict bodily control ('good governaunce' l.526) as inseparable from adherence to the true faith. Protestant propagandists, like the physician William Turner, frequently harnessed the horror and fear associated with actual bodily disease (particularly syphilis and plague) to render their messages more meaningful. William Turner's *A newe booke of Spirituall Physik for dyverse diseases of the nobilitie and gentlemen of Englande* (1555), for example, represents Roman Catholicism as 'the pokkes' (syphilis) spread throughout Europe by 'a certeyne hore in Italy' (the Whore of Babylon astride her beast) strewing monstrous corruption in her wake.[20] Because of Protestant interpretation of the Book of Revelation, 'beasts', and beast-like behaviour, inevitably, for some, had Roman Catholic associations.

So far, we are still in the realm of metaphor and polemic, but it was not long before medical theory and precepts about bodily care in Protestant regimens were being adjusted to accommodate and underpin these perceptions, and to rectify the nation's spiritual, moral, and social diseases. 'The Haven of Health', Protestant England (but also the title of Thomas Cogan's medical book of 1584), like English bodies, was construed as constantly vulnerable; its defences were under unremitting threat from Romish infection: the body must be fortified against it, and strict bodily regimen, including temperance, sobriety and restraint in matters of Venus, were the linchpin of the Protestant prescription for regenerating and maintaining the nation's health. For Cogan, a physician and Manchester grammar school teacher, dietary temperance was one with godliness: 'And no doubt but that meane and temperate dyet, in the feare of God, is more commendable than all the delicate fare in the world, and ought of the godly to be esteemed as a thing that best contenteth nature, and preserveth health.'[21] By the 1580s, staying 'healthy' had enormous spiritual and moral implications;

disease had become a culpable and blameworthy affair closely associated with over-indulgence. Cogan sermonised in his regimen:

> Now what a reproch is it, for man whome God hath created after his own likenesse, and endued with reason, whereby he differeth from beasts, to be yet beastlike, to be moved by sense to serve his bellie, to follow his appetite contrarie to reason?[22]

The physician Phillip Barrough similarly stressed that the body, as 'that best workmanship of God', must be subjected to close vigilance and control 'to correct, reforme and amend it.'[23] John Calvin's injunction in *The Institution of Christian Religion* (1536), to know and be displeased with 'our selves', had clearly taken on a physical as well as a spiritual dimension by this period; indeed, knowing one's complexion, and subjecting the body to rigorous ordering practices, had risen to the status of a Christian and national obligation for the Protestant godly circa 1600. As James Manning's medical regimen of 1604 entitled, *I Am For You All Complexions Castle*, explains: it is the 'duty' of man to 'look after his castle', to keep the 'cage' of his soul as 'cleane' as he can, 'neither breake or dissolve the same, least his soule, as an untimely bird, flie unto the hill.'[24] Bodily regimen is, for this minister, a deeply spiritual and disciplinary matter; the text proceeds to rail:

> Seeing then the lawe of God, thy owne soule, nature, the law of man, parents, king, and country, commaund, and call unto thee to endevour to preserve thy bodie, by the almightie his meanes left unto the ... and by his meanes to correct excesse of bad humours, and to amend their confusion ... Therefore it is most necessarie for thee to know thy complexion, to know what humours abound in thee, or are deficient ... causing alteration or confusion.[25]

If the soul and the country are to be saved from 'confusion', the regrettable animal tendencies of the body ('rage', 'sleepiness', 'phrensie' and 'wantonness'[26]) produced by 'bad humours', must be closely addressed and corrected.

It is probably true to say that the maxim, 'We are what we eat', was never so significant in England until this period: the individual's corporal composition and health, his morals, behaviour, salvation; and the spiritual, moral and social health of the nation, all largely depended, according to these regimens, upon careful attention to dietary rules. What people ate and drank, when, and in what quantities, were perceived to have profound and far-reaching consequences. Thus Thomas Newton's translation of Levinus Lemnius's (a noted Dutch physician) regimen, *The Touchstone of Complexions* (1576), intricately details the medical mechanisms whereby through a change of diet and temperance the body can be 'refourmed into better' and sinful behaviour averted. It describes how 'Immoderate gurmandyze, surphet, and dronkennesse' produces humoral disorder, leading to loss of reason, domination by 'the spirit animal', and ultimately to sin and damnation:

> For when the naturall and vitall facultie, together wyth the natur-all and inwarde Spirites waxe somewhat stronge, and partlye by aboundaunce, partly by the qualitye of meate and nourishment, have attayned strength and power: they reject and cast away the brydle of reason, and draw the spirit animal also ... into their faction and disordered rebellion. Wherby it happeneth, that when any lewde devyse or wilful thoughte aryseth in the minde of man, he is prone to runne into dissolute riot, libidinous lust, filthy and shameful pleasures.[27]

According to Lemnius' medical system, some 'nourishments and meates ... engender good bloude and juyce' and through 'holesome diet and order' a distempered body and soul can be restored to their 'former integritie'.[28] A special hazard of over-consumption is unbridled lust: 'For who is hee, that being thoroughly whittled in drinck, doth not beastly rushe into venerous luste, and filthy desires? For when the body is bumbasted wyth drincke, and belly-cheere, the privities and secrete partes do swel, and have a marvey-lous desire to carnal coiture'.[29]

Medical texts such as Lemnius's, which stress the crucial import-ance to social health of individual temperance and restraint of the animal passions, reveal how a resurgence of interest in Platonism in the Renaissance was exerting a considerable influence on medical paradigms. Indeed, the intemperate beasts evident in late sixteenth-century medical tracts (and in the drama of the period) are recog-nisable versions of *The Republic of Plato*'s unjust, despotic and tyrannical types – those unfit for husbandry and rule because of their lack of self-mastery (the ruination of bodies, souls, households and states, caused by 'despotism of appetites' is stressed in another seminal text for the Renaissance, Xenophon's *Oeconomicus*[30]). The *Republic* describes how 'full-fed with meat and drink', the control of reason is withdrawn and the 'wild beast' under the influence of a 'master passion' goes on the rampage:

> When a master passion is enthroned in absolute dominion over every part of the soul, feasting and revelling with courtesans and all such delights will become the order of the day. And every day and night a formidable crop of fresh appetites springs up, whose numerous demands quickly consume whatever income there may be. Soon he will be borrowing and trenching on his capital; and when all resources fail, the lusty brood of appetites will crowd about him clamouring. Goaded on to frenzy by them ... he will look out for any man of property whom he can rob by fraud or violence. Money he must have, no matter how, if he is not to suffer torments.[31]

This is surely echoed in the behaviour of Husband in *A Yorkshire Tragedy* who, having squandered away all his resources, frenziedly and violently screams at his wife, 'Money, money, money, and thou must supply me' (scene 2, l.58), and again 'Money, whore, money, or I'll – [Draws his dagger]' (scene 3, l.71). Shortly prior to the first outburst Wife had been anxiously ruminating:

> 'tis set down by Heaven's just decree
> That riot's child must needs be beggary.
> Are these the virtues that his youth did promise,
> Dice, and voluptuous meetings, midnight revels,
> Taking his bed with surfeits? – ill beseeming
> The ancient honour of his house and name.
>   (scene 2, ll.4–9)

Husband's 'idle' lifestyle and surfeiting have caused the decline of his house – its 'beggary' – but 'worse' is to follow. Wife frets aloud about her husband's horrific transformation:

> Bad turned to worse!
> Both beggary of the soul as of the body;
> And so much unlike himself at first
> As if some vexed spirit had got his form upon him.
>   (ll.35–8)

Indeed, some 'vexed spirit' has got 'his form upon him', for as the audience witnesses in the final scene, the devil, who has made Husband act this 'unnatural tragedy' of rioting, whoring and murder, 'glides' from his body (scene 8, l.18). Servant, who reckons he has been trying to restrain a 'monster' rather than his 'master' (scene 5, l.41), provides a commentary for the audience (like Wife) on Husband's unexpected change of character, his damnation and devilish transformation:

> A man before of easy constitution,
> Till now hell's power supplied to his soul's wrong.
> Oh, how damnation can make weak men strong.
>   (ll.61–2)

This is cautionary drama, warning all Husbands ('Let every father look into my deeds', scene 8, l.59) that unbridled appetites lead to the ruin of houses, and 'worse', can lead to possession by the devil, and 'monstrous cruelty' (scene 7, l.12).

Devils gliding in and out of bodies may seem merely sensationalist 'mumbo-jumbo' and highly 'implausible' today, but the phenomenon was quite within the realm of medical orthodoxy, and thus of credibility circa 1600. Thomas Newton's translation of Lemnius provides graphic descriptions of how poorly regimented bodies – those 'full of ill humours'[32] – are more susceptible to invasion by bad spirits. In the airy, mysterious world of this medical book, man is continuously beset by 'external spirites recoursing into his body and mind':

> Now, for so much as Spirits be without bodies, they slyly and secretly glide into the body of man, even much like as fulsome stenche, or as noysome and ill ayre, is inwardly drawen into the body: and there not onely incense and pricke a man forward to mischiefe, but also like most pestilent Counsellers, promyse to the partye reward and impunitye ... the Devill ... is most subtile and crafty .... Yea, his fetch is slyly to insinuate himselfe into our mindes, cogitations, counselles and willes.[33]

According to Lemnius's medical theory, evil spirits read the 'inward disposition' of an individual through signs in his 'eyes, countenaunce, gesture' and assess the best time to catch him 'unwares and unprovyded'; and, if the body is insufficiently disciplined through proper regimen, it is possible to catch disastrous moral contagion (which can lead to damnation) in the same manner as a cold or plague – through 'evil', tainted air. Thankfully, however, not all airy spirits are up to no good: 'And furthermore as pure subtyle ayre breatheth into lyving Creatures and into greene herbs, a lively and holsome spirite: so likewise the good Angels imparte holsome ayre, and with a pleasaunt sweete inspiration refresh our inward minds.'[34]

The lively spirit world of *The Touchstone of Complexions* is by no means unique; indeed, Paul H. Kocher's assertion, in his influential book *Science and Religion in Elizabethan England* , that 'by the end of the sixteenth century the idea of the devil had been pretty well washed out of the medical books' seems to bear little relation to that which one finds in the vernacular regimens.[35] In his treatises, John Cotta ('Doctor in Physicke'), dwells at length on the power of the imagination to infect others and declares that 'evil spirits' are sent 'partly to quicken and stirre up the godly and holy man, and to trie and proove him thereby.'[36] Puritan physicians like Cotta felt that Galenic physicians neglected the workings of the soul, and the forces of evil on the body; interestingly, physicians were often brought in to arbitrate in witchcraft disputes in this period. In a manner similar to Cotta, the divine, William Perkins, describes the fifth of Satan's five powers as 'the procuring of strange passions and torments in mens bodies'.[37] Robert Burton's bulky medical tome, *The Anatomy of Melancholy* (1621), contains a fascinating and lengthy 'Digression' on the variety of 'Spirits, Bad Angels, or Devils, and how they cause Melancholy'.[38] Practising alchemists such as John Dee also emphasised the supernatural aspects of the universe that contributed to 'dis-ease'; as Charles Webster succinctly describes: 'The esoteric aspects of alchemy blended well with currents of religious thought which were gaining ground during the Reformation and with the neo-Platonic philosophy which was beginning to attract the intelligentsia.'[39] Indeed, by 1600, the body as represented in texts inhabiting a variety of overlapping categories (medical, religious, philosophical, political) appears highly unstable, its boundaries indistinct; sometimes, as in Lemnius, its borders seem to dissipate altogether in a Christianised-Neoplatonic-type universe of spirit:

> Now, man at the hands of his Creatour, being furnished wyth such excellent gifts and garnishments of minde, as first to be

endued wyth a natural and internall Spirite, and then to be moved and inspyred with a Divine Spirite, hath also (not withstanding) externall spirits recoursing into his body and mynde.[40]

Such porous bodies are inevitably depicted as highly vulnerable and susceptible to invasion by hostile circumambient forces. William Vaughan's *Directions For Health* (1600) addressed to the author's sister provides an engaging example of this; Vaughan concludes his instruction with the advice: 'Pray fervently to God, before you sleep, to inspire you with his grace, to defend you from al perilles & subtelties of wicked fiends ... & let your night cappe have a hole in the toppe, through which the vapour may go out.'[41]

The occult moral universe of these treatises seems remarkably pertinent to an understanding of 'motivation' in late Elizabethan and Jacobean domestic tragedy, where characters seem to catch passions and spirits (which goad them on to good or evil) like they might catch a dose of flu – through close contact and 'infected' breath. *In The Witch of Edmonton*, for example, Winnifride suggests that Sir Arthur's breath is morally tainted and contagious and responsible for her 'former deeds of lust' (I.i.189); Elizabeth Sawyer, accused of witchcraft, complains that she is 'shunned/ And hated like a sickness' (II.i.100–1). Alice Arden in *Arden of Faversham* accuses her lover of corrupting her through 'ticing speech', witchcraft and sorcery (scene 1, l.96; scene 8, ll.78–9); a charge which Mosby lays at Alice's door: 'thou unhallowed hast enchanted me' (scene 8, l.94). Feeble excuses for bad behaviour these might appear to us, but for early seventeenth-century audiences such explanations were real possibilities: the task for them was to try to identify which 'seeming angels' were really devils. Anne Frankford's sudden desire for Wendoll, her 'unexplained' adultery with a man who feels 'some fury pricks [him] on', is perfectly understandable in the context of the lines:

O Master Wendoll,
Pray God I be not born to curse your tongue
That hath enchanted me! This maze I am in
I fear will prove the labyrinth of sin.
(II.iii.158–161)

As the servant Nicholas fears, Anne has been corrupted by the devilish Wendoll ('This fiend with an angel's face' (V.iii.111)) who, like

Satan watching Eve in Milton's *Paradise Lost*, meditates on Anne's 'divine perfections' before spoiling them (II.iii.11). Once Anne's 'infection' is revealed to Frankford, he seeks to put barriers between her 'infectious thoughts', and their children , fearing 'her adult'rous breath may blast their spirits' (IV.iv.124–5). Repentant, Anne appears to try to rid her body of disease – reform it into a better – through self-starvation: this was surely the ultimate bodily and spiritual discipline for those who believed, with many physicians of this period, that over-eating and subsequent humoral disorder would have rendered the body susceptible to the influence of 'evil' in the first place. Robert Burton's *Anatomy* confirms, for example, that fasting is 'the physic of the soul, by which ... viscious and predominant lusts and humours are expelled'.[42] But *A Woman Killed With Kindness* is also interested in the 'holsome' spirit world and its influences. If Wendoll is a bad angel, Susan is the antithesis; her virtue is as contagious as Wendoll's sin:

> Oh, what a look did fly
> To strike my soul through with thy piercing eye!
> I am enchanted, all my spirits are fled,
> And with one glance my envious spleen struck dead.
>   (III.i.90–4)

The explanation of Sir Francis Acton's 'sudden infatuation with Susan' is quite simply 'Fascinatio' (infection via the eye). Galenic medical theory posited that eye infections ('opthalmia') were passed from person to person via 'noxious rays' falling upon the observer's naturally receptive eye; late sixteenth-century theory developed this as a possible route for the transmission of spirits too. Discoursing on the power of beauty to 'fascinate', Burton relates, 'The rays, as some think, sent from the eye, carry certain spiritual vapours with them, to infect the other party, and that in a moment.'[43]

Cumulatively, these writings suggest that by the early seventeenth century, the borders of the human – the ramparts of the castle – were imagined as vulnerable places, easily penetrated by airy circumambient forces. Sometimes, these spirits introduced positive, 'refreshing' qualities into the recipient body and soul (see above, Lemnius's 'good Angels'), but they were most often envisaged as hostile, in the worst case scenarios bringing about monstrous behaviour in their hosts, and violating the sanctity of the home and the community. According to the medical regimens only constant vigilance, self-scrutiny and self-discipline can maintain body, soul and community intact. Intemperance (closely associated with pleasure and 'laughyng') has replaced 'sorrow' (in Paynell's and Elyot's regimens) as the greatest 'enemy to life' and anxiety about physical and moral infection polluting the soul, is intense. I have argued that the combined religious and intellectual currents of Protestantism, Neoplatonism, Paracelsianism and alchemy encouraged this change in perception of the body and its environment through the course of the sixteenth century, but insights from cultural theory offer additional ways of understanding this shift.

III

In *The Civilizing Process* Norbert Elias analysed the transformation in manners (social bodily rituals as prescribed in conduct books) which occurred in the Renaissance; and asked the crucial question why a preoccupation with 'uniform good behaviour', associated with the humanist concept of 'civilite', became so acute in the sixteenth century.[44] Elias argued that the information contained in the conduct books 'exposes to view ... an accessible segment of a much more far-reaching process of social change' and that these treatises were 'direct instruments of "conditioning" or "fashioning", of the adaptation of the individual to those modes of behaviour which the structures of his society make necessary.'[45] For Elias, the transformation in manners – the increased embarrassment, shame, and closer and more private attention to social bodily rituals suggested by sixteenth-century manuals – could be attributed almost entirely to a change in the structure of society, which in turn necessitated a change in social behaviour. Elias designated the sixteenth century as a 'fruitful transitional period' between two great epochs characterised by 'more inflexible social hierarchies'; a period in which 'the social circulation of ascending and descending groups and individuals speeds up.'[46] For the first time men could be 'fashioned' into gentlemen – made not born – and conduct books written by eminent humanists like Desiderius Erasmus instructed an emerging strata of educated lay-persons in 'humane' and noble conduct. It can reasonably be argued that Renaissance medical regimens (and some literary texts, for example, Edmund Spenser's *The Faerie Queene*) were similarly participating in this process. 'In-humane' behaviour – the antithesis of what the humanists prescribed – was inevitably demonised and labelled bestial and 'monstrous' in all such texts.[47]

The seminal influence of Elias's hypotheses on later twentieth-century cultural and literary theory is readily apparent, but it is the developments of Elias's rudimentary insights into the body-society axis, in the work of the anthropologist Mary Douglas, which are most pertinent to this study. Crucially, in *Natural Symbols*, Douglas argues that there is a continual exchange of meanings between the two kinds of bodily experience – physical and social – so that each reinforces the categories of the other. Her analysis of the way the body is perceived in different cultures leads Douglas to conclude:

> There can be no natural way of considering the body that does not involve at some time a social dimension ... Interest in its apertures depends on the preoccupation with social exits and entrances, escape routes and invasions. If there is no concern to preserve social boundaries, I would not expect to find concern with bodily boundaries .... I now advance the hypothesis that bodily control is an expression of social control.[48]

For Douglas, bodily symbolism exhibiting a preoccupation with boundaries indicates a culture anxious to protect social boundaries and fearful of unwanted intrusions; one that is experiencing a strong sense of group identity, but which is short on rules ('strong group, weak grid').[49] This would certainly seem a reasonable description of sixteenth century English society – neither feudal nor bourgeois, but, in Elias's terms, in a state of transition and social fluidity; one searching for new structures, definitions and limits. It was a society, too, in which Protestantism was playing a considerable role in shaping a distinctive 'godly' English nation. Furthermore, Douglas identifies a 'witch cosmology' associated with bodily symbolism such as we find at the turn of the seventeenth century where 'the emphasis is on valuing the boundaries, guarding the orifices, avoiding improper mixtures.'[50] It is 'confused social experience' which, in Douglas' view, leads to witch-hunting and the witch hunter 'expresses himself in bodily restraint.'[51] Again this seems relevant to late sixteenth-century and early seventeenth-century England where hysteria about witchcraft – as the papers from the celebrated Mary Glover case reveal – was rife.[52]

These insights from cultural theory provide a helpful additional approach to understanding the structures of behaviour and motivation depicted in the domestic tragedies. The social space of these plays is certainly precarious and transitional: old values associated with loyalties, family ties and charity come into conflict with hard-nosed early capitalism. In *Arden of Faversham*, as in *The Witch of Edmonton*, supernatural happenings are exacerbated by greed and lack of charity (especially on the part of new entrepreneurs like Arden) in the absence of alternative alleviating structures for poverty. All these plays, too, are preoccupied with social risings and fallings, with transformations in social status which appear conducive to evil influences entering the home. As Husband in *A Yorkshire Tragedy* gambles and whores away his inheritance things go from bad to worse: the devil gets his form on him. In *Arden of Faversham* Mosby's highly effective social climbing is represented as intimately connected with the breach in decorum in the Arden household, and in *The Witch of Edmonton*, Frank Thorney's desire to extricate himself from the 'misery of beggary and want' consequent on his family's bankruptcy, leads him to commit evil deeds. Wendoll in *A Woman Killed With Kindness* is portrayed as in a similar in-between social niche: 'a gentleman/ Of a good house, somewhat press'd by want' (II.i.30–1). In these plays men who inhabit the borders between social groups are dangerous: they are associated with moral, spiritual and social dis-ease. Indeed, social instability, psychic instability and domestic instability seem to be closely related in the worlds of the domestic tragedies. One message of such plays is undoubtedly that heads of households would do well to beware of befriending socially ill-defined, inbetween types who are seeking to gain entry into their domestic and social terrain. This is an interesting development of a motif about dubious friends from earlier plays; for example, the Protestant morality, *Enough is As Good as a Feast*, which warned its audiences: 'it is not all Golde, that like Golde dooth shine/ No more are all freends that friendship pretend:/ As it approved with many in the end.'[53]

IV

Douglas's analysis of bodily symbolism can produce fruitful insights into early modern cosmology and its medical and dramatic representations, yet her approach neglects, indeed erases, biological events (in favour of social events) which, I wish to argue, exert an equally profound shaping effect on bodily perceptions. The deliberations of that great advocate of empiricism, Francis Bacon, on the parameters of the psychic contagion controversy in 1605, help to foreground this aspect:

> *Fascination* is the power and act of Imagination intentive upon other bodies than the body of the imaginant ... wherin the school of Paracelsus, and the disciples of pretended Natural Magic have been so intemperate, as they have exalted the power of the imagination to be much one with the power of miracle-working faith; others, that draw nearer to probability, calling to their view the secret passages of things, and specially of the contagion that passeth from body to body, do conceive it should likewise be agreeable to nature, that there should be some transmissions and operations from spirit to spirit without the mediation of the senses; whence the conceits have grown, now almost made civil, of the mastering spirit, and the force of confidence, and the like.[54]

As Bacon confirms, speculation about the machinations of minds was intense in the first decade of the seventeenth century, and Paracelsian medicine had, in his view, led to 'intemperate' claims. Yet he identifies another source of theories about the transmission of spirits which he associates with greater 'probability': those who derive their ideas from the observation of 'contagion'. Hypotheses about 'operations from spirit to spirit' were evidently most scientifically respectable when, as in Lemnius's and Vaughan's medical texts, they derived from theories about the transmission of physical infection.

The disease which was attracting most attention in this respect was, undoubtedly, bubonic plague: a devastating, life-threatening infection associated with extreme pain, which was endemic in London during the last decade of the sixteenth century and the first decades of the seventeenth century (when the domestic tragedies were first staged). In 1593 and 1603 plague was particularly virulent and reached epidemic proportions in the capital; in 1603 it killed some 25 000 Londoners.[55] The medical regimens reveal that physicians speculated furiously about how this terrifying and mysterious disease was caught, most by 1600 favouring transmission by close bodily contact coupled with infection of the air (in fact plague was passed to man through the fleas of black rats, something which remained unknown to science until the late nineteenth century). A medical treatise by the physician and man-of-letters, Thomas Lodge, provides a graphic account of 'contagion' as he understood it in 1603:

> *Contagion*, is an evil qualitie in a bodie, communicated unto an other by touch, engendring one and the same disposition in him to whom it is communicated ... For very properly is he reputed infectious, that hath in himselfe an evil, malignant, venemous, or vitious disposition, which may be imparted and bestowed on an other by touch, producing the same and as daungerous effect in him to whom it is communicated.[56]

Lodge was certainly not a Paracelsian, in fact, his adherance to Roman Catholicism led to a brief period of imprisonment, but this medical discourse of the plague speaks simultaneously of moral and physical contagion and the 'malignant' effects of both. Bubonic plague encouraged, too, a discourse of 'borders' with policing: in Lodge's treatise, as in most others from this period, infected people were to be kept outside the city walls (and punished by magistrates if they infringed them) and shut-up in their homes. Inevitably too, marginal types – the poor living in the slum tenements at the borders of the city (the liberties and suburbs) – were closely associated with the spread of plague contagion. The official form of prayer for plague in 1603 stressed the importance of close self-government: 'Now the chief remedy to be expected from men is that everyone would be a magistrate unto himself and his whole family.'

The terror inspired by the plague is evident in this tract by the minister James Balmford:

> From the heart proceed (as Phisitions say) vitall spirits, whereby man is made active and couragious. If they by feare be inforced to retire inward, the outward parts be left infirme; as may appeare by the palenesse and trembling of one in great feare, so that as enemies easily scale the walles of a towne abandoned by souldiers; so the Plague ... doth find readie passage into the outward parts of a man ... [thus] feare (adversarie to faith) pulleth to the wicked the evill which he feareth.[57]

According to Balmford, and many other commentators on the 1603 plague, 'feare' itself could result in infection. Inevitable anxieties about plague contagion encouraged the perception of a vulnerable body whose 'walles' might be easily scaled if the inward spirits were 'wounded' by insufficient spiritual and physical regimen. In fact prayers, self-control and social controls (shutting the suspected carriers of infection 'in' and 'out') were this society's major bulwarks against a terrifying disease phenomenon.

EPILOGUE

This was a period in English cultural history in which imagination and trepidation – alone – could appear to some to act like a magnet attracting physical or psychic contagion across fragile bodily borders surrounded by hostile forces.[58] The domestic tragedies discussed above, which – significantly, I have argued – emerged from a context in which anxiety about fearful plague contagion was justifiably rife, participate in the highly topical and medically sanctioned debates about the transmission of evil, and the relationship of this to personal bodily regimen, and to disturbing bestial and monstrous behaviour. Like the medical regimens and conduct books they are also functioning (partly through exhibiting the animalistic behaviour of 'inhumane' others) to define and fashion 'humane' behaviour. Searching for explanations based on modern ideas of psychological realism to account for 'sondry mutations in mens minds', such as Anne Frankford's fascination with Wendoll and Sir Francis Acton's with Susan, is undoubtedly misplaced in this context. Far from a growth of rationalism as England advances apace towards the scientific enlightenment, the vernacular medical books provide evidence of a far more complex story which has crucial implications for the way we understand the portrayal of character, and of misfortune, on the late Elizabethan and early Jacobean stage.

Notes

1.   Thomas Newton, *The Touchstone of Complexions* (London, 1576), f.20ᵛ. Newton's was a free translation of a medical regimen by the Dutch physician Levinus Lemnius. Tom Coryat in his *Crudities* (1611) calls Lemnius an 'admirable sweete schollar, and worthy ornament of learning', p. 649. Lemnius is repeatedly cited as an important source

of medical authority in Robert Burton's *Anatomy of Melancholy* (1621), ed. Holbrook Jackson (1641 edition, London: J. M. Dent & Sons, 1972); all references are to this edition.

2. All references to the anon. *Arden of Faversham, A Yorkshire Tragedy* and Thomas Heywood's *A Woman Killed With Kindness* are to Keith Sturgess (ed.), *Three Elizabethan Domestic Tragedies* (1969), (Reprinted Harmondsworth: Penguin Classics, 1985). All references to William Rowley, Thomas Dekker and John Ford, *The Witch of Edmonton* are to Peter Corbin and Douglas Sedge (eds), *Three Jacobean Witchcraft Plays* (Manchester: The Revels Plays, Manchester University Press, 1986).

3. On the issue of 'realism' see Sturgess, 'Introduction', particularly pp. 7–9, 19; Rick Bowers, '*A Woman Killed With Kindness*: Plausibility on a Smaller Scale', *Studies in English Literature*, 24:2 (1984), 293–306; Diana E. Henderson, 'Many Mansions: Reconstructing *A Woman Killed With Kindness*', *Studies in English Literature*, 26 (1986), 277–94, especially 277, 290. Henderson provides a useful summary of prior views of the play.

4. Henry Hitch Adams, *English Domestic or Homiletic Tragedy 1575–1642* (New York: Columbia University Press, 1943), pp. 156–7.

5. Laura G. Bromley, 'Domestic Conduct in *A Woman Killed With Kindness*', *Studies in English Literature*, 26:2 (1986), 259–76, 259. Bromley provides a summary of earlier responses to this aspect of the play, 277. Kathleen McLuskie, *Renaissance Dramatists* (Hertfordshire: Harvester Wheatsheaf, 1989) discusses the play's 'complete failure to explore the motivation or the process of the relationship between Wendoll and Anne', p. 135. Catherine Belsey, 'Desire's Excess and the English Renaissance Theatre' in Susan Zimmerman (ed.), *Erotic Politics: Desire on the Renaissance Stage* (New York and London: Routledge, 1992) remarks that 'In *A Woman Killed With Kindness* desire exceeds marriage in a curiously unmotivated way', p. 96.

6. Henderson asserts, for example, that Heywood's 'adherence to contemporary notions of realism' led to his complete exclusion of 'all devils, spirits and gods', 'Many Mansions', 279, 290.

7. The explanations have been remarkably ingenious: David Cook, '*A Woman Killed With Kindness*: An Unshakespearean Tragedy', *English Studies*, 45 (1964), argued that Frankford's lack of passion 'impelled Anne into adultery', 361. Bromley asserted that Heywood simply 'is not interested in individual psychology', 'Domestic Conduct', 261. Bowers found plausibility here but 'on a smaller scale' which calls for 'simplistic' emotional responses, '*A Woman Killed With Kindness*', 295. Hardin Craig, *The Enchanted Glass: The Elizabethan Mind in Literature* (Oxford: Basil Blackwell, 1952) argued that 'an Elizabethan conception of psychology was behind the behaviour of Anne and Wendoll', Wendoll's 'passion' led him astray: in positivist fashion Hardin Craig elides the fact of Wendoll's devilish powers, his being pricked on by some 'fury'; indeed, he produces an account which lays blame firmly at Anne's door, pp. 130–1.

8. Adams, *English Domestic or Homiletic Tragedy*, p. 146.

9. On the function of myths and constructs in medicine see, Meyer Fortes, Foreword, *Social Anthropology and Medicine*, ed. J. B. Loudon, (London: Academic Press, 1979); and P. Wright and A. Treacher (eds), Introduction, *The Problem of Medical Knowledge* (Edinburgh: Edinburgh University Press, 1982).
10. Thomas Paynell, *Regimen Sanitatis Salerni* (1528), sigs. B1^r, B2^{r-v}.
11. Thomas Elyot, *The Castel of Helth* (1534), f.66^r and 45^r.
12. Elyot, *Castel of Helth*, f.1^r.
13. Elyot, *Castel of Helth*, f.3^r.
14. See Charles Webster, 'Paracelsus: medicine as popular protest' in Ole Peter Grell and Andrew Cunningham, (eds), *Medicine and The Reformation* (London: Routledge, 1993).
15. R. Bostocke, *Auncient and Later Phisicke* (1585), pp. 80, 127.
16. Bostocke, *Auncient and Later Phisicke*, p. 90.
17. William Bullein, Preface, *Bulwarke of Defence* (1562), sig.C2^v.
18. Bullein, *Bulwarke of Defence*, f.lxvij^r.
19. References are to, *A Preaty Interlude Called, Nice Wanton* (1560) in John Manley (ed.), *Specimens of the Pre-Shakespearean Drama*, (Boston: Ginn & Company, 1897).
20. William Turner, *A newe booke of Spirituall Physik for dyverse diseases of the nobilitie and gentlemen of Englande* (1555), f.74–5.
21. Thomas Cogan, *The Haven of Health* (1584), f.2^r.
22. Cogan, *Haven of Health*, f.3^v.
23. Phillip Barrough, *Method of Physick* (1583), sig. A6^r.
24. James Manning, *I Am For You All Complexions Castle* (1604), p. 2.
25. Manning, *I Am For You*, p. 6.
26. Manning, *I Am For You*, p. 2.
27. Newton, *Touchstone of Complexions*, f.14^{r-v}.
28. Newton, *Touchstone of Complexions*, f.5^r, f.3^v.
29. Newton, *Touchstone of Complexions*, f.10^v.
30. Translated from Greek into English 'at the desyre of mayster Geffrey Pole', as *Xenophons Treatise of Householde* in 1534, and reprinted numerous times through the sixteenth century.
31. *The Republic of Plato*, translated by Francis MacDonald Cornford (1941), (Reprinted, Oxford: Oxford University Press, 1945), pp. 298–9.
32. Newton, *Touchstone of Complexions*, f19^v.
33. Newton, *Touchstone of Complexions*, f.22^{r-v}.
34. Newton, *Touchstone of Complexions*, f.23^r and f.24^r.
35. Paul H. Kocher, *Science and Religion in Elizabethan England* (California: Huntington Library Publications, 1953), pp. 256–7.
36. John Cotta, *The Triall of Witch-craft* (1616), f.26^v.
37. William Perkins, *A Discourse of Witchcraft* (1608), p. 124.
38. Burton, *Anatomy of Melancholy*, see note 1 above, p. 180.
39. Charles Webster, 'Alchemical and Paracelsian Medicine' in Webster, (ed.), *Health, Medicine and Mortality in the Sixteenth Century* (Cambridge: Cambridge University Press, 1979), p. 314.
40. Newton, *Touchstone of Complexions*, f.21^v.
41. William Vaughan, *Directions For Health* (1600), p. 75.
42. Burton, *Anatomy of Melancholy*, p. 342.

43. Burton, *Anatomy of Melancholy*, p. 85.
44. Norbert Elias, *The Civilizing Process: The History of Manners*, translated by Edmund Jephcott (1936), (Reprinted, Oxford: Basil Blackwell, 1978), pp. 73–80.
45. Elias, *Civilizing Process*, pp. 83–4, 108.
46. Elias, *Civilizing Process*, pp. 73–9.
47. 'These seeming beasts are men indeed'; Edmund Spenser, *The Faerie Queene* (1596), II xii, 85. In J. C. Smith and E. De Selincourt (eds), *The Poetical Works of Edmund Spenser* (1912), (Reprinted, Oxford: Oxford University Press, 1924).
48. Mary Douglas, *Natural Symbols: Explorations in Cosmology* (London: The Cresset Press, 1970), pp. 65, 70.
49. Douglas, *Natural Symbols*, pp. 65–70.
50. Douglas, *Natural Symbols*, Preface, p. ix.
51. Douglas, *Natural Symbols*, Preface, pp. viii, xii.
52. See Michael MacDonald, *Witchcraft and Hysteria in Elizabethan London: Edward Jordon and the Mary Glover Case* (London: Routledge, 1991).
53. Anon., *Enough is As Good as a Feast* (1570), sig.D2ᵛ.
54. Francis Bacon, *The Advancement of Learning*, ed. G. W. Kitchin, (London: J. M. Dent & Sons Ltd.,1861), p. 119.
55. Paul Slack, *The Impact of Plague in Tudor and Stuart England* (1985), (Reprinted, Oxford: Clarendon Press, 1990), p. 151.
56. Thomas Lodge, *A Treatise of the Plague* (1603), sig.B2ᵛ.
57. James Balmford, *A Short Dialogue Concerning the Plagues Infection* (1603), p. 15.
58. Undoubtedly, there were many sceptics, too, such as Ben Jonson, whose plays (notably *The Alchemist* (1610)) parody and ridicule alchemists, mystics and Paracelsians.

4

Midwifery and the New Science in the Seventeenth Century: Language, Print and the Theatre

Julie Sanders

In a satirical broadsheet of 1603 entitled 'Tittle-Tattle; Or, the Several Branches of Gossipping' the stereotypical role of women in the community as gossips and scandalmongers is vividly represented (Fig. 4.1). Women are depicted as chattering with each other in various locales; from the marketplace to the water conduit and from there to the river; in the bakehouse and the alehouse. These are all outside activities, public exchanges of sorts, but there is one other section of the illustration that accompanies the broadsheet which takes place in an interior space, that of the childbirthing room, where the midwives and gossips are shown in dialogue around the childbed. Female communities are shown in this satirical print as being centred on the activity of gossip, and the semi-professional medical role of the midwife is effectively belittled in its implied alignment with the idle chatter or 'tittle-tattle' of the title.

Part of the means by which the New Science constructed understandings of itself in the seventeenth century involved the harnessing of popular satire in this manner in order to denigrate the importance of women's roles in practising medicine. If women were mere gossips then men spoke the language of the New Science, an empirical discourse born of experiment and debate, not tradition and tittle-tattle.

Social and medical histories of the early modern period frequently tell of an erosion of women's power in practising medicine, arguing that this erosion was encouraged and sometimes even directly shaped by emergent male empirical science.[1] Anne

75

4.1 From *Title-Tattle; Or, the Several Branches of Gossipping* (c. 1603).

Laurence has observed that 'by the end of the [early modern] period there was less scope for women to occupy career positions than there had been. There was a serious attack by men on female midwives; and male midwives achieved a prominent position during the eighteenth century.'[2] Laurence's account is admirably non-sensationalistic, but perhaps underestimates the extent to which this erosion of both the professional and amateur positions of women midwives was achieved by means of a conscious male penetration of the female space of the birthing room, a penetration which was both physical and discursive.

The 'Tittle-Tattle' broadsheet represents in some sense a visual enactment of the conscious cultural marginalisation of the female practice of medicine in this period. The childbed scene of the birthing room is consigned to the corner of the frame, excluded from the original street scene. The supposed scene of privacy and of non-observed female communion is nevertheless being circumscribed and made visible by the misogyny of the broadsheet, and this circumscription through language – print – is the subject of this essay.

I

The period of childbirth and the subsequent, often lengthy, 'lying-in' provided a rare, socially sanctioned space of female autonomy in the seventeenth century. Just before giving birth the pregnant woman would enter the birthing room and would not officially re-emerge into society until she had been 'cleansed' of the so-called pollutative effects of childbirth in the churching ceremony during which the new mother entered church veiled in order to be symbolically purged and re-admitted to society.[3] When a woman was due to give birth not only would the midwife be summoned but also a group of female attenders: these could be friends or family of the expectant mother and usually included her own mother. It was the task of these women to calm the patient; they provided the 'caudle' or hot spiced drink that soothed her during labour; they offered advice, often derived from direct experience; and, significantly, they protected the female space from male intrusion, hanging heavy curtains over any windows or doors, and blocking keyholes. The space, constructed by patriarchy, was taken over by the very women whom patriarchy had marginalised, and this exclusive and enforced female experience can, paradoxically, be seen as the root of the male anxiety surrounding childbirth that led to the eventual penetration of this space by male doctors and more generally by the discourse of the New Science.[4]

Fear of women's ability to exploit this female space of the birthing room was culturally rife. The ability to tamper with the 'evidence' of childbirth which this private space provided them with added to the social myths of subversion that built up around midwives. They were credited with the ability to practice magic and witchcraft, or, more pragmatically, with the provision of birth control and abortifacients to women in the community who were in need. The imaginative power of the space of the birthing room was, then, potent and feared and helped to shape popular understandings of the midwife.[5]

In truth, the majority of midwives in the period were socially respectable, educated women whose practice of midwifery came about through the circulation of written testimonials authored by significant members of their local community or indeed of the communities they were entering, since these women frequently ventured out into the provinces and did not practise only in their own localities.[6] Such spatial and social mobility may in itself have been threatening to the practitioners of the New Science. Midwives were figures of considerable social standing; many were employed on repeated occasions by particular families (the clientele representing a range of social classes), and such repeated employment suggests a trust in, and a validation of, their work. Many midwives also acted as significant witnesses in trials for rape, infanticide, and bastardy, a fact which re-writes the stereotypical notion of the 'midwife on trial' which again stems from popular superstitions relating to witchcraft. Such power helps to suggest why male science sought to enter and to control the social and professional spaces of the seventeenth-century midwife which, ironically, patriarchy itself may have helped to create.

One of the ways in which the male scientific community began to harness midwifery and the space of the birthing room for its own purposes was through language. This practice did not only take the form of associating midwives with witchcraft and occult herbalist practices which would obviously marginalise their status in communities where they practised; male scientists also confronted the traditional, often orally disseminated, experiential remedies of (frequently female) medical practitioners in rural communities with the obfuscatory language of experimental science. Jonathan Sawday has recently described this innovation as the 'masculine discourse of science and reason', suggesting that '[a]t some point during the seventeenth century, the great super-structure of Renaissance medical practice and theory – the world of interlocking metaphors of affinity and dissimilarity... – began to crumble, to be replaced by the technological regime in which a new, labouring body was created.'[7] Women were as a result, he argues, excluded from this brave new world even more than they had been from the older medical regime, on class as well as gender grounds: '[t]he female occupation of midwife ... was soon to become a male prerogative. The network of traditional remedies which surrounded the body (male as well as female) and which were administered mainly by women, though they lingered on, were to become the primary health-care system of the rural poor, as opposed to the wealthy, who now had access to a growing urban and commercial system of health maintenance.'[8] The professionalisation of medicine and medical discourse effectively excluded women from a world they had previously gained access to due to that world's continuing involvement with traditional and local (and by implication amateur) practices which were handed on within communities rather than disseminated through the world of textbooks.

During the course of the seventeenth century the separation of the discourses of New Science and traditional medicine became more pronounced. An increasingly technological and mechanical approach to the discipline refashioned it as a self-consciously masculine, professional discourse, and the similarly masculinised world of print disseminated the practice. During the seventeenth century a number of male-authored texts advising on the best practice on midwifery were published, and a female-authored text did not appear until 1671: Jane Sharp's *The Midwives Book*. A significant issue to note about her work is that it is directly addressed to 'her Sisters, the Midwives of England'.[9] The counterpart male texts are invariably jointly addressed to surgeons and midwives – that is to say, to both male and female communities. The male texts serve to include, and to control the female practitioner. Sharp uses plain language in an attempt to reach her informally educated audience, resisting therefore the discursive blockings that Sawday suggests enabled the New Science to consolidate its power.

The objective of social control that lay behind a number of the male medical textbooks is clearly evident in the language of *The*

Accomplisht Midwife (1673). Originally published in French by Francis Mauriceau, this text was translated and altered by its English adaptor Hugh Chamberlen who was 'Physician in Ordinary to His Majesty'. The Chamberlen family played an important part in altering perceptions of the art of midwifery in the seventeenth century. When in 1616 women midwives petitioned James I to allow them to form a society, the Chamberlen brothers supported them. They were significant in this debate partly because they had invented the obstetrical forceps. In 1634, however, they sought to gain control of the midwives' profession for themselves, a project which failed but which created considerable bitterness and division and, as a result, the family kept the exact design of their forceps a closely guarded secret.[10] This may explain the rather confrontational tone of Hugh Chamberlen's translation of Mauriceau's text.

The novel nature of the incursion of *The Accomplisht Midwife* into female matters is made explicit: 'we do not usually discourse of Women with Child, nor of their different Labours', but so too is the aim of governing such women. The professional limitations of the female midwives are stressed: 'The principal thing worthy their observation in this Book; is accurately to discover what is properly their work, and when it is necessary to send for advice and assistance, that so many Women and Children may be preserved.'[11] The emphasis is on the superior ability of male medical practitioners – who were trained in professional institutions – to preserve and save in the face of female limitations: 'Nor can it be so great a discredit to a Midwife (let some of them imagine what they please) to have a Woman or Child saved by a Man's assistance.' Professional boundary lines are being drawn, and the midwife's role clearly circumscribed.

However, not all male writings on midwifery were necessarily hostile to female practice: Nicolas Culpeper famously defended traditional practice in his *A Directory for Midwives, or A Guide for Women in Their Conception, Bearing, and Suckling Their Children* (1651): indeed Chamberlen's text is in part a retort to Culpeper's influential work. This was a highly popular text in the period, reprinted many times, and it is significant to note that Jane Sharp's text, which according to Elaine Hobby was designed to 'teach her fellow-midwives anatomy, a knowledge which has been denied them because they cannot attend the universities or register for apprenticeships', echoes Culpeper's vocabulary at various points.[12] Rather than excluding them, Culpeper emphasises the role of neighbours and the local community in birthing, and indeed goes so far as to suggest the limit to male understanding of the female body, a direct reversal of those texts which sought to exclude the midwife. Writing on the formulation of the child in the womb, he notes: 'This is the difficultest piece of work in the whole book, nay in the whole study of anatomy because such anatomies are hard to be gotten, most women that lie on their death-beds, when they are with child, miscarry before they die ...'[13]. He suggests the lack of anatomical understanding amongst male doctors:

> Myself saw one woman opened that died in child-bed not delivered, and that is more by one than most of our dons have seen, yet they are as confident as Aesop's crow was that he was an eagle, but he was made a mocking stock to the boys for his labours; and so will they be shortly for their foolish model of physic, that I may give it no worse name.[14]

Jonathan Sawday has credited the increase in the practice of dissection and the detailed anatomising of the interior body with instituting the discourse of New Science, the same discourse that Culpeper and Sharp attempt to resist. But this discourse would, despite their efforts, lead by the end of the seventeenth century to the rise of the male midwife and to his colonization of the birthing room.

II

The birthing room had, however, already been penetrated prior to the emergence of the New Science of the late seventeenth and early eighteenth centuries by literature, by male writers who were fascinated by imagining the 'goings-on' behind the keyhole at childbirth. This essay therefore concludes with a discussion of some of the ways in which seventeenth-century literature can be seen to be reflecting and indeed responding to the cultural and linguistic debates taking place over medical practice and in particular midwifery. My particular focus will be on one of Ben Jonson's Caroline plays, *The Magnetic Lady* (1632) which not only concerns itself with a midwives' conspiracy and the anxious off-stage space of the birthing room, but also raises the question of the social and cultural belittling of women through the discourse of gossip and their exclusion from the professional science that is the subject here. Jonson, in fact, seems at first glance to echo the work of the 'Tittle-Tattle' broadsheet with which I began this essay.

A number of early modern texts on midwifery cite as their precedent the writings of Louise Bourgeois (1563–1636) who had been midwife to Marie de Medici at the French court and who, in 1609, had published her *Observations diverse sur la sterilité*. Whilst a number of male-authored texts cite her as a precedent and influence, their revisions of her work also suggest further attempts at literal and linguistic control of this otherwise threateningly female domain of childbirth.

In seventeenth-century France there was a proliferation of *'caquets de l'accouchée'*, texts which 'recuperate the femaleness of the lying-in through the presence of the voyeuristic male narrator.'[15] This narrator was usually placed behind one of those curtains or screens which had been erected to shield events from men's eyes; thus he (and the readers) gained access to the private talk of women, which was invariably figured as sexual and scatological. The controlling male gaze and narrative resubordinated female experience to the sphere of male interpretation and circulation, not here of science, but of the printing house.[16]

What the male eavesdropper gains is access to the gossip of the bedside: *caquet*, the term used to denote this type of literature, quite literally means the sound that a hen makes when laying an egg, but has in French become an equivalent to culturally loaded accounts in English writings of the 'clucking' of housewives. Within the *caquets* there is a sense in which once male access to the birthing room is gained female gossip is defused of any threat.[17] There were also *anti-caquets* authored by women in this period and the appearance of these texts suggests an attempt by members of the female community to protect and preserve their customs, and seems to confirm the significance the birthing room, that space for autonomous exchange, held.[18]

Marina Warner has suggested that the lyings-in allowed women a temporary control of their own narratives: 'Gossip was perceived to be a leading element in women's folly, and in the sex's propensity to foment riot.' She also notes that the 'changes in the meaning of the word "gossip", however pejoratively weighted, illuminate the influential part of women in communicating through official and unofficial networks, in contributing to varieties of storytelling and in passing on their experience in narrative.'[19] The term 'gossip' originally referred to a baptismal sponsor, male or female: a 'god-sib'. By as early as the fourteenth century the term had become almost exclusively female in its application and 'applied ... to female friends invited by women to the christening of her child.'[20] At the end of the sixteenth century the word acquired the meaning of 'midwife'; that meaning is now obsolete but as the 'Tittle-Tattle' broadsheet indicates the gossip and the midwife were part of a culturally linked discourse and ideology in the period.

In 1626 Ben Jonson had framed *The Staple of News*, his play about emergent print culture, with a meta-theatrical on-stage audience of female gossips, highlighting the interrelations between authorised male printed discourse and the 'tattle' of women. Jonson was acknowledging women's role in the communication of information, not simply parodying their worthless gossip in support of the male-dominated press-shops: the print-house and its propaganda, after all, explode in Act IV.[21] As Warner notes, '[w]omen dominated the domestic webs of information and power; the neighbourhood, the village, the well, the washing place, the shops, the stalls, the street were their arena of influence ...'[22] This more empowered understanding of the social exchange implicit in the activity of gossip facilitates a more nuanced version of the role and function of gossip and midwifery in Jonson's *The Magnetic Lady*.

III

The Magnetic Lady, written just two years before the midwives' petition and the Chamberlen family's moves to acquire a monopoly over the practice of the craft, is utterly domestic in its dramatic location. The play takes place in one house, a house which is controlled by women. Since Jonson's plays at this time were explicitly engaged with questions of community and neighbourhood, his decision to depict a female domestic household community in this play should not go unremarked.[23] In the play a midwife's plot to conceal a birth and thus protect the hidden identity of the mother is arranged in order to secure a considerable family legacy. Lady Lodestone, an aristocratic estate owner, has a niece called Placentia who, on her marriage, is due to inherit her late parents' fortune. In the meantime, her avaricious guardian-uncle, Sir Moth Interest, has the money in his care. When the play commences Lodestone is in the process of choosing a suitable husband for her niece: Placentia herself is attended by her nurse Keep, her mother's resident female advisor, Polish, and Polish's daughter, Pleasance. When we first see them altogether on-stage they are suggesting gleefully to Placentia whom she should marry.

The plot, however, truly thickens when Placentia falls ill. Two more characters enter, figures connotative of medical and religious institutions – Dr Rut and the Parson Palate – both of whom are quick to offer prognoses and diagnoses of Placentia's sickness. Both, however, in their obsession with wind and stereotypical scientific theories on 'green-sickness' (the supposed hysterical illness which befell virgins who were not married off quickly enough) miss the truth of Placentia's complaint – her pregnancy.[24] A convoluted plot-line ensues in which, in order not to damage Placentia's marital prospects, various midwives and female attenders at the premature birth of her child seek to cover up the event. The birth is induced it seems by one of Captain Ironside's violent interjections at the dinner table – male language here causing, rather than attacking, the seclusion of the women. Polish is at the forefront of these attempts to cover up the birth because, as the audience learns before the resolution of the play, she has in fact swapped her real daughter for Lady Lodestone's niece in the hope of inheriting a portion of the family fortune.

The depiction of the midwives' conspiracy should not be read as a straightforward misogynist confirmation of the need to control, even to evacuate, female spaces such as the birthing room. The alternative of the professional doctor in the play is scarcely a reassuring depiction of male empiricism, and does not therefore function as an overt appeal for the New Science to take over. Medicine, like the church, is shown to be flawed and cor-ruptible once at play within the cultural domain. Jonson, like Culpeper later, seems to be proposing the need for women to control the birthing space.

However, neither can a proto-feminist account of the midwives' conspiracy be given that somehow releases the previously con-strained female agency in the play. Gossip Polish and Mother Chair the midwife (her name suggestive of flesh – *la chair* – and the birthing stool[25]) are also fairly reprehensible characters, as apt to slander each other as male members of the community in their on-stage diatribes, and are shocking in their lack of care for their medical charge in all but the most materialistic terms. The function of themes such as medicine and gossip in the playtext require a deeper reading that contextualises them within the framework of contemporary concerns around midwifery and the agitations for the New Science, and as such Jonson's play can be interpreted as commenting upon such concerns.

One important discursive debate engaged with in *The Magnetic Lady* is that which links women, midwives and witchcraft. The heated altercations between Nurse Keep and Gossip Polish, as each is quick to blame the other for the imminent collapse of their carefully rehearsed plot, employ the stereotypical masculinist definitions of midwives as witches and bawds: 'Out thou catife witch!/Bawd, Beggar, Gypsy: Anything indeed/But honest woman' (IV.iv.1–3).[26] Even while they are practising the old, traditional 'non-scientific' arts of midwifery they are claiming access to the language which excludes their roles.

It has become a commonplace of critical interpretations of seventeenth-century witch-hunts and witchcraft accusations that midwives were regularly prosecuted for performing occult practices and for dabbling in the herbal lore that was the province of the early modern witch as it was constructed by contemporary patriarchal, theological and legal discourse.[27] The direct association of witches and midwives in the period had come about through one particularly influential text: the *Malleus Maleficarum* written by Heinrich Kramer and Jacob Sprenger, two Dominican monks,in 1486, a text which is often described as a 'handbook for witch hunters', and which directly associated the midwife's craft with black magic and the occult.[28] This tract is cited in many writings on this theme, and yet Diane Purkiss has recently questioned the centrality of that text to early modern culture, describing twentieth-century constructions of the witch story as a 'myth of the burning times', an attempt by radical feminism to find a holocaust of its own against which to define the movement. The potent figure of the herbalist/healer/midwife/witch living on the edge of the community is, she says, as much a product of our own needs in the late twentieth century as of historical fact, with the witch figure acting as 'a spectacular collage of everything which feminist historians and others see as the opposite of medical patriarchy …'.[29]

As we rewrite the history of midwifery and of witchcraft, so we must reconsider our assumptions about the operation of cultural stereotypes within drama as well as contemporary communities. When Nurse Keep rails against Polish's involvement in cradle-changing, she describes it in terms of an offence against all the infants of the 'neighbourhood' (IV.iv.44). Midwives were responsible, powerful members of those communities and Jonson's play, for all its recognition of their subversive potential within a patriarchal context, never suggests any supernatural or occult power on their behalf: the mal-practice is truly worldly.

There is a need to read the treatment of midwifery in *The Magnetic Lady* from the vantage point of contemporary medical debate and its harnessing of popular superstition about the special powers of midwives or wisewomen (*sage-femme* was in French the term for a midwife) for scientific reasons: that is to say, in order to marginalise and demonise their activities and therefore allow for male incursions into their territory. Texts like *The Magnetic Lady* in their socialising of midwives and witches as 'real' members of 'real' communities may well be more forward thinking in their approach to epistemology and the rewriting of the operation of traditional beliefs than we have previously acknowledged.

One way in which to confirm the idea that *The Magnetic Lady* was a playtext engaging with the problematic and shifting status of the midwife within the medical profession in the early to mid-seventeenth century is to look at the language. What midwives' manuals we have prior to the Restoration are in the main, as noted above, authored by men. There are exceptions, of course: the *Countess of Lincoln's Nursery* (1622) offers some surprisingly radical advice to aristocratic women on the advantages of breast-feeding.[30] Jane Sharp's aforementioned *The Midwives Book* was not published until 1671; and the polemical Catholic Elizabeth Cellier wrote her pamphlet petitioning for a college of midwives in London in 1688.[31] The problem remains of controlling the desire to 'read back' too much from these texts to the productions of earlier decades, but nevertheless the associations between the plain speech of Sharp's text (itself a reworking of earlier writings) and Jonson's chosen network of metaphors within the play are striking; they suggest that he was quite consciously employing the common parlance of midwifery to authenticate and invigorate his drama, and that the play is consequently less 'masculine' than has previously been stated. Jonson may indeed be acknowledging the local power of such figures as midwives and female healers and questioning the motives of male denigrations of their work.

Jane Sharp, in the wake of Culpeper, described the reproductive act in the following terms: 'The womb is that field of nature into which the seed of man and woman is cast, and it hath an attractive faculty to draw in a magnetic quality, as the lodestone draweth iron, or fire the light of the candle; and to their seed runs the woman's blood also ...'[32] The 'magnetic' themes of *The Magnetic Lady* thus take on a redolence additional to that outlined by Helen Ostovich in her account of contemporary (male) theories of magnetism, a redolence that is potentially female.[33] It is the womb that functions as the attractant vessel, and it is the magnetic allure of Lady Lodestone that does indeed literally draw iron by the end of the play with her marriage to Captain Ironside.[34]

Jonson's names directly signal his engagement with the contemporary debates about midwifery and the practice of medicine. It is not only Placentia's first name which is self-referential; her surname of Steele is connotative of remedies for false swelling or green-sickness (the very illness she was diagnosed as suffering from by Dr Rut).[35] But she is, of course, false Steele, being in truth Polish's daughter, and the extravagant claims of male medical discourse are made to seem spurious as a result of these parallels.

But, as noted, a proto-feminist defence of midwives against the onslaught of male medicine is not to be found in *The Magnetic Lady*; neither though is the misogynistic, anti-populist text that has been promoted by what limited criticism there is of this play. In its place Jonson is engaged with the complex reconfigurations and redefinitions of his own community, cultural and theatrical, and not least medical, and from these literary incursions into the birthing room we may perhaps read back into the wider socio-political community and understand that the innovations of the New Science, linguistic and actual, were both ongoing and questioned throughout the seventeenth century. Within Jonson's play there is the possibility of recognising the celebration of the role of the midwife and the criticism of the New Science (represented in the form of Dr Rut), and in this celebration and criticism we can perhaps see represented a questioning of the exclusion of the woman from the birthing room. Even within the development of the New Science Jonson and others represent experiential medicine – so often figured as gossip – as central. Where *The Magnetic Lady* might seem to echo 'Tittle-Tattle' it in fact overturns the whole concept of the place of female conversation within the realms of medicine and repositions the birthing room at the heart of the community which is both domestic and medical.

Notes

1. See, for example, Roy Porter, *Disease, Medicine and Society in England, 1550–1860* (London: Macmillan, 1987); Jean Donnison, *Midwives and Medical Men: A History of Inter-Professional Rivalries and Women's Rights* (London: Heinemann, 1977); Edward Shorter, *A History of Women's Bodies* (Harmondsworth: Penguin, 1982).
2. Anne Laurence, *Women in England, 1500–1760: A Social History* (London: Weidenfeld and Nicolson, 1994), p. 107.
3. Adrian Wilson, 'The Ceremony of Childbirth and its Interpretation', in Valerie Fildes (ed.), *Women as Mothers in Pre-Industrial England* (London: Routledge, 1990), pp. 68–107.
4. In the seventeenth century male midwives only entered the scene as a last resort when surgery became necessary since they were allowed to use the tools of obstetrics such as forceps. See Audrey Eccles, *Obstetrics and Gynaecology in Tudor and Stuart England* (London: Croom Helm, 1982).
5. For the historical counterbalancing of these myths, see David Harley, 'Historians as Demonologists: The Myth of the Midwife Witch', *Journal of the Society for the Social History of Medicine* 3 (1990), 1–26; Diane Purkiss, *The Witch in History: Early Modern and Twentieth Century Representations* (London: Routledge, 1996). Useful for considering the dissemination of cultural practice and belief is Pierre Bordieu, *The Field of Cultural Production* (Cambridge: Polity Press, 1993).
6. See David Harley, 'Provincial Midwives in England: Lancashire and Cheshire, 1660–1760', in Hilary Marland (ed.), *The Art of Midwifery: Early Modern Midwives in Europe* (London: Routledge, 1993), pp. 27–48.
7. Jonathan Sawday, *The Body Emblazoned: Dissection and the Human Body in Renaissance Culture* (London: Routledge, 1995), p. 230.
8. Sawday, *Body Emblazoned*, p. 230.
9. Reproduced in extract form in Charlotte F. Otten (ed.), *English Women's Voices, 1540–1700* (Miami: Florida International University Press, 1992). See also Kate Aughterson (ed.), *Renaissance Women: Constructions of Femininity in England: a Sourcebook* (London: Routledge, 1995).
10. I am indebted for this account to Elaine Hobby, *Virtue of Necessity: English Women's Writing, 1649–88* (London: Virago, 1988), pp. 183–4.
11. F. Mauriceau, *The Accomplisht Midwife, Treating of the Diseases of Women with Child, and in Childbed*, translated by H. Chamberlen, London, 1673, sig.A4.
12. Hobby, *Virtue of Necessity*, p. 185.
13. Nicolas Culpeper, *A Directory for Midwives, or A Guide for Women in Their Conception, Bearing, and Suckling Their Children* (London, 1716), p. 23. Reproduced in extract form in Aughterson, *Renaissance Women*, pp. 59–60.
14. Culpeper, *Directory for Midwives*, p. 23, in Aughterson, *Renaissance Women*, p. 60.

15. Donna C. Stanton, 'Recuperating Women and the Man Behind the Screen', in James Grantham Turner (ed.), *Sexuality and Gender in Early Modern Europe: Institutions, Texts, Images* (Cambridge: Cambridge University Press, 1993), pp. 247–65, quotation, p. 250. Bakhtin employed these multi-authored texts to talk about the transition from the open 'grotesque' and essentially low-cultural female gathering of the childbed – where talking and eating in huge quantities were very much the order of the day – to the post-Renaissance world of 'private' bourgeois manners: Mikhail Bakhtin, *Rabelais and His World* translated by Hélène Iswolsky (Bloomington: Indiana University Press, 1984), pp. 105–6. According to Stanton, this passage reveals not only Bakhtin's gender-blindness in his theoretical writings but also the ideological agenda that underwrites them. Stanton, 'Recuperating Women', p. 248.

16. Margreta de Grazia, in 'Imprints: Shakespeare, Gutenberg, and Descartes', in Terence Hawkes (ed.), *Alternative Shakespeares 2* (London: Routledge, 1996), pp. 63–94, demonstrates how the opposed spaces of the (male) printing house and the (female) birthing room feed into the metaphorical language of early modern drama. Sawday has also drawn lines of connection between representations of the womb in the period and the blank text, the *tabula rasa* of the printing house: see Sawday, *Body Emblazoned*, p. 215.

17. Stanton, 'Recuperating Women', p. 259.

18. Indeed, as David Harley has persuasively argued, we need to revise our reading of women as passive in these matters. Changes in midwifery practice may have been as much due to changes in taste on the part of women as to patriarchal intervention.

19. Marina Warner, *From the Beast to the Blonde: On Fairy Tales and Their Tellers* (London: Chatto and Windus, 1994), p. 33. See also Bernard Capp, 'Separate Domains?: Women and Authority in Early Modern England', in Paul Griffiths, Adam Fox and Steve Hindle (eds), *The Experience of Authority in Early Modern England* (London: Macmillan, 1996), pp. 117–45.

20. Warner, *From the Beast to the Blonde*, p. 33.

21. See my 'Print, Popular Culture, Consumption and Commodification in *The Staple of News*' in Julie Sanders, Kate Chedgzoy and Susan Wiseman (eds), *Refashioning Ben Jonson: Gender, Politics and the Jonsonian Canon* (London: Macmillan, 1998) pp. 183–207.

22. Warner, *From the Beast to the Blonde*, p. 34.

23. See, for example, my '"The Collective Contract is a Fragile Structure": Local Government and Personal Rule in Jonson's *A Tale of a Tub*', *English Literary Renaissance*, 27 (1997), 443–67.

24. *The Magnetic Lady* II.ii.30–2. The edition of the play used is in C. Herford and P. and E. Simpson (eds), *Ben Jonson: The Complete Works*, 11 vols (Oxford: Clarendon Press, 1925–52), Vol VI. Further references to the play are contained in parentheses in the text.

25. See Helen Ostovich, 'The Appropriation of Pleasure in *The Magnetic Lady*', *Studies in English Literature, 1500–1700*, 34 (1994), 425–42. It is

worth noting that the French associations with the trade and the figure of Louise Bourgeois would have had particular relevance in the 1630s when Marie de Medici's daughter, Henrietta Maria, was the Queen Consort of England.

26. See Jim Sharpe, 'Women, Witchcraft, and the Legal Process', in Jenny Kermode and Garthine Walker (eds), *Women, Crime, and the Courts in Early Modern England* (London: UCL Press, 1994), pp. 106–24. See also Malcolm Gaskill, 'Witchcraft and Power in Early Modern England: The Case of Margaret Moore' in the same volume, pp. 125–45.

27. Keith Thomas and Alan Macfarlane's work in the 1970s promulgated the theory that witches were members of the village community who became scapegoats for cultural and financial transitions. Thus, they suggested, villages cast out old, poor, often single women as the support network of poor relief diminished, justifying their action and assuaging their guilt by means of the devil and the supernatural. See Keith Thomas, *Religion and the Decline of Magic* (1971) (Reprinted, Harmondsworth: Penguin, 1991) and Alan Macfarlane, *Witchcraft in Tudor and Stuart England: A Regional and Comparative Study* (London: Routledge and Kegan Paul, 1970). For feminist critiques of that stance, see Marianne Hester, *Lewd Women and Wicked Witches* (London: Routledge, 1992); Anne Llewellyn Barstow, *Witchcraze: A New History of the European Witch Hunts* (New York: Harper Collins, 1994); Annabel Gregory, 'Witchcraft, Politics, and "Good Neighbourhood" in Seventeenth-century Rye', *Past and Present*, 133 (1991), 31–66; Christina Larner, *Witchcraft and Religion: The Politics of Popular Belief* (Oxford: Blackwell, 1984). See also Richard Horsley, 'Who were the Witches? The Social Roles of the Accused in European Witch-trials', *Journal of Interdisciplinary History*, 9 (1979), 714–5; and David Harley, 'Ignorant Midwives: A Persistent Stereotype', *The Society for the Social History of Medicine Bulletin*, 28 (1981), 6–9. Kathleen McLuskie, in *Renaissance Dramatists* (Hemel Hempstead: Harvester Wheatsheaf, 1989) differentiates between high cultural and popular cultural constructions of the witch. See in particular Chapter Three: 'Women and Cultural Production: The Case of Witchcraft', pp. 57–86.

28. See Ann Giardina Hess, 'Midwifery Practice and the Quakers in Southern Rural England in the Late Seventeenth Century', in Hilary Marland (ed.), *The Art of Midwifery* (London: Routledge, 1993), pp. 49–76, quotation p. 88. Jim Sharpe suggests that white magic was prosecuted as frequently as black magic and that twentieth-century accounts of witchcraft are distorted on this point.

29. Purkiss, *The Witch in History*, p. 19.

30. Reproduced in Otten, *English Women's Voices*.

31. Elizabeth Cellier, *To Dr — an Answer to His Queries, Concerning the College of Midwives* (1688), reproduced in Otten, *English Women's Voices*.

32. Otten, *English Women's Voices*, pp. 197–8. See also Sawday's account of this in print terms in *The Body Emblazoned*, p. 215.

33. For the relevance of contemporary discussions of magnetism and *The Magneticall Advertisement* by William Barlow which is directly cited in *The Magnetic Lady* see Ostovich, 'The Appropriation of Pleasure'.
34. The use of the womb and childbirth as a metaphor was a common trope for Renaissance male writers to describe their own art of creation and production. See Katherine Eisaman Maus, 'A Womb of His Own: Male Renaissance Poets in the Female Body', pp. 266–89, in Grantham Turner, *Sexuality and Gender*.
35. Culpeper, *A Directory*, pp. 233–5.

5

Calling Creatures by their True Names: Bacon, the New Science and the Beast in Man

Erica Fudge

And therefore it is not the pleasure of curiosity, nor the quiet of resolution, nor the raising of the spirit, nor victory of wit, nor faculty of speech, nor lucre of profession, nor ambition of honour or fame, nor inablement for business, that are the true ends of knowledge ... but it is a restitution and reinvesting (in great part) to man of the sovereignty and power (for whensoever he shall be able to call the creatures by their true names he shall again command them) which he had in his first state of creation.

Francis Bacon, *Valerius Terminus of the Interpretation of Nature* (1603)[1]

In seventeenth-century ideas of the philosophy of science 'mythic' pronouncements were demonised as unscientific, irrational and vulgar, while induction and experiment were proposed as the new ways of realising human potential and power in the study and control of the natural world. Within this scheme Francis Bacon is regarded as the 'Father' of the new movement, offering, in numerous works, a philosophical basis for future investigative endeavours. It is somehow fitting that this Father should represent the movement of the New Science as being not only from myth to proof, but from infancy to maturity.

'Knowledge is power' is a well-known paraphrase of one of Francis Bacon's aphorisms. What is often forgotten in post-Foucauldian writings is the way in which Bacon asserts that power should be used to change and dominate in very concrete ways: to call the creatures by their real names (as Adam did) is to understand – to 'know' – them; to know the creatures is to wield power over them; and to wield power over them is to remove humans from their 'infantile' place in post-lapsarian society and to return them to their original position of superiority on earth. Power in Bacon's terms, means exploitation, and exploitation is proof of humanity. Within this scheme, experimentation – whether dissection or vivi-section – becomes the ultimate means of exploitation, and, consequently, of domination. The human reduces the animal to the status of an object while increasing his own status. To experiment on animals – a means of understanding, 'naming', them – is to place the human in a God-like position (something which emerges most clearly in Bacon's *New Atlantis*, discussed below). In his work, however, Bacon sets up a notion of humanity which, I will argue, is deeply contradictory: by analogy, the child-like is revealed as absolutely formative in the creation of the adult, but at the same time, the adult – a term which becomes the synonym for the human within Bacon's philosophy – is represented as breaking all links with the child.

This essay examines the method of Francis Bacon's New Science, and relates this to the understanding of non-human animals which can be traced in his works. The denial of the fable, the mythic 'old science', which was vital to the establishment of the New Science, represents a paradox in Bacon's methodology: within his work the fable is analogous with childhood and becomes a dangerous and problematic notion for the scientist. Childhood both defines humanity and reveals humanity's closeness to the animal, and as such this essay argues that Bacon's denial of the learning of childhood represents his inherent failure to separate the human from the animal which is one of the central premises of his scientific endeavour.

I

In Bacon's thought the application of reason, and, by extension, the control of the natural world is what makes a human, and, in order to exist, this application of reason requires an application of his theory: requires, in fact, 'a new birth of science; that is, in raising it regularly up from experience and building it afresh.'[2] The Baconian human is re-born, re-created, if you like, through Bacon's ideas. Tangible proof becomes central and the methods of experimentation are used to avoid the potential failings of the human mind acting alone. Within the mind's three-fold make-up of history/poetry/philosophy[3] (an idea to which I return), the ideal is the application of philosophy which is, implicitly, in Bacon's thought, based on the rationality of proof.

To the immediate and proper perception of the sense therefore I do not give much weight; but I contrive that the office of the sense shall be only to judge of the experiment, and that the experiment itself shall judge of the thing.[4]

The experiment will prevent the exaggeration and myth-making which has occurred in earlier scientific work because experiment offers up nature as she exists:[5]

For I admit nothing but on the faith of eyes, or at least of careful and severe examination; so that nothing is exaggerated for wonder's sake, but what I state is sound and without mixture of fables or vanity.[6]

All of this – Bacon's movement away from fable to experimentation – might appear to have little reference to the place of animals in early modern England, but the implications of this quest for knowledge are of great significance. Bacon states '[h]uman knowledge and human power meet in one'[7], and it is this potential of knowledge which has implications for human-animal relations.

Science, in Bacon's terminology, is about power, and it is power directed over the natural world. In fact, this is the only form of power which Bacon advocates in his scientific writings (in the moral and political works power over other humans is, of course, a central issue). Three different possibilities for the use of science are presented, and two, which represent power over other humans, are dismissed, and only the third is regarded as the true reason for knowledge. The three are: 1. the extension of the power of the individual, 'which kind is vulgar and degenerate'; 2. the extension of the power of one country over others, '[t]his certainly has more dignity, though not less covetousness'; and 3. the extension of the whole of the human race, an ambition 'without doubt both a more wholesome thing and a more noble than the other two'.[8] This is reiterated in other works: in *The New Atlantis* (1627) the intention of Salomon's House – established for 'the study of the Works and Creatures of God' – is clear:

> The End of our Foundation is the knowledge of Causes, and secret motions of things; and the enlarging of the bounds of Human Empire, to the effecting of all things possible.[9]

The Fall caused a massive diminution of human power, and it is the truly religious role of science to restore man's rightful position within the universe.[10] In this way, animals become merely the tools of human inquiry, and, given a spiritual rationale, experimentation on animals could continue, and increase, with little moral questioning:[11]

> most sure it is, and a true conclusion of experience, that a little natural philosophy inclineth the mind to atheism, but a further proceeding bringeth the mind back to religion.[12]

The notion of dominion reverberates throughout Bacon's works. In one of his earliest pieces focusing on natural history, *Valerius Terminus of the Interpretation of Nature* (1603), Bacon places his theory of dominion in specifically biblical terms. His reading of Genesis argues for an original innate and benevolent understanding between the species: 'being in his creation invested with sovereignty of all inferior creatures, he was not needy of power and dominion.'[13] This all changes after the Fall when learning is needed to restore man to his position as sovereign and commander of creation (see quotation at the head of this essay). The fact of naming, of calling creatures by their true names, is a clear recognition by Bacon of the religious implications of the New Science. Bacon is offering a method of returning humanity to its original status. In *The Masculine Birth of Time* (also 1603) this is reiterated in a phrase which sums up the aims of the New Science: 'to stretch the deplorably narrow limits of man's dominion over the universe to their promised bounds ...'.[14] The New Science is presented as a way of restoring humans to their prelapsarian position.

The attempt to extend the limits of human dominion would appear to be a truly democratic and anti-nationalistic endeavour; *all* of humanity is included within Bacon's scheme. However, a close reading of *The New Atlantis* offers a revision of this sense of democracy. Bacon's democratic noises hide (not too well) a clearly élitist reality. Some of the discoveries of Salomon's House are not revealed to outsiders: 'we have consultations, which of the inventions and experiences which we have discovered shall be published, and which not', and even the state itself does not automatically learn all the 'secrets'. Alongside this internal control, the rest of the world, likewise, is not given access to the findings of the College; in fact, the whole of New Atlantis is kept secret from all outsiders, Bacon's narrator is the first to be told the details of the island.[15]

The exercise of power, then, becomes the exercise of power by the few trained in the methods of Baconian science. But this élitism does hide one form of democracy: this power always extends itself over the whole non-human animal world. Indeed, in *The New Atlantis* Bacon presents experimentation which sounds very much like the contemporary practice of genetic engineering: the alteration of appearance and reproductive faculties, the creation of new hybrids.[16] All these interferences with 'God's work' are absolutely central to Bacon's scheme, because here man truly becomes god-like.

In 1608 Bacon implied that this pseudo-divinity was a natural attribute of humanity. In *The Refutation of Philosophies* the speaker states:

> We are agreed, my sons, that you are men. That means, as I think, that you are not animals on their hind legs, but mortal gods. God, the creator of the universe and of you, gave you souls capable of understanding the world ...[17]

It is the word 'capable' which should be emphasised here. It is this *potential* which Bacon is attempting to fulfil. There are two versions of humanity here: the fallen, dangerously animal, unknowing, postlapsarian creature, and the mortal divine.

Once again a distinction between the animal and the human is made, but this time rather half-heartedly via the possession of the soul.[18] But the suggestion that the difference of the human from the animal is based wholly on the soul in Bacon's thought should be regarded as highly questionable. Timothy H. Paterson notes the significance of Bacon's parenthesis in *Valerius Terminus*, 'Immortality (if it were possible) ...', and argues that it might 'suggest a blurring of the distinction between the indefinite prolongation of life and immortality.'[19] Most importantly both for Bacon's argument, and for my own, in the differentiation of the human from the animal the emphasis is laid on the possession of under-standing. Within Bacon's thought the humanist overtones of educa-tion are replaced with the New Science, an endeavour which is once again perceived to be difficult and yet ultimately, and power-fully, worthwhile.

> My dear, dear boy, what I propose is to unite you with *things themselves* in a chaste, holy, and legal wedlock; and from this asso-ciation you will secure an increase beyond all the hopes and prayers of ordinary marriages, to wit, a blessed race of Heroes or Supermen who will overcome the immeasurable helplessness and poverty of the human race, which cause it more destruction than all giants, monsters, or tyrants, and will make you peaceful, happy, prosperous and secure.[20]

In this description the human race and its poverty are left behind and a new race is born – 'a blessed race of Heroes or Supermen'. The sense here is that the New Science will enable the development of the full potential of the race through an understanding and dom-ination of the natural world. In fact, dominion, with its inevitable consequences for the natural world, is *the* means to fulfil human po-tential: the exploitation of animals is a necessity.

Such a role for science was explicitly reproduced in Thomas Sprat's ultra-Baconian *History of the Royal Society* (1667). Here the exercise of power over other humans is placed below the exercise of power over the natural world when Sprat contrasts the endeav-ours of colonialism with the endeavours of science and gives the priority to science. The Royal Society represents at first 'An *Enterprize* equal to the most renoun'd Actions of the best *Princes*', but Sprat goes on to state:

> For, to increase the Powers of all Mankind, and to free them from the bondage of Errors, is greater Glory than to enlarge *Empire*, or to put Chains on the necks of Conquer'd *Nations*.[21]

The actions of the Society's members represent a throwing off of the chains that tie humanity to the baser parts of creation, the baser parts of creation here including some humans themselves.[22]

However, this notion of the removal of the human from the animal through domination and subjugation respectively raises more problems in Bacon's thought. If humanity as it exists in the post-lapsarian world has to improve to reach this status – that is, has to free itself – then its status as human in this process of gaining freedom is questioned and postlapsarian man is closer to the beast than is proposed. The idea of humanity's apparently innate humanness is threatened by the Fall; paradise is always lost.

In *Of the Wisdom of the Ancients* in his interpretation of the myth of Pan, which he reads to signify a vision of the natural world and man's place within it, Bacon states:

> the body of Nature is most truly described as biform: on account of the difference between the bodies of the upper and lower world. For the upper or heavenly bodies are for their beauty and the equability and constancy of their motion, as well as for the influence they have upon earth and all that belongs to it, fitly represented under the human figure: but the others, by reason of their perturbations and irregular motions, and because they are under the influence of the celestial bodies, may be content with the figure of a brute.[23]

This division of the universe into human/constant and animal/irregular hides a complication. Far from offering a pure and totally divided binary, Bacon presents one which has already broken down. The slippage of the terms constant/irregular, and, importantly, human/animal is figured in the term 'biform'. Not only does this term relate to the binary nature of the world, it also presents nature itself as made up of mixed elements:

> there is no nature which can be regarded as simple; everyone seeming to participate and be compounded of two. Man has something of the brute; the brute has something of the vegetable; the vegetable something of the inanimate body; and so all things are truly biformed and made up of a higher species and a lower.[24]

Man is no longer separate, but dwells dangerously close to the animal.

In *The Advancement of Learning* (1605), Bacon divided the 'parts of human understanding' into three, each with its own category of learning: 'History to his Memory, Poesy to his Imagination, and Philosophy to his Reason'.[25] Within this scheme, poetry is viewed as a diversion from the path of true learning, and an application of the weaker human faculty to the work in hand. One element of man is figured as faulty and untrustworthy, and the notion of real learning is constituted by a new interpretation of reason. Rationality is proof of humanity. This division of the human mind against itself creates massive problems within Bacon's ideas. There is an element of the understanding which must be denied, and this element, as he shows in many of his works, is what links the adult with the child he once was. In the desire to separate the species the constant link between the old science and the new science, the child and the adult, and ultimately, the animal and the human re-emerges again and again, and the notion of the rights of human dominion over the natural world are constantly under question. As Brian Klug has noted: 'the animal within us, like the animal outside us, is part of nature: something which human reason should suppress or master.'[26] The freedom proffered by Bacon hides a new form of oppression: the 'beast within', like the beast without must be denied.

II

Bacon's relationship with the fable links his notion of science with his notion of humanity and would appear to be straightforward: in 'The Plan' of *The Great Instauration* (1620) he remarks that 'fables and superstitions and follies which nurses instil into children do serious injury to their minds.'[27] The vulgar (it is the nurse and not the parent who passes on the fables) imprint vulgar ideas on the formative mind, and the damage is almost irrecoverable:

> No one has yet been found so firm of mind and purpose as resolutely to compel himself to sweep away all theories and common notions, and to apply the understanding, thus made fair and even, to a fresh examination of particulars. Thus it happens that human knowledge, as we have it, is a mere medley and ill-digested mass, made up of much credulity and much accident, and also of the childish notions which we at first imbibed.[28]

A similar idea had been stated earlier in *Thoughts and Conclusions on the Interpretation of Nature or a Science of Productive Works* (1604), where Bacon wrote,

> [i]nfants as they learn to speak necessarily drink in a wretched hotch-potch of traditional error. And however much men as they

advance in wisdom and learning ... they can never shake off the yoke.[29]

As a corrective, Bacon advocates a deliberate, and conscious, move away from medieval works of natural history, such as bestiaries, Albertus Magnus's *Book of Secrets*, Alexander Neckam's *De Naturis Rerum*, and attempts to create a new, more empirically based science.[30] Taking off from sixteenth-century works by, among others, Conrad Gesner and William Turner,[31] Bacon attempts to provide a new methodology for the examination of the natural world, an examination which, in his works, has massive implications for the place and status of humanity.

The reasons which Bacon gives for his attack on fables are simple: the 'Idols of the Theatre', as he calls received ideas in *Novum Organum*, represent reality like the playhouse stage – 'worlds of their own creation after unreal and scenic fashion'.[32] This is figured as childlike, and it is the job of the scientist to understand and control nature as she exists in reality, not in fiction: 'it is not good to stay too long in the theatre.'[33] The fable and the myth represent for Bacon sham philosophy: in *Thoughts on Human Knowledge* written in 1604 he states:

> a Natural History resting on insufficient research and insufficient testing begets two faults and, as it were, two diseases or corruptions of theory. The first results in sophistry, the second in poetry. Take first a man, who, on the basis of commonplace observations, constructs a specious theoretical system and relies for the rest exclusively on his discursive and argumentative ingenuity. His discoveries may be so fortunate as to win a great reputation, but he himself is nothing more than a survivor of the old school. Take again a man who conducts a thorough and carefully controlled investigation of the portion of the field. If he is puffed up by this and allows his imagination free play he may be led to interpret the whole nature after the pattern of the little bit he knows. His philosophy then passes into the realms of fancy or dreaming and consigns him to the category of the poet.

The scientific endeavour must be carried out accurately for it to have any real meaning. If other methods are used, natural history becomes 'as unstable as water and as gusty as wind'.[34]

The rejection of the sense of the inherent truth of ancient learning is central to Bacon's philosophy; 'generally speaking science is to be sought from the light of nature, not from the darkness of antiquity.'[35] The so-called ancients are reinterpreted by Bacon as the exact opposite – '[f]or the old age of the world is to be accounted the true antiquity; and this is the attribute of our own times, not of that earlier age of the world in which the ancients lived': the moderns are the real ancients.[36] This, however, is merely academic: as he notes in *Novum Organum*, 'truth is to be sought for not in the felicity of any age, which is an unstable thing, but in the light of nature and experience, which is eternal'.[37] It is the method and not the period which gives a work its real significance, but the idea of the increased age of his own time over the ancients can be seen as a reiteration of the notion of maturity which he proposes as part of the endeavour of the New Science.

In works of scientific enquiry, Bacon would therefore appear to be proposing a straightforward dismissal of the role of fables, but in *Of The Wisdom of the Ancients* (1609) he presents a very different view of the role of fables and myths. In this work he argues that

> the truth is that in some of these fables, as well in the very frame and texture of the story as in the propriety of the names by which the persons that figure in it are distinguished, I find a conformity and connection with the thing signified, so close and so evident, that one cannot help believing such a signification to have been designed and mediated from the first, and purposely shadowed out.[38]

Fables bear a hidden truth which Bacon is able to uncover, a notion which is an overturning of the interpretation of the role of fables which appeared in *The Advancement of Learning* in 1605 where he argued that

> I do rather think that the fable was first, and the exposition devised, than that the moral was first, and thereupon the fable framed ... but yet that all the fables and fictions of the poets were but pleasure and not figure.[39]

This change of mind was noted by one seventeenth-century commentator on Bacon: in *Mythomystes* (1632) Henry Reynolds, in a defence of the fabling tradition in English poetry, says of Bacon:

> What shall we make of such willing contradictions, when a man to vent a few fancies of his owne shall tell vs first, they are the

wisdome of the Auncients, and next, that those Auncient fables
were but meere fables, and without wisdom or meaning til their
expositours gaue them a meaning.[40]

For Paolo Rossi, a twentieth-century critic, this change of heart is to
be regarded as an evolution of Bacon's ideas.[41] This fails to acknowledge Bacon's re-assertion of the unscientific nature of mythic ideas
which appear in works which not only precede, but also follow *Of
The Wisdom of the Ancients*, not least in *Preparative Towards a Natural
and Experimental History* (1620) where they are dismissed as 'slight
and almost superfluous'.[42] To search for an unequivocal development in Bacon's thought is obviously more problematic that Rossi
allows for.

In a more recent study Timothy H. Paterson offers another interpretation which posits that *Of the Wisdom of the Ancients* is 'radically
insincere' and that Bacon's 'belief in the real existence of such
"ancient wisdom" [is] wholly and deliberately feigned.'[43] This, as
Paterson notes, is something which most critics might shy away
from, arguing: 'the very possibility of radical authorial irony or
insincerity' is a direct attack on our notion of the author as a source
of meaning.[44] If Bacon is being insincere then it is for the interpreter
to recognise the place of this text in the Bacon canon, just as it is for
the Baconian investigator to recognise the place of the non-human
in the creation; to 'be able to call the creatures by their true names'.
There is an application of reason required: the interpreter of
the Baconian text is recognising the realities of Bacon's meaning, in
the same way that the scientist is recognising God's meaning in the
natural world.

In *Of the Wisdom of the Ancients* Bacon interprets classical myths as
revealing meanings which back-up his scientific endeavour, but he
also argues that the fable 'will follow any way you please to draw
it', that 'meanings which it was never meant to bear may be plausi-
bly put upon it.'[45] Such contradictions lead Paterson to claim that

it seems to me simpler, far more plausible, and more consistent
with Bacon's obvious stature as a thinker to assume that he
always meant what he said in speaking of the pretended existence of ancient wisdom as primarily a means of adding prestige
to his own thoughts through a conscious deception, and that he
wrote *Wisdom of the Ancients* intending precisely that deception of
many of his readers.[46]

Bacon, recognising the continuing power of ancient ideas, interprets them – ironically, within the context of his other works – to back up his own ideas about the role of natural history in society. In this text fables literally 'serve to disguise and veil the meaning, and they serve also to clear and throw light upon it'[47]; 'infantile' notions are presented as both useless and useful, and it is for the reader to recognise the irony of this duplicity.

If Paterson's notion of the irony of *Of the Wisdom of the Ancients* is correct then this text must be read as a contradictory document: it contains a recognition of the pervasiveness of the learning of the ancients, of fables, a recognition of interpretation as both a maturing and humanising skill, and, paradoxically, a call to move away from such poor science. Paterson cannot but offer the work as ironic in his attempt to view Bacon's complete works as consistent. I want to argue, however, that the confusion over the place of the fable represents the confusion over the issue which Bacon places as analogous to the fable: childhood.

As has been noted, Bacon saw childhood as playing a crucial role in the creation of the adult intellect, but childhood was, more often than not, abusive to human potential. As Leah Sinanoglou Marcus has noted, 'many intellectuals viewed the new science with alarm: to follow it they were obliged to undergo the painful process of cutting off their own mental roots, of wrenching apart a continuum from childhood belief to its adult elaboration.'[48] This is where a contradiction emerges in Bacon's thought: if the analogy of the fable and childhood is extended, the dismissal of the fable from the New Science is parallelled in the dismissal of childhood in the formation of the adult. The reasons why such a dismissal is made are central to this essay, as they present the most important implications of Bacon's work within the context of human-animal relations in the early modern period, and offer up a site of significance in seventeenth-century culture where the attempts to separate the human from the animal break down.

III

The child was often placed alongside the animal in discussions of education. Leah Sinanoglou Marcus notes that 'As early as an Anglo-Saxon school-book, children asked why they desire learning reply, "Because we do not want to be like beasts, who know nothing but grass and water"; and as late as a fifteenth-century text, boys are still repeating, "Withoute connyng we ar as rude bestes which know not goode fro evyll".'[49] By 1617 Puritan despair over the status of postlapsarian humanity made the link even more explicit and inevitable: John Moore asked;

> How full of ignorance is the time of our infancie? how light and wanton are wee, growing to be striplings? how rash and head-long is the time of our youth? ... What is an infant but a bruit beast in the shape of a man? and what is a young youth but (as it were) a wilde untamed Asse-colt unbridled?[50]

Education was figured as necessary and as the duty of the parent: William Gouge argued that 'God hath laid it as a charge upon parents, that they should see their children well trained up.'[51] It is vital that the child leave the animality of childhood and emerge as a good adult. The link between the two stages of human develop-ment – between the child and the adult – is obviously (and un-avoidably) there, and yet the link is shown as requiring more than the mere existence of nature. Just as in Bacon's model of science where the adult must be re-educated so that the fables – the imagin-ative ideas – which are instilled during childhood are removed in order to leave room for the scientific endeavour to take root, so in contemporary attitudes to children there was a sense in which the things of childhood were animal-like and had to be trained out of the child in order that the child become an adult. Gouge states;

> Too much sport maketh [children] wilde, rude, unfit to be trained up to any good calling, and spendeth their spirits, and wasteth their strength too much. Yet many parents care not how much time their children spend in sport, and how little in learning: they thinke it duls their children too much to bee held to schoole, or to any learning: whereas indeed too much play infatuates them more, and learning would much sharpen their wits.[52]

The child must be introduced into adult society through learning or through work, but both entries of the child into the world of their parents reveal the difficulty of the move. The child does not automatically, naturally become an adult, such a process requires nurture, requires training. With this sense of the child's difference from the adult comes a sense of danger: as Keith Thomas writes;

We accept that playing is a natural stage in a child's development and are not usually in a hurry to accelerate the process of growing up. But in the early modern period it was more usual to feel that children's play was at best a waste of time and at worst a very bad preparation for adult life.[53]

The separation of the adult from the child which is implicit in Bacon's scientific theory – traceable through the analogous relation of the fable (bad science) with childhood (bad human) – is made explicit in his essay 'Of Parents and Children'. But here Bacon links the dangers of childhood to adult lack of knowledge in another way:

> The perpetuity by generation is common to beasts; but memory, merit, and noble works are proper to men: and surely a man shall see the noblest works and foundations have proceeded from childless men, which have sought to express the images of their minds, where those of their bodies have failed: so the care of posterity is most in them that have no posterity. They that are the first raisers of their houses are most indulgent towards their children; beholding them as the continuance not only of their kind but of their work; and so both children and creatures.[54]

The posterity of ideas, the 'noblest works', are given only to those without a biological posterity. The child is seen in this essay (like the fable in his scientific writings) as a distraction from the true exercise of humanity. The child is a creature.

Bacon's theory of the destructive role of the child is, of course, hardly a commonplace one in the period, and he does acknowledge that, for many, children are a true pleasure, that parents are 'indulgent'.[55] Such an idea can be traced in a less negative way in the writings of some of Bacon's contemporaries, where, far from representing the child as a distraction, it is for many the desired posterity. William Gouge argued that 'the Lord hath given [children] to parents as an inheritance', Anne Bradstreet saw her children as 'my dear remains', while Ben Jonson wrote in memory of his dead son;

> Rest in soft peace, and, asked, say here doth lie
> Ben Jonson his best piece of poetry.[56]

For these writers children represented the parents' true fulfilment on earth and were not, as Bacon proposes, the distraction from that fulfilment. The unnaturalness of Bacon's proposals for natural philosophy become clear.

So within Bacon's writings there are two dangers to be found in the idea of childhood. In his scientific writings the child represents a stage of humanity which must be dismissed in order that true humanity (which is achieved, and expressed through the gaining of knowledge, and through the exercise of power over the natural world) can be reached. In the essay 'Of Parents and Children', on the other hand, it is not the adult's place as a (former) child which is regarded as endangering and undermining the endeavours of the New Science, it is the distraction of raising the child to be an adult which is destructive.

Within this contradiction it is unsurprising that, as he writes in *Novum Organum*, 'No one has yet been found so firm' as to truly remove themselves from the learning of the past – 'all theories and common notions' – because that learning is so completely, for Bacon, tied up with childhood. The child presents Bacon with a no-win situation: the child is an inevitable and natural stage of human existence, even though childhood seriously compromises Bacon's ideals of adult existence, but training – raising the child to be a good adult, removing it from the potential for beastliness – is itself destructive of the adult's potential for achieving his 'noblest works'.

Within Bacon's scientific writings the child is placed with imagination, the adult with reason, and this is perhaps, where the contradiction in *Of the Wisdom of the Ancients* exists: Bacon had aligned fables with childhood, and wanted to excise fables from the New Science. His analogy complicated this. To deny fables was implicitly to deny the link between the child and the adult, a denial which was massively problematic in a number of ways; of course the child and the adult it became were linked, and it is the role of the adult to ensure that this link is the right one.

Bacon's way around the contradiction was to offer the fable/child as having some deeply hidden relation to the development of science/adult, a link which would only ever bolster the methodology of the New Science:

> I find a conformity and connection with the thing signified, so close and so evident, that one cannot help believing such a signification to have been designed and mediated from the first ...[57]

In this sense *Of the Wisdom of the Ancients* is not a text of authorial irony, or deliberate authorial contradiction, it is a text which is needed within the establishment of Bacon's scientific ideas because it responds to and allows for the analogy of the fable and the child. Within this text some of the problems which Bacon creates for himself are explored: the fable is part of science, just as the child is part of humanity. But the fable is a hidden form, unlike science which is ultimately visible – '[f]or I admit nothing but on the faith of eyes' – and the child remains somehow both outside of and a part of the ideal Baconian human: it remains a natural animal, but a potential (hidden) human.

Within the logic of his ideas, while setting up the possibility of human perfection based on human separation from the natural world, Bacon was unable to remove the human link to that world. Proving a satisfactory difference between the species, a Baconian ideal, was, then, proving almost impossible. Biformity might mean a state of binary oppositions in the universe, but it was also an admission of the closeness of the beast. To 'call the creatures by their true names' was to exercise reason and dominion over them and to be fully human, but to call humans by their true names was to recognise the animality of humanity. Ultimately, and inescapably, Bacon's man, despite all of the proposals within his scientific works, would always be at least part animal. The border which Bacon created to separate the human from the beast ultimately reveals the inseparability of the species.

Notes

1.   In *The Works of Francis Bacon*, ed. James Spedding, Robert Leslie Ellis and Douglas Denon Heath, (1859), (Reprinted, Stuttgart: Friedrich Frommann, 1963), III, p. 222.
2.   Bacon, *Works*, IV, p. 94.
3.   See Bacon, *The Advancement of Learning*, (1605), in *Works*, III, p. 329.
4.   Bacon, *Works*, IV, p. 26.
5.   Referring to nature as 'she' – Mother Nature – is an important part of the representation of the scientific endeavour in Bacon's writing: understanding is often closely aligned with rape, subordination and domination. See Carolyn Merchant, *The Death of Nature: Women, Ecology and the Scientific Revolution* (London: Harper Row, 1980).
6.   Bacon, *Works*, IV, p. 30.
7.   Bacon, *Works*, IV, p. 47.
8.   Bacon, *Works*, IV, p. 114.
9.   Bacon, *Works*, III, p. 156.
10. Charles Webster has noted the puritan support for Bacon's ideas:

the Calvinist God was distant and inscrutable, but the patient and accurate methods of experimental science, penetrating slowly towards an understanding of the secondary causes of things in the search for a gradual reconquest of nature, represented the form of intellectual and practical endeavour most suited to the puritan mentality.

Webster, *The Great Instauration: Science, Medicine and Reform 1626–1660* (London: Duckworth, 1975), p. 506.

11. In this way Robert Boyle's personal debate about animals and his rights to use them as experimental tools places Bacon's ideas within a very important framework. Boyle recognises the potentially questionable act of putting a sentient creature through painful experiences, but can defend, and reassert his rights to do this through the claim that he is carrying out a religious inquiry. See Malcolm R. Oster, '"The Beame of Divinity": Animal Suffering in the Early Thought of Robert Boyle', *British Journal for the History of Science*, 22:2 (1989), 151–179.

12. Bacon, *Works*, III, p. 217.

13. Bacon, *Works*, III, p. 217.

14. In Benjamin Farrington, *The Philosophy of Francis Bacon: An Essay on its Development from 1603 to 1609 with New Translations of Fundamental Texts* (Liverpool: Liverpool University Press, 1964), p. 62.

15. Bacon, *Works*, III, p. 165.

16. Bacon, *Works*, III, p. 159.

17. Bacon, in Farrington, *Philosophy of Francis Bacon*, p. 106.

18. The problem of using the soul as the distinguishing characteristic of humanity is the subject of Michael Newton's essay in this collection.

19. Timothy H. Paterson, 'Bacon's Myth of Orpheus: Power as a Goal of Science in *Of the Wisdom of the Ancients*', *Interpretation*, 16:3 (1989), 434.

20. Bacon in Farrington, *Philosophy of Francis Bacon*, p. 72.

21. Thomas Sprat, *The History of the Royal Society* (1667), (Reprinted, London: Routledge, 1966), 'Epistle Dedicatory', n.p.

22. Once again, however, the presentation of the Royal Society as an organisation which aimed to free humanity disguised a highly élitist institution. Restrictions on membership were based predominantly on economic rather than intellectual arguments and thus excluded many: see, Michael Hunter, *The Royal Society and its Fellows 1660–1700: The Morphology of an Early Scientific Institution* (Chalfont St Giles: British Society for the History of Science, 1982), p. 8.

23. Bacon, *Works*, VI, p. 170.

24. Bacon, *Works*, VI, pp. 710–11.

25. Bacon, *Works*, III, p. 329.

26. Brian Klug, 'Lab Animals, Francis Bacon and the Culture of Science', *Listening*, 18 (1983), 66.

27. Bacon, *Works*, IV, p. 30.

28. Bacon, *Works*, IV, p. 93.

29. Bacon in Farrington, *Philosophy of Francis Bacon*, p. 74. This emphasis on the role of childhood in the formation of the human mind is

repeated in many of Bacon's works: see, for instance, *Valerius Terminus*, III, p. 231.

30. In his poem, 'To the Royal Society' Abraham Cowley regards Bacon as a Moses figure, leading his people to the promised land. He writes;

> Bacon *at last, a mighty Man, arose,*
> *Whom a wise King and Nature chose*
> *Lord Chancellour of both their Laws,*
> *And boldly undertook the injur'd Pupils caus.*

Old learning is injurious, the New Science will correct the hurts of the past. Bacon is figured as a prophet, a teacher, and, perhaps, a father figure. Cowley, in Sprat, *History of the Royal Society* sigs.B2ᵛ and B1ᵛ.

31. For discussions of the significance of the work of Gesner and Turner, see: Whitney R. D. Jones, *William Turner: Tudor Naturalist, Physician and Divine* (London: Routledge, 1988); Charles E. Raven, *English Naturalists From Neckam to Ray: a Study of the Making of the Modern World* (revised edition, London: Abelard and Schuman, 1959); and Keith Thomas, *Man and the Natural World: Changing Attitudes in England 1500–1800* (London: Penguin, 1983), pp. 51–91.

32. Bacon, *Works*, IV, p. 55.

33. Bacon, *Works*, III, p. 346.

34. Bacon in Farrington, *Philosophy of Francis Bacon*, pp. 41–2.

35. Bacon in Farrington, *Philosophy of Francis Bacon*, p. 69.

36. Bacon, *Works*, IV, p. 82.

37. Bacon, *Works*, IV, p. 60.

38. Bacon, *Works*, VI, p. 696.

39. Bacon, *Works*, III, p. 345.

40. Henry Reynolds, *Mythomystes, Wherein a Short Survay is taken of the Natvre and Valve of Trve Poesy and Depth of the Ancients above ovr Moderne Poets* (1632), in J. E. Springarn (ed.), *Critical Essays of the Seventeenth Century: Vol I 1605–1650* (Oxford: Clarendon, 1908), p. 177.

41. Paolo Rossi, *Francis Bacon: From Magic to Science*, translated by Sacha Rabinovitch (London: Routledge, 1968). Rossi states that

> [t]he elusive ambiguity of Bacon's attitude to classical mythology derives then: from the value he attributed to fables as a means of popularising his plan for scientific reform; from his belief in ancient, forgotten wisdom that must be recaptured; and from his notion of the fable as a primitive form of expressions used by an uncivilised humanity incapable of rational thought. And this confluence of variously inspired motives can only be reconciled in the light of Bacon's pragmatism. (pp. 127–8)

42. Bacon, *Works*, IV, p. 255.

43. Paterson, 'Bacon's Myth of Orpheus', 429.

44. Paterson, 'Bacon's Myth of Orpheus', 430.

45. Bacon, *Works*, VI, p. 695.

46. Paterson, 'Bacon's Myth of Orpheus', 430.

47. Bacon, *Works*, VI, p. 698.
48. Leah Sinanoglou Marcus, *Childhood and Cultural Despair: A Theme and Variations in Seventeenth-Century Literature* (Pittsburgh: University of Pittsburgh Press, 1978), pp. 92–3.
49. Marcus, *Childhood and Cultural Despair*, p. 11.
50. John Moore, *A Mappe of Mans Mortalitie* (1617), p. 43.
51. William Gouge, *Of Domesticall Duties* (1634), p. 449.
52. Gouge, *Of Domesticall Duties*, pp. 536–7.
53. Keith Thomas, 'Children in Early Modern England', in Gillian Avery and Julia Briggs (eds), *Children and Their Books: A Celebration of the Work of Iona and Peter Opie* (Oxford: Clarendon, 1989) p. 63.
54. Bacon, *Works*, IV, pp. 390–1.
55. For a useful summary of the historical debates about parent-child relations in pre-industrial society see Linda A. Pollock, *Forgotten Children: Parent–Child Relations from 1500 to 1900* (Cambridge: Cambridge University Press, 1983), especially pp. 1–67.
56. Gouge, *Of Domesticall Duties*, p. 457; Anne Bradstreet, 'Before the Birth of one of her Children', in Germaine Greer *et al.* (eds), *Kissing the Rod: An Anthology of 17th Century Women's Verse* (London: Virago, 1988), p. 135, line 22; Ben Jonson, 'On My First Son' (1603), in George Parfitt (ed.), *Ben Jonson: The Complete Poems* (London: Penguin, 1975), p. 48, lines 9–10.
57. Bacon, *Works*, VI, p. 696.

6

Cartographic Arrest: Harvey, Raleigh, Drayton and the Mapping of Sense

Stephen Speed

> Just as in a very small commonwealth [there is] the same judge, king, adviser, so in larger they are separate, and politicians [can acquire] many examples from our art.
>
> William Harvey[1]

The body, the body corporeal, was for many the chosen metaphor for the experience of the English early modern world. In its commonplace details, its mutable features and significances, its elaborate evidence of universal tendencies and local distinctions, the figure of the body, as both a real and imaginary entity, provided a ready map for reading, interpreting and comprehension. Yet the very idea of a map, with its implicit dependence upon the survey of a stable terrain, fixed referents and measurement, seems to contradict the palpable flux and fluidity of life. Maps are full of references and indications but they are not peopled. In order to get around an actual body, to explore its viscera, its textures and tissues, a map was certainly needed by the seventeenth-century anatomist. But that intellectual orientation, that kind of 'mental map', no more than a text or an illustration would have exhausted the reality that would be confronted in the Anatomy Theatre.[2] A mental map, as with any map, implies a rationalisation of space and of time: its signs and images are also temporal indices. It permits the grasping of an outline, a shape, some sort of location, but not the contexts, customs, histories, languages, experiences, hopes and desires that course through the body, even after death. The latter would have pierced the logic of topography and spilt over the edges of the anatomist's 'map'.

Beyond those edges, and abstract, one-dimensional indications, the space of the vibrant, everyday world and its challenge of complexity was to be acknowledged, however, by William Harvey: 'Anatomy [is] philosophical, medical, mechanical.'[3] From within that world he would discover the gendered body, the body of ethnicity, the material particle of a particular social formation, of a shifting embodiment and periphery of power, of culture, of discourse: the body that was both a fixed object of anatomical design ('The body is divided') and simultaneously topographical and historical: the site of transitory events, movements, memories. This was also a significant space for analysis, critical thought and comprehension. I want to use this essay to reflect on this space and the opportunities that I believe it provided for Harvey – and for fellow 'mental mappers' like Walter Raleigh and Michael Drayton – in reconsidering the scope and sense of early modern cultural discourse. In particular, I want to suggest how social and cultural sense became not a goal but a discourse, not a closure but a trace in an endless passage of critical thought that could only aspire to a temporary arrest, to a self-conscious drawing of a limit across the diverse possibilities of the contemporary world.

The idea of both lived and intellectual complexity, of Edgar Morin's '*La pensée complexe*', introduces the notion of a social ecology of being and knowledge.[4] Here both thought and everyday activities move in the realm of uncertainty: linear argument and certainty break down. Harvey found himself orbiting in a perpetual paradox around the wheel of being: sense could be bestowed on the body, a 'solid and certain knowledge', yet certainty would remain unguaranteed: '[T]ake on trust nothing that I say of the generation of animals.'[5] The experience of cultural complexity, most sharply on display in the baroque patterns of Harvey's lecture notes – the *Prelectiones anatomie unversalis* (1616-?) – weakened established schemata and paradigms concerning the body; it destabilised and decentred existing knowledges and theories. The narrow arrow of linear progress that was elsewhere fired by Francis Bacon was here detoured by the open spiral of hybrid signs, perceptions, inscriptions, and what Luke Wilson has assessed Harvey's *Prelectiones* as having amounted to: 'an accumulation of data and an induction of universals from particulars, a hypothesizing and testing of hypotheses – a presentation continually modifying itself in its very act of presentation.'[6] It was a corporeality that was multiformed, heterogeneous, diasporic. The body provoked a creative disorder, an instructive confusion, an interpolating space in which the imagination carried the anatomist in every direction, even towards the previously unthought. There, in the anatomy theatre, in the dissonance and interrogation that lay between what Donna Haraway has called 'situated' and 'disembodied' knowledges, the very location of history would be disturbed.[7]

I DISSONANCE AND HISTORY

[T]hus acid humors, acid *sawces*; wherefore if too much heartburn, pains, fainting, vertogo, epilepsy, &c.; wherefore in me myself nausea and sneezing; wherefore fever little increased in epilepsy; wherefore hiccuping from absorbed or compressed humor; wherefore *Sir William Rigdon all yelleow*; wherefore *J. simpson of Chalis*, detention of spirit; wherefore Sal[amon] Albert[i] *from compression of the ribs*. **WH** Sneezing; wherefore by valetudinarian diet of lessened sharpness; many are always complaining; *Lady Croft*. In certain ones by voluntary motion: *porcupin hedghog turkey cocktoo, ruff Bird in ye Ballat*. In men: in wakefulness; early in the morning, *lord how you look as gamesters, sick leane dog, Begger sick*; the hair arose in horror. Hence use of mordicative medicines against dry ulcers.
8, Sensitivity: in man especially for pudendum, root of penis, nipples where &c.
Two notable nerves, *Nan gunter &c.*; I believe had produced a callous: the *mad woman pins in her arme; Mary pin her cross-cloth; beginning with the* incantation *as* boys in palm in the hand.

William Harvey[8]

Hiccuping from an 'absorbed and compressed humor' is caused by the spleen dilating: it leads 'in me myself [to] nausea and sneezing ... wherefore *Sir William Rigdon all yelleow*'. He suffered from jaundice due to a biliary obstruction by gall stones followed by infection. Sir William Rigden, of Dowsby, Lincolnshire, was born in 1558 and knighted on 23 July 1603. His will, dated 25 October 1610, was proved on 20 November 1610, so that he must have died between those dates. His executor and heir was his son Robert, who entered Cambridge in 1605, married Mary, the daughter of John Argent, and died 12 May 1657. Argent (*c.* 1560–1643), MD (Cantab.), 1595, was fellow of the College of Physicians, 1597, and President from 1625 to 1633. To him, in his official capacity as President too, and as 'the writer's particular friend', Harvey dedicated his *De motu cordis* (1628), stating that he had 'for nine years or more confirmed it [the circulation of the blood] in your presence by numerous ocular demonstrations'[9]: '*Sir William Rigdon*' signifies a difference, a particular history and context, a cultural and linguistic ambiguity.

There are animals too: '*in a frogg* only the throat is touched' by a sneeze, while for a '*porcupin hedghog turkey cocktoo, ruff Bird in ye Ballat*', 'voluntary motion' occurs when stimulated. The ruff-bird (*machetes pagnax L.*) is described as a game-bird by Thomas Browne. During the spring months the male has a handsome ruff of feathers round its neck which it can erect or depress at pleasure; 'Ballat' is an old spelling of 'ballad'; *Lord how you look like gamesters'* refers to the exhausted appearance of men who have spent the night gaming; '*sick leane dog, Begger sick*' playfully invokes a discourse of expenditure; '*Lady Croft*' was the wife of Sir James Croft, KT., of St Osyth, Essex, a pensioner of Queen Elizabeth's bodyguard and grandson of the Controller of the Queen's Household ('*Lady Croft*' died of nervous exhaustion); '*J. simpson of Chalis*' died from the 'detention of spirit' in the spleen; 'Sal[amon] Albert[i]' died 'from compression of the ribs' (the reference comes from 'Themica medica: de singultu', in *Tres Orationes* (Nuremberg, 1595); '*Nan gunter*' is Anne Gunter, who claimed to have been bewitched. It was a celebrated case in London in 1604–5 and the subject of official investigation by the College of Physicians. Drs Wilkinson, Dunne and John Argent led the investigation, before the Star Chamber, and James I took over. It is here in the *Prelectiones*, in the anecdotal chit-chat and splintered reportage of everyday life, that voices and stories from different temporalities and cultures become mixed up and written down. Most of the references are to well-known deceased and to objects of curiosity, revisionary criticisms of Galen and Aristotle, in praise of Vesalius ('visionary teacher'). These are supplemented by reminiscences and references derived from personal experience and culled from other texts. The bulk of the writing is in Latin, with occasional phrases in formal English, and much in colloquialism. It is a mélange of detail that stretches from Greece to England, from Padua to Tyburn, from the nausea of its writer to the jaundice of a deceased patient. Composed of connective rhythms and local inflections, the *Prelectiones* propose instances of blending, re-blending, translating and transforming a shared tonality into particular voices and situations. They help to articulate the dissonance of the experiences of a particular time and place: to be alive *and* to be dead, to be an anatomist *and* to be a body.

Such examples, easily found in similar but distinct passages in the *Prelectiones*, do not suggest a neat integration with an existing College hegemony or the mainstream of seventeenth-century culture, but rather with the shifting, mixing, contaminating, experimenting, revisiting and recomposing that the wider horizons and the intra-cultural networks of everyday life both permit and encourage. They present the dialectical connection of certain social constructs with certain syntaxes of discourse which in turn impel irresistible signs of the transformation of social reality.

II   TO TRACE A DESIGN

Yf I could shew what I hav seen yt weare att an end between physicians and philosophers.

William Harvey[10]

The labyrinthine and vertiginous quality of everyday life not only led to the particular cultural and linguistic connections of the *Prelectiones*. It also undermined the presumed purity of thought of a particular tradition of learning. In entertaining this encounter, and thereby abandoning a distanced monologue for more immediate dialogue, Harvey's thinking curved downwards into the everyday world and a different register. To 'travel' in this zone without charts was for a self-styled 'discoverer',[11] to experience dislocation and a lack of intellectual mastery of the body/world: '[How] unsafe, and base, a thing it is to be tutored by other men's commentaries without making trial of the things themselves.'[12] The illusions of cultural and personal identity long organised around the privileged voice of Galenic orthodoxy would become swept up and broken down in a movement of self-discovery that could not yet, however, permit the Cartesian institution of self-identity between thought and reality.

To inhabit this world, intellectually and culturally, individually and socially, is as Bacon put it, to struggle to continue in its continuation: crucial to 'the uses of human life' is not an opinion to be held, but a work to be done.[13] The discoverer does not dominate in thought , but lets go and loses himself in order to explore and find parts of that uncharted self: here 'Nature herself must be our adviser; the path she chalks must be our walk.'[14] This may open up the possibility of an eventual inertia of the masculinist 'I', of a Baconian severity of identity coherence, but it more immediately leads to the amplification of diverse voices, an encounter with an *other* side, and 'since Nature's book is so open and legible' – negates the possibility of reducing diversity to the identical.[15] At the same time, and in a crucial sense, knowledge takes a holiday, a sabbatical, from ideas of truth and meaning as unitary and transcendental entities. Against the virility of a self-assured, strong thought where, as Bacon says, true discoverers 'propose not to devise, mimic, and fabulate worlds of their own, but to examine and dissect the nature of this very world itself', the *Prelectiones* suggest a weaker mode of thinking about the body that though empirical is, all the same, multi-directional, transitive and permeable.[16]

The intellectual condemnation by William Harvey of traditional epistemology, although more subdued than Bacon, is still withering: the renunciation of anatomical drawings which predecessors such as Vesalius, Piccolomini, Laurentius and Bauhin had pragmatically supported; the rejection of the 'reading of books' and the 'opinions of philosophers'.[17] Given here is the impression not of coming closer to the truth of the body, but to a neurosis (or the diagnosis of a neurosis). Still, there remains the critique of those knowledge formations as amounting to 'deceitful eidola' and 'vain fancies' or, more strongly, as 'sick men's fantasies'.[18] The most salient features of that critique are: that representation and argument are tainted by 'equivocation',[19] and that it produces (as Bacon argues) 'a false representation of the reality.'[20] *Tradition* can no longer provide for the truth, only a diversion; it has been reduced to a discourse of abstraction, (rituals, rites, protocols) blindly absorbed in the implications of precedence.

To this Harvey can oppose some countervailing observations: sensory experience is the web in which people are embedded and in which the sense, the truth of their being, is revealed by their eyes: thus the false assertions of the past 'instantly vanish like phantoms of the night when the light of anatomical dissection dawns upon them.'[21] There, in the Theatre, 'the Reader himself, with his own eyes, shall discover the contrary by ocular inspection and find that contrary conformable to reason.'[22] In this way, the rational justification of the empiricist logic and project, suitably translated into subjectivist terms of autopsia, involves a shattering of tradition and the secularisation of knowledge. This, in turn, leads to a concentrated reception in which all in the Theatre become anatomists – acquire 'experience and skill in anatomy' – and learn to move around the inside languages of the body.[23] It leads to a potential democratisation of the use of signs and images, and the space for an unexpected politics of critical thought and the body.[24]

The Harveian critique of traditional epistemology reveals it as being ultimately concerned with the philosophical fate of Man (*sic*) and the distillation of the body in the abstract. It has little to say about how *real* anatomists are getting by and making sense of the *real* body in the seventeenth century; about how sense is being grasped from what can be seen, touched and physically transformed. Invariably presented by its adherents as a homogeneous totality, without contradictions or room for subtle, subaltern or alternative voices, tradition cannot speak to the actual intentions, aims, hopes, desires and fears involved in using and constructing a sense about the body.

But what if contradictions lie not between tradition and Harvey's 'new and if I mistake not [...] surer path to the attainment of knowledge', but in the very conditions of the culture and society that permit them to co-exist?[25] This is what Harvey seems to be saying when he insists that his 'new' and 'surer path' has emerged out of the old, as internal contradictions have led to new developments, new possibilities and a widened intercourse between those caught up in the social relations of everyday life. He writes,

> It has pleased me to set down these things as a foretaste so that you may understand by what helps I myself was assisted and upon what considerations I was induced to communicate to the world my observations and experiments; and that you yourself, treading the same path, may be able not only to be an impartial umpire between Galen and Aristotle, but also, laying aside all cavillings and verisimilar conjectures, that you may find out many things as yet unrevealed to others, and perchance more precious, by embracing the practice of viewing Nature with your own eyes.[26]

This proposes a step away from the traditional intellectual mission to maintain clear distinctions between authority and (common) sense, privilege and everyday society, and reflects an enhanced awareness that knowledge, thought and experience are integral to the production of contemporary culture.

This debate, and its consequences, increasingly figures in the passage of English early modernity. It is a significant and often contradictory theme in Edmund Spenser's monumental epic, *The*

Faerie Queene (1590). It was inaugurated on the Continent by Cusanus around 1450, and his opposition to an art of conjecture that did not lead to empirical experiment, while being resisted, for example, by Sidney distinguishing between the rational and a 'liberty of conceit'. It was precisely such distinctions that had allowed the sphere of anatomical learning to be treated so long as an autonomous realm, a source of eternal values, untouched by immediate history and the dirty hands of society, power and desire.

It is from this debate that the College of Physicians inherits its largely transcendental, or metaphysical, view of the body, an atemporal reality separate from the everyday world. Whereas Harvey's argument that comes from below, as it were, from inside the details and different histories of society, and the changes induced in society, suggests an opposed view. Here knowledge about the body, its attendant values and aesthetics, is not timeless but, rather, inexorably caught up in time, in the restless movement and shifting tides of the world. Here 'Disputatious authors differ much among themselves.'[27] Here there are no eternal values, no pure states, just different knowledges: everything, including Harvey's own knowledge of the body, is destined to emerge, develop and die within this movement.

This sense of the mutability of sense itself introduces a further complexity to the debate. The classical subject – the semantic centre and habitat of a stable conception of knowledge and aesthetics – has yet to take the stage. In the early 1600s, Harvey confronts the liberation of differences under the newly dawned sign of a pragmatic empiricism:

> Let us conclude, confirming all these things with one example, that everyone may believe his own eyes. If any one cut up a live Adder ...[28]

Here, reaffirmed by Harvey is a significant critical shift in which understandings and interpretations of the body (anatomical, figurative, *real*) are no longer tied to a reading that rests upon traditional appeals to a unique or homogeneous truth that will guarantee critical thought – and not even one, in the last analysis, *entirely* provided by one's own eyes:

> Now the reason for all this is that in vision or in the act of seeing, each particular by itself was clear and distinct; but the object

being removed (as if, for example you shut your eyes), this same particular is abstracted in the imagination or laid up in the memory and appears obscure and confused.[29]

And yet, despite the eye's inconstancy – of knowledge derealised in a blink – there is still the evocation of the idea of an ontological truth that comes to be inscribed in the being of the discoverer; in the continual becoming and mutation of being in the languages in which he is cast (in the sense of unceasing, unfolding self-discovery). In such a manner, does the Harveian critique of tradition come to be based on tradition itself, on the rules of the game and its languages of being, on what Harvey calls the 'way of the Anatomists.'[30] Just as the discourse of discovery is expressed through tropes of discovery, as, for example, in Bacon's *Novum Organum*, nothing is entirely fixed: analyses are constantly forced to change focus and attention, while remaining attached to elements of tradition that privilege certainty: 'It behoves him, who is ever is desirous to learn, to see anything which is in question', Harvey counsels.[31] There are no longer unambiguous positions that are eternally and wholly true, but shifting constellations of meaning, openings and visual possibilities. It is here, simultaneously and endlessly amid the flow of critical thought, that flashes of sense, of a 'solid and certain knowledge', as Harvey will put it, temporally come to rest.

Such an enframing of life produces enquiries attentive to the different histories, nuances and narratives that call into being the present, and which become inscribed in the *Prelectiones*. There the commonplace, and apparently homogeneous, material of a knowledge formation, reveals its complex stories and alternative ways of making sense of the body, while still drawing upon the vocabularies of established lexicons and languages.

In remaining subject to those languages, nevertheless are established trajectories of concerns and desires that are neither necessarily determined nor captured by the system in which they develop. It is in this sense, as Harvey underlines, that all can become anatomists, moving across a system that is too vast to be each their own, but in which they are fully involved, translating and transforming bits and elements of knowledge into local instances of sense. It is this very mutability of mental mapping that makes the languages and texts that comprise the *Prelectiones* – the names, histories, memories, cultures – habitable: as though they compose a space borrowed for a moment by a transient, a traveller, a discoverer;

[According] to Aristotle greater fluidity of the bowel in one body; but, on the other hand, in another body, providing [there are] many concoctions, such as are distinguished by fat, great spirit and tenacity; they are unable to stand for long on one [foot]; *waddle like a puffin*; wherefore 'Solomon' Ecclesiasticus 19:28, gait, laughter and attire. For some employing measured, regular step walk [in the manner in which] the executioner approaches; others move about here and there in a disorderly confusion like ducks; wherefore those of disorganised habits, pertinacious *dogged fellowes*. Wherefore 3 kinds of dwarfs; [1] very small, proportioned pigmies; [2] dwarfs, sm[all] body, shapeless, *vgly*; [3] those in whom the spine is curved, humped, limbs rather long; *gibber Gobbo Nang*.[32]

And because an autonomous space of perception is lacking 'solid and certain knowledge' can only be achieved across such a network of already established intellective forces and representations. And it is in such historical details, in the often unremarkable and overlooked everyday fragments of sense, that the ideological knot of tradition and the 'new' and 'surer path' can be re-woven while critically getting beyond both the condemnation of tradition and its abstractions.

This all suggests that there is no exterior truth to be salvaged from the body and from the immediate world of anatomy; that somehow beneath the surface and inside the sign there lurks a deeper and final truth waiting to be discovered. The argument, central to both Harveian and Baconian critiques of representation (as falsity, simulacrum), is that surfaces and appearances are simply the deceptive, seductive and mystifying manifestations of an underlying reality: the distantiation of the human condition. But this reduction to a hidden value – the value of bodily authenticity supposedly masked by false appearances – denies the ontological reality of signs, appearances and as everyday life. It denies the fact that they, too, are sites of sense, of meaning. To not appreciate this opening, this particular possibility, will still allow the anatomical discoverer to take his sabbatical – but from the very ideological critique that directs his attention.

III   AWAY

[T]he fruit thereof (as it seemeth) was long before fallen from the tree, & the dead stocke only remained.

Walter Raleigh[33]

The idea of letting go, of taking a holiday from the discourses that constrain, is how Walter Raleigh prefaces his Guiana journal. Two decades before Harvey's own *excursus*, Raleigh refers to having undertaken 'these travels, fitter for bodies lesse blasted with misfortunes, for men of greater abilitie, and for mindes of better incouragement, that thereby, if it were possible, I might recover but the moderation of excess, & the least taste of the greatest plenty formerly possessed', and he muses on how, 'If I had knowen other way to win, if I imagined how greater adventures might have regained, if I could conceive what farther meanes I might yet use.'[34] He uses his recent encounter with the other of Guiana not to presume to explain that alterity, but rather to go beyond himself, his own language and sign culture, and thereby disturb and question the apparent stability of the political and symbolic order of which he is part. Here George Puttenham's concept of 'METAPHORA, of the Figure of TRANS-PORTE' will become realised as a trope of distantness.[35] Here differences, although recognised, remain as differences, irreducible to the same. They will exist as a supplement, an excess that causes knowledge, and this discoverer, to vacillate.

In writing his journal, Raleigh relies on Spanish texts about the New World: he uses information gained from discussions with his captive, Don Antonio de Berreo, the governor of Trinidad; appends to his text relevant Spanish documents that had been intercepted at sea. He records not a ship's log, but a recollection, a fragmented narrative, a fiction. Raleigh himself acknowledged this deep-seated ambiguity in his writing, underlining the infinite and whirling play of language that carries with it the strange sensation of losing oneself as sense is transformed, rewritten, and proliferates in interpretation. Further, when he writes that, '[I] was very desirous to understand the truth of those warlike women, because of some it is beleeved, of others not', he is registering not the actual flush of desire, but its reconstruction, to the elements that constitute the space of memory in the present.[36] What is important for Raleigh is not so much what happened – the rumours, the women – as the particular account of the narrative that he now presents to his reader(s). It is that material which is *real*; *reality*, what actually might have happened, is no longer immediately available. It has been rewritten and displaced by a construction that comes to be represented in the second order of a discourse that simultaneously claims authentic status and yet reads like a travelogue composed to assuage a hostile reception committee.[37]

Guiana – embodied as a 'countrey that hath yet her maydenhead' – offers Raleigh, retrospectively, the possibility of undoing his own reality, and, if only intellectually, to pre-empt the position, or topology, of himself as a subject, together with his (tarnished) authority. What was taken for granted prior to Guiana, considered *natural*, hence universal, is now, after the event, revealed to be local and historical. This Raleighean awareness does not emerge from excavating beneath the surfaces of appearances so much as from putting surface to surface, sign to sign, culture to culture, and there in the lateral or horizontal plane, registering the difference. There are the ethnographic, cultural and social differences that Raleigh has discovered in appearances – as in the towns of the Incas which were 'built like the towns of the Christians',[38] in the islands in the Orinoco 'many of which were 'as bigge as the yle of Wight, and bigger, and many lesse';[39] in the Tivititas who live on these islands; in the ornamental and fragmented arrangement of their food; in the painted ideogram; in the event which resembles 'a great market or faire in England';[40] in the transitory instance of his 'Indian interpreter, which I carried out of England';[41] signs that, as Thomas Wilson puts it, in being 'twoo waies taken', suggest that the rational is merely one system among others.[42]

For Raleigh, the plenitude of cultural differences and identities, of these minimal expressions of the here and now (*hic et nunc*), provide a space of pure fragments in which it is language itself that is foregrounded in a veritable digression from meaning. Although Raleigh may modify these differences, attempt to abolish their multiplexity and install stereotypes – 'Amazones', 'marvellous great drunkards' [the Guianians] – there always remains just a trace, a designation of words, where sense is, as it were, unfinalised. Back home in England, with censure in place and a text to write, there are just repetitions without origins, events without causes, memories without peoples, a language without moorings, and a gulf of temporality that yet may provide for a consoling significance.

Signs and language can be set free from immediate referents. This is what Raleigh's *Guiana* permits him on his return to contemplate. This is not to say that his 'mental mapping' pronounces the end of meaning, of sense. What his journal opens up is the opposite of a resigned nihilism, that is, simply the mood and mode of a travel-writer who fears his time is almost up: written after the end of Guiana, it now proposes an excess of sense. In the journal of the *Discoverie*, signs are cast loose from their meanings in one system of thought, and transmuted through language, culture and history, acquire other, sometimes unrecognisable, even incomprehensible, ones elsewhere. Such a semiotic movement, of setting sign to sign, and appearance to appearance, on the surfaces of language and culture, does not avoid the question of significance, but supplements, extends and complicates it.

IV   MUSING ON TRADITION

Steale thee to the top of an easie hill, where in artificiall caves, cut out of the most natural Rock, thou shalt see the ancient people of this Ile delivered thee in their lively images.

Michael Drayton[43]

The perspectives on contemporary life as suggested by both the *Discoverie* and the *Prelectiones* can be compared with a project which unlike those of Raleigh and Harvey is not determined to break through the appearances of the world and the arc of everyday life and movement. At virtually the same moment as the anatomist embarks on his course of discovery, this project results in a mapping of Britain, confident in its figuration and formation too, that is, however, prematurely foreclosed in an insistence on seeking an ultimate finality, an anchorage and shelter in the realm of *authentic* being and tradition.

Picking up some of the key words and concepts that Michael Drayton employs in *Poly-Olbion*, and running them against the grain of his own topology, we might consider what further sense emerges:

Of ALBIONS glorious Ile the Wonders whilst I write,
The sundry varying soyles, the pleasures infinite (Where heate
Kills not the cold, nor cold expels the heat,
The calmes too mildly small, nor winds too roughly great.
Nor night doth hinder day, nor day the night doth wrong,
The Summer not too short, the Winter not too long).[44]

Drayton's declared aim is to chart 'every mountain, forest, river, and valley, expressing in their sundry postures their loves, desires, and natural situations'; to map by way of allegory, that is, a Britain naturalised, and thus authenticated as timeless and true; a Britain, moreover, where the moderation of the natural climes registers limits to, or negations of, other unbeneficent identities.[45] But what if this insular (and insulated) landscape is not about continuity but discontinuity? What if there is not an uninterrupted inheritance that reaches into the present from the past, but instead bits and pieces that exist in the present as traces, as elements not of an unique tradition but of different histories that are continually being recomposed? In other words, what if there has already occurred a historical shift in the very understanding of *tradition* and its identification with a unitary sense of belonging? There is, after all, a major difference between tradition defined by an apparent uninterrupted faith in an imagined *community* (Drayton), and the recognition of complex identities forged in discontinuous, heterogeneous histories in a contingent world (Raleigh and Harvey). In the latter case, we are forcefully reminded of Walter Benjamin's observation that 'discontinuity is the foundation of an authentic tradition.'[46] For Drayton tradition and roots will remain important in themselves, as though stable tokens of a vanished authenticity. For Raleigh and Harvey, however, they acquire significance as part of a flexible and composite inheritance that is drawn upon, rewritten and modified in assembling an effective passage through the present. For them, unlike for Drayton, roots become routes.

Drayton wants to keep Britain as it is. But if the Faustian double-bind – the drive to finality and authentic being at whatever cost – is integral to Drayton's sense of Britain, he remains reluctant to put those terms, and hence the very idea of Britain itself, into question. Despite his beatific landscape, (and because of it) his mental mapping leaves us with a Gaunt-like impression that Britain was once a noble country that has somewhat fallen by the wayside, and that, therefore, in order to salvage it, there is a need to get back, or at least celebrate, its sources, its well-springs: a 'God-like' hero (Brutus) credited with its founding; the 'most renowned Knight' Arthur, with its safeguarding; more recent 'great monarchs' like Elizabeth with prescient rule; seamen-explorers, including Robert Dudley and Sherley, with mercantile wealth; 'the valient *Cicill*' with wise administration. And yet of course there is never any going back. Genesis exists in the present only as traces in memories, elements that can be reconstructed through historical and topographical representations; myths, stories and accounts that are encountered, interpreted, and hence become positioned, inscribed and located, in the present. There can be no return to the scene of beginnings and their presumed origins.

The actors charted by Drayton in his epic map – the Muse, Eliza, the *peoples* inhabiting the villages, countryside, sundry festivities and fairs – are all abstract unities, unified (pre-Cartesian) subjects. It is as though they are merely the (by)products of cartography, early modernity and early capitalism, and not their labourers and producers. The only producers that Drayton's map permits are those nymphs, shepherds and satyrs populating the countryside which are capable of riding the storm of political, economic and intellectual development. In a decidedly idealised and nostalgic view of Britain, attention is continually drawn to the voice, implacably male and Jamesian, that manages to rise above the maelstrom and cast it into the canon of significant expression.

Finally, there is the tragedy of the body. For Drayton the drama of corporeality is played out in the familiar identification of body with island, island with Britain: the vivification of the many forests, hills, and rivers into a single living thing. Agreed, the figuration of the body – harmoniously composed of members and parts – offers an imaginatively persuasive resistance to the cultural stagnation, fragmentation and discontinuity which profoundly disturbs Drayton and some of his contemporaries. All I would suggest is that when we look further into the particular histories and discourses that make up early modernity, we discover that the oft-cited crises of the times set problems and proposals that could also permit the moving beyond of a nostalgic appeal for a lost unity, coherence and unified sense of tradition. For Harvey, as for Raleigh they presented heterogeneous matrices of sense, with languages of images and signs intent on transforming the traces and fragmented inheritances of the past, together with other more immediate borrowings and suggestions, into a meaningful present.

V   RUINS AND RUNES

Naturally, all this is a prelude, part of a reflection gathered from looking at fragments of a particular cultural discourse, and at the histories, prospects that framed such work. I have tried to unpack some of the analytical baggage that I believe was carried around in this landscape, and which passed, at moments of arrest, as critical thought. Assuredly, these mappings of sense offer today the chance to consider further senses of cartography itself, its languages, figurations and possibilities, a learned power by another name. To so query is not only to reveal in the undoing of its discourse, other, more open, more politically nuanced ways of formulating questions and prospects. To move through its ruins, and into the subsequent openings, is to enter into another type of dialogue altogether. This also involves putting aside the intellectual comfort afforded by the rational clarity of conventional schematics and abstract theoretical unities, and likewise implies an imaginative itinerary that can entertain the murmurs and echoes of previous idioms and dialogues. By that route, in paying attention to such multiple voices, ethnographic details, diverse stories and not always commensurable realities, are we drawn beyond ourselves and the critical world we inhabit.

Notes

1. William Harvey, *Prelectiones anatomie unversalis* (1616–?), translated and published as *William Harvey: Lectures on the Whole of Anatomy* edited and translated by C. D. O'Malley, F. N. L. Poynter & K. F. Russell, (Berkeley: University of California, 1961), p. 214. The lecture notes were used by Harvey over a considerable but indeterminable period of time: unlogged supplementations and amendments preclude the precise dating of the manuscript. For a discussion of the composition of the notes and of Harvey's work in general see Geoffrey Keynes, *The Life of William Harvey*, (Oxford: Clarendon Press, 1966). In this essay Harvey's annotations referring to personal observations are signalled **WH**; Harvey's native idiolect is italicised; enclosures within brackets i.e. [...] indicate extensions made to the original script by the translators and editors.
2. The concept of 'mental mapping' that I employ here mainly as a heuristic device is indebted to John Gillies's discussion of imaginative projections and 'poetic geographies' in *Shakespeare and the Geography of Difference* (Cambridge: Cambridge University Press, 1994), pp. 40–69.
3. Harvey, *Lectures*, p. 22.
4. Edgar Morin, *La méthode. 1. La nature de la nature* (Paris: Éditions du Seuil, 1977).
5. William Harvey, *Exercitationes de generatione animalium* (1651) published as *Disputations concerning the generation of animals*, translated by Gweneth Whitteridge, (Oxford: Oxford University Press, 1981), p. 13.
6. Luke Wilson, 'William Harvey's Prelectiones: the Performance of the Body in the Renaissance Theatre of Anatomy', in *Representations* 17, Winter 1987, 75.
7. Donna J. Haraway, *Simians, Cyborgs, and Women: the Reinvention of Nature* (London: Free Association Books, 1991), p. 188.

8. William Harvey, *Exercitation anatomica de motu cordis et sanguinis in animalibus*, (Frankfurt, 1628) translated by Gweneth Whitteridge as *An anatomical disputation concerning the movement of the heart and blood in living creatures* (Oxford, 1976), p. 44.

9. Harvey, *Lectures*, p. 42.

10. On this point see Andrew Wear, 'William Harvey and the Way of Anatomists', in *History of Science*, 21 (1983), 234.

11. Harvey, *Lectures*, p. 89.

12. Harvey, *Disputationes*, p. 8.

13. Francis Bacon, 'Of the Proficience and Advancement of Learning Divine and Humane', in *The Philosophical Works of Francis Bacon*, edited by J. Spedding, R. L. Ellis & D. D. Heath, 14 vols, (Stuttgart: Frommann, 1962–63), vol. IV, p. 406.

14. Harvey, *Disputationes*, p. 9.

15. Harvey, *Disputationes*, p. 9.

16. Francis Bacon, 'Plan of the Work (Distrubutio Operis for the Instauratio Magna)' in *The Philosophical Works of Francis Bacon*, vol. IV, pp. 25, 28, 32–3.

17. Harvey, *Disputationes*, p. 9.

18. Harvey, *Disputationes*, p. 15.

19. Harvey, *Disputationes*, p. 15.

20. Harvey, *An anatomical disputation*, p. 32.

21. Harvey, *Disputationes*, p. 8.

22. Harvey, *Disputationes*, p. 8.

23. Harvey, *Disputationes*, p. 13.

24. The intensity of the controversy surrounding Harvey's work – 'Frivolous and unexperienced persons do scurvily strive to overthrow by logical and far fetch'd arguments' (Harvey) – is gauged in Keynes, *The Life of William Harvey* and Louis Chauvois, *William Harvey: His Life and Times: His Discoveries: His Methods* (London: 1957).

25. Harvey, *Disputationes*, p. 13.

26. Harvey, *Disputationes*, p. 13.

27. Harvey, *Lectures*, p. 23.

28. Harvey, *An anatomical disputation*, p. 86.

29. Harvey, *Disputationes*, p. 11.

30. William Harvey, *Exercitationes anatomicae* (London: 1653), translated and published as *Two anatomical exercitationes concerning the circulation of the blood* (London: 1661), p. 74.

31. Harvey, *Two anatomical exercitationes*, p. 87.

32. Harvey, *Lectures*, p. 33.

33. Walter Raleigh, 'The Discoverie of the large, rich, and beautifull Empire of Guiana, with a relation of the great and golden citie of manoa (which the Spainards call El Dorado) and the provinces of Emeria, Aromaia, Amapaia, and other countries, with their rivers adjoyning', in *The Principle Navigations Voyages Traffiques & Discoveries of the English Nation*, composed by Richard Hakluyt (1598–1600), (Glasgow: James Maclehose & Sons, 1903–5), vol. x, p. 339.

34. Raleigh, 'The Discoverie', p. 339.

35. George Puttenham, *The Arte of Poesie* (London, 1589), III xvii.

36. Raleigh, 'The Discoverie', p. 366.
37. '[To] appease so powreful a displeasure' [of Howard and Cecil] Raleigh gives as the principal reason for undertaking the voyage and for producing the report. Hakluyt, *The Principal Navigations*, pp. 366, 339, 374, 382, 371, 409.
38. Raleigh, 'The Discoverie', p. 374.
39. Raleigh, 'The Discoverie', p. 382.
40. Raleigh, 'The Discoverie', p. 371.
41. Raleigh, 'The Discoverie', p. 409.
42. Thomas Wilson, *The Rule of Reason*, (London, 1551), p. 163.
43. Michael Drayton, *Poly-Olbion*, in *The Works of Michael Drayton*, ed. J. William Hebel, 5 vols. (Oxford: Shakespeare Head Press, 1931–41), vol. IV, Song 1, 16; vol. I, 27–8.
44. Drayton, *Poly-Olbion* vol. IV. Song I, 16.
45. Drayton, *Poly-Olbion* vol. I. 27–8.
46. Walter Benjamin, 'The work of art in the age of mechanical reproduction', in Walter Benjamin, *Illuminations*, translated by H. Zohn (New York: Schocken Books, 1969).

7

'The Doubtful Traveller': Mathematics, Metaphor, and the Cartographic Origins of the American Frontier

Jess Edwards

I

New England's Prospect, written by the Puritan settler William Wood, and published in London in 1634, is a member of that class of texts produced to encourage early American colonisation. In it, Wood tells a story clearly intended to disperse English fears about the Indian menace. 'The doubtful traveller', he records, 'hath oftentimes beene much beholding to ... [the Indians] for their guidance thorow the unbeaten wildernesse.'[1] 'My selfe', he continues, illustrating his point,

> with two more of my associates bending our course to new *Plimouth*, lost our way, being deluded by a misleading path which we still followed, being as we thought too broad for an *Indian* path ... which begat in us a security of our wrong way to be right, when indeed there was nothing lesse: the day being gloomy and our compasses at home ... happily we arrived at an *Indian* *Wigwamme* ... the son of my naked host ... took the clew of his travelling experience, conducting us through the strange labyrinth, of unbeaten bushy wayes ...[2]

Wood's experience in the 'wilderness' is registered here both as exemplary and as exceptional. Exemplary in its illustration of Indian

128

helpfulness; exceptional, in that without the temporary absence of the *compasses*, there would have been no need for such help, and indeed no story. Mathematical orientation, the absent compasses imply, renders the traveller independent of any given environmental contingency, and returns him home with predictable, and therefore unremarkable consistency. Where experience, in its infinite variations, always has a story to tell, mathematics is self-identical and mute.

The indeterminacy of Wood's anecdote between the exceptional and the exemplary is clearly predicated on the simultaneous availability and dispensability of the mathematical overview, or 'prospect'. This essay will take such an indeterminacy to be paradigmatic of a more general vacillation in early modern technologies of environmental negotiation and representation between geography and history; consistent, mathematical 'description' and contingent narrative. It will look to show that this element of 'doubtfulness' in a story such as Wood's, in which the alternative of mathematics is implied, finds its structural complement in maps which consistently imply the alternative of narrative. Ostensibly, the primary function of such doubtful maps and stories is to record, and indeed to project the distinct experience had and to be had by a traveller in a particular environment. More fundamentally, however, I argue that they also work to constitute a negotiable boundary between geography and history. We have noted that the story told above marks its own exceptionality in the unusual dependence of the compass-less colonial traveller on Indian experience. Within the generally descriptive context of his 'prospect' of New England, Wood's story of being lost also seems singular in that it does not make any attempt to represent the environment in which it takes place. In fact, however, my argument suggests that, far from being exceptional, the story has simply dropped a veil and revealed a basic function of the geographic in general.

A little further on I examine a map which, in very much the manner of Wood's story, wears its vacillatory heart upon its sleeve. And just like Wood's story, rather than addressing history and geography directly, this map encodes their relation in a negotiation between the universality of European science and the particularity of Indian experience. It is precisely this encoding that encourages me to take the element of 'doubt' in Wood's story, and ultimately in the map, as paradigmatic not just of a particular problematic of representation, but more generally of the full Janus-aspect of that early

modern 'attitude' persistently designated 'colonial' in recent discourse. Such an attitude, which has been described at various levels,
from the psychic to the economic, is held to look both apprehen-
sively and acquisitively upon empirical novelty, whether human or
environmental, with a view to bringing such novelty within the
universal limits of intellectual comprehension, but without dissipat-
ing its newness. It is frequently presumed that a newly mathematical geography was serviceable to early modern colonialism.[3]
Critical accounts which make such an assumption rightly point to
the capacity which mathematics affords for the simplification of the
empirically complex; and for the forgetting of embarrassing and
anxious stories of appropriation, often proving their argument with
colonial maps which, in particular limit cases, certainly appear to be
empty of anything but mathematics. I argue, however, that the
service paid by mathematics to colonialism is somewhat more
complex, involving in fact the very vacillation between universal
and particular; between identity and difference that 'Colonial
power' is supposed to manifest in the demands it makes of its
colonised 'other' – again, whether human or environmental.[4]

If the compasses in Wood's story can be taken, as I take them, as a
metonym for the mathematical 'perspective' in general, the story also
bears an equally important metaphoric burden: one which plays a
significant role in mediating precisely the 'colonial' demand for both
identity and difference; consolidation and gain – a demand which is,
at the same time, that for both intellectual consistency and the contingent particularity of new experience. Wood, as he puts it – lacking
the clear view of mathematics – misrecognises the 'labyrinth' of
Indian territory for his own, consolidated colonial domain. Reduced,
by his carelessness, from familiar intellectual judgement to contingent empirical sense, he is first, without knowing it, lost; and then –
discovering anew the hospitality of the Indian – finds that his
misleading senses in fact misled him aright, and that he is, as he had
presumed in the first place, at home. At the same time as he finds he
can, after all, trust sensory experience, Wood finds that he can, after
all, trust the Indian. In the exemplary terms of this anecdote-turned
allegory, the labyrinth of corporeal experience turns out to be not a
prison but a fortress, and its guardian – by whom Wood finds himself
'hosted'; or into whom he finds himself metamorphosed – not the
Minotaur, but Ariadne; not monstrous, but humane.

    In temporarily surrendering the intellectual overview of mathe-
matics, and taking up the hospitality of his own particular place in

the *terra incognita* of corporeal sense and experience, Wood has then, in effect, merely taken a detour leading back to home and to the desk or cupboard from which this overview can safely be retrieved.[5] His labyrinthine quest, or adventurous metamorphosis, seems to have left him fundamentally unchanged. This has, nonetheless, been an important detour. In its course, the novelty; the particularity of the un-colonised, marked off for incorporation within the universalising frame which the compasses will no doubt soon impose, has been taken account of, yet not dissipated. And significantly, the space that has been allowed for this novelty; this particularity – space allowed as an exceptional dispensation attributable to the exceptional nature of the detour itself – is the space of narrative, and within it, the space of such a metaphor as the 'labyrinth'. How unexceptional this whole manoeuvre is, the remainder of this essay demonstrates.

In conventional histories of art, the defining moments in the evolution of a 'modern' European cartography, one suited to serve colonialism in the manner that we often find described, are those through which it came to be established on a mathematical foundation. One such moment is comprised in the fifteenth-century adoption of mathematical methods for projecting global geography onto two-dimensional maps, as described by Ptolemy.[6] Another, perhaps still more significant for my purposes, is comprised in the sixteenth-century development of a method for applying the laws of surface geometry to the practice of local surveying: a method subsequently known as 'triangulation'.[7] Without discussing the substance of these methods, we can appreciate their constitution of a universal framework – one, in Ptolemy's words, of 'just proportion' – within which not just a global, but even the most local subject might be contained.[8] The paradox of such mathematical delimitation is, of course, that whilst on the one hand it defines its content; makes it more discrete; more evidently itself, on the other it accommodates it within a universal economy, and thus in a sense disperses its integrity.[9]

At the same time as this mathematical framework contains, tempers the particularity of its subject – shows off its universal aspect – it tempers the particularity of the cartographer who represents this subject. The cartographer may engage with the particularity of his subject; may have a correspondingly particular experience of this subject; may indeed have particular skills and aptitudes suited to relaying this experience. However, to the extent that he communicates by way of the universal language of mathematics, this particular experience and these particular skills are superfluous, neutral, unproductive in relation to his cartographic meaning (rather as the Indian's experience and skills would have been, had Wood not forgotten his compasses).

The mathematics in early modern cartography comes, in fact, to be the principle of its truth, to precisely the extent that it is not necessarily implicated in any given instance of cartography, or indeed in the range of extra-mathematical skills and materials that constitute cartography as a practical craft and the cartographer as a craftsman. And the liberality, literally the 'largeness', or generosity if this mathematical foundation in relation to cartography is confirmed in its being shared with other renovated Renaissance crafts: notably architecture and painting. Each of these disciplines, founded on common ground, can serve to flesh out aspects of an archetypal model of early modern mathematical cartography, and I shall use them briefly to this end.

II

In architecture, the advent of a liberal foundation or framework is marked, as Spiro Kostof has described, in the increasing prominence, and ultimately the semi-autonomous authority over the building process, of an individual whose principal qualification for such authority is mathematical knowledge.[10] The Roman architect Vitruvius, through his newly translated treatise *De Architectura*, famously provided the blueprint for a revived classical style in the Italian Renaissance. He also supplied the blueprint for the liberalisation of the architect's role, distinguishing between the theoretical knowledge 'common' amongst scholars – to which the architect is privy – and the practical skills 'proper' to specialist craftsmen whom the architect commands.[11] This well-known liberalisation of the role of the architect is attended by the ascendancy, and ultimate autonomy, of the mathematical planning; the 'design' phase in the work of architecture. It is attended, indeed, by the ascendancy of the design itself, as a medium radically independent of the building, and as a fully 'sufficient' representation of any given building, whether or not it has yet been built.[12]

The liberalisation of painting may be said to arrive with the advent of the mathematical perspective method refined and promulgated by

Leon Battista Alberti – again, of course, in fifteenth-century Italy. Once more, without detailing Alberti's rules, we can appreciate their subordination of the particularities both of the craft of painting, and of the artist's own experience of a subject, to the universal foundation of mathematics.[13] It can safely be posited that the division of labour between knowledgeable scholar and skilful craftsman that is marked in Vitruvian architecture, and often described by its proponents as a division of head from hand, is reproduced within the person of Alberti's painter, as it is within the mathematical cartographer.[14] The personae of Renaissance painter and cartographer are constituted, in other words, in terms both of a primary, universal element of intellectual government, and of a subordinate, particular element of mechanical (manual) execution. It also seems plausible to suggest that the design which marks the boundary between common knowledge and proper skills in Vitruvian architecture; between liberal science and practical craft, and which in itself is taken as sufficient to signify the building, has its structural counterpart in the mathematical plans which both painter and cartographer treat as *a priori* in relation to the distinguishing details of their subject and of its particular re-presentations. The design, in each case, divides the artist's intellect from his experience; his head from his hand.

The commitment of the Renaissance artist to a neutral foundation in his art is, then, evident. Upon this foundation is grounded his authority to represent and reproduce the world about him truly; in 'just proportion'; according to absolute principles uncorrupted by secular phenomena and concerns. Accordingly, in Leonardo's words, mathematics is, and should be, 'the bridle and rudder' of art.[15] However, equally conspicuous in the founding texts that I have mentioned, and closely attendant upon such votes of confidence in the authority of mathematics, are scruples which cast *doubt* upon its sufficiency. Vitruvius warns that though the architect must be a scholar, and never a mere elevated master mason, he must neither only be a scholar, nor be too deeply immersed in scholarship. Should he be so, his patron risks obtaining the mere 'shadow' of a building.[16] It is best that the architect have just a 'dip' into both mathematics and, for instance, the skills of masonry – enough for him to mediate between patron and craftsman.[17] With this warning, Vitruvius defends the liberal profession of architecture not just as liberal, but, indeed, also as a profession, marking out a territory somewhere between that of the general scholar, and that of the artisanal specialist.[18] And if the position of the artist can appear to be one of suspension between common knowledge and proper skills, that of his design can seem equivalently poised. In his writings on perspective, Alberti, in what seems very much a mere Vitruvian 'dip' into mathematics, advises that the painter should think, for instance, of the geometric point, or '*signum*', not so much as mere signifier of the ideal Euclidean principle of indivisibility, as the 'mathematician' would, but more as 'somehow a kind of thing *between* the mathematical point and ... finite particles like atoms' (my emphasis).[19]

I cannot stress sufficiently the significance of the compromise between universal concept and particular quantity. Whilst we can be sure that it is the *mathematician's* point that is in play in art, its particular embodiment as sign – whether in the artist's, or in the architect's or the cartographer's preliminary 'design' – is clearly superfluous, unproductive, neutral in relation to the meaning which mathematics guarantees. Any mathematical scholar could sketch in the mathematics of such a plan. If the design conceived in these purely mathematical terms is important in itself, it is so only to the extent that it is *exemplary* of a radical separation from the domain of craft. Alberti's perspectival design, however, is important in itself in quite another sense. Possessed of an equivocal concreteness 'somehow', in Alberti's words – that is, indeterminately – between concept and quantity, it is not just neutral in relation to the domains which it divides, but it also bids to participate in each of them, and to realise out of their relation its own *exceptional* identity. Without discarding the neutrality of the signifier, and the correspondent integrity of the concept to which it refers – there still is a mathematical point as such, to which the painter's point will be different – Alberti simply disregards it for the purposes of painting; leaves it, like Wood's compasses, at home. And over the virtual gap thus opened in the otherwise punctual relation between mathematics and meaning, the mathematical artist, with his dip into both common knowledge and proper skills, can claim his exclusive, professional proprietorship.

Since the indeterminacy of Alberti's mathematics allows the artist to enjoy his own, professional domain of operation, and yet not sacrifice the absolute, liberal authority of mathematics, it is unsurprising that from Alberti onwards, right through at least to the English seventeenth century, an extensive canon of writings on mathematics and artistic applications is testimony to a pervasive desire that such indeterminacy should remain unresolved. This

desire bridges otherwise distinct agendas promoting the enlarge-
ment of mathematical education in the late sixteenth and seventeenth centuries. In his highly influential 1570 preface to the first
English Euclid, for instance, the speculative mathematician John
Dee, who seeks to link the sphere of liberal science with that of
hitherto debased manual crafts, defines the subject matter of mathematics as '(in a manner) middle ... immaterial, and neverthelesse,
by material things able *somewhat* to be signified' (my emphasis).[20] It
is this indeterminate 'middle'-ness; this partial signification that
inspires Dee's mystic awe at the impenetrable capacity of 'things
Mathematicall' for both 'a marveilous newtrality ... and also a
strange participation between things Supernaturall ... and things
naturall'.[21] In the still earlier, and again seminal writings of the sixteenth-century anti-scholastic Robert Recorde, which seek to flatten
out the depth of such ruminations as Dee's to a generous, pragmatic
plain-ness which might make such knowledge truly common,
Alberti's painterly point has become 'that small printe of penne ...
which is not moved'.[22] And where Recorde's generosity is refined
into a politer humanism, more suited to the leisure of gentleman-
amateur practitioners than the working knowledge of the craftsman, the point can be considered, in the words of a French text
translated in 1633, amongst 'things of small consequence, as ...
the foote of a *fly*'.[23] In its airy triviality, even this last, recreational
mathematics is actually still, like Alberti's practical, professional
science, balanced between the uncivil retirement of scholarship, and
the illiberal graft of craft, however it may disdain regard for either.[24]

If the notion of an indeterminate, only virtually material mathematics constitutes design as a medium through which the artist may
mediate exclusively a division of labour, it also, through honouring
yet blurring the distinction between mathematics and the 'natural'
world, allows him to limit access to the natural world itself, as a
sphere of reference for artistic re-presentation. I have noted that the
knowledge requisite to produce a 'sufficient' design in architecture,
painting and cartography is common to all scholars – to anyone with
a liberal education. Such is contemporary confidence in the universal
truth of mathematics, that the Renaissance artist knows his subject,
in a sense, before he encounters it. In framing such a subject in
geometry he merely *expresses* its natural form, finding what is
already there. As such, it is intrinsic to the geometric design that it
should make no difference between geometry commemorated in the
world, as in an architectural painting; or geometry projected on to it,

as in designs for a new building, farm or city. In this way design turns temporal discreteness into punctual identity – in its medium, its executor, and its subject. It presumes a language so luminously self-evident that its meanings are exchanged immediately, without the necessary delay of hermeneutic detours through the physical, the figural, the historical. Without such detours, whose particular routes mark off the individual work of art, the individual artist, and the individual subject, clearly we have only mathematics. And if there is nothing new to be found in the subject of pure mathematical design, there is nothing particular to be contributed by the artist – only common, mathematical knowledge. But just as mathematical art always seems both to insist upon yet also to qualify the neutrality of its medium, there is always a limit to the attenuation of discreteness in its subjects: a limit which once again leaves room for artistic discretion, and for the discrete artist himself. This is most evidently the case with the mathematical map.

Whilst the 'truth' of early modern cartography comes unquestionably to reside in its capacity to express the geometric 'meaning' of its worldly subjects – their 'just proportion' – the extra-mathematical particularity of such subjects is, of course, always retained. If it is not quite the case that any (neutral) signifier will do to signify mathematical form, neither is it quite the case that the natural (in the broadest possible sense) subject in which this form is expressed is neutral in relation to artistic meaning, and thereby can be any subject. The map is never only a design; the subject of cartography never only mathematics. And yet the retention of the natural is invariably subject to a logic which leaves the sufficiency of mathematics, in comprehending the cartographic subject, intact. This paradoxical logic is the same ('logocentric') logic which makes the material embodiment of the sign dispensable to meaning, and cartography's most superficial aspect – the map – figures it especially powerfully as the logic of the supplement.[25]

A map, we might with some justification say, always has a margin – as surely, indeed, as a mind always has a body, and as the knowledgeable architect, painter or cartographer always has a crafty, dextrous hand. This margin, particularly generous in the early modern period, is the proper location – in the words of a recent historian of cartography – for 'matter not forming part of the map itself':[26] matter constituting, in early modern artistic terminology, the *parergon* (literally, 'around the work'). Such matter finds one of its most familiar forms in the key which supplements the map's self-evidence with explanation. Equally familiar, perhaps, are the ornamental devices – sometimes pictorial, sometimes emblematic, sometimes still more abstract – which whilst they appear to add to the map's meaning, to tell us *more* about the cartographic subject, are nonetheless registered as unnecessary to it. We might believe in this unnecessity or not: it is certainly open to argument whether, as I would suggest, the key exposes the necessary entanglement of cartographic representation in particular discursive communities with their own priorities and conventions, or whether ornament always tends, in its parades of heraldry or exotic commodities, to demonstrate the inseparability from cartographic art of rather less than neutral sources of marginality and interest. There are, however, less familiar forms of marginality, which – to exactly the extent, in fact, that they are obscured – still more starkly expose the necessary fall of a neutral cartographic mathematics into the world. Most striking amongst these is the information and guidance sought from local inhabitants by the surveyor of an unfamiliar terrain, upon which he depends not just to represent it, but even to find his way, where mathematics leaves him little better than transcendently lost. Treatises in surveying advise the artist in mitigating the contingency of such guidance – he must, for instance, ask local authorities to choose for him the oldest and most honest inhabitants of a region.[27] If anything, however, such attempts make still more glaringly apparent a rupture in the universal, self-sufficient authority of mathematics, into which seeps the discreteness of history and locale, and the artistic discretion which must negotiate these vagaries. The danger which this rupture constitutes is implicitly acknowledged by cartography in that whilst local testimony may be absent even from the borders of the map itself, the strictly ordered process, as described in surveying manuals, according to which the artist collects such information in his field book, uses it to help him conduct and transcribe his triangulation, and then erases or discards it, clearly, nonetheless, follows a logic of marginalisation.[28]

To return to the story with which this essay began, we might then say that the avowal of exceptionality in Wood's anecdote about Indian helpfulness is disingenuous. Mathematics *always* needs empirical supplementation in cartography, whether or not one leaves one's actual compasses at home. We might, in fact, as I suggested, regard Wood's story as working simultaneously through colonial and cartographic anxieties. The supplement of the empirical, it implies, is both unnecessary, and always available; the instance of native helpfulness to the map or/and cooperative identity with the colonial project both exceptional and exemplary. In this light the story might fruitfully be compared with a contemporary cartographic representation of early colonial America mentioned cursorily in my introductory remarks: John Smith's 1612 'Map of Virginia' (Fig. 7.1). Smith's representation of what in an accompanying 'History' he calls a 'plaine wildernesse as God first made it'[29], is an exceptional instance of its genre only in that the frontier between particular native, empirical guidance – as figured by some very corporeal, ornamental Indians – and an *a priori* mathematical frame – as figured by a mathematical instrument manifesting the purely intellectual presence of the cartographer – is not just left implicit within the cartographic technology, but is actually embodied on the surface of the map, and not just 'ornamentally'. Smith's 'History', expanding upon a key presented in the margins of the map itself, explains: 'In which mappe observe this, that as far as you see the little crosses … have been discovered; the rest was had by information of the savages, and are set down according to their instructions.'[30] Here, then, once again, is the negotiation between European Science and Indian experience; between geography and history. Smith, like Wood, has, at a certain, avowedly exceptional point in the inauguration of a colony, and the making of a geography, been obliged to leave his compasses at home.

I have suggested that whilst it is in evident conflict with his claim to undetermined liberal truth, the cartographer's resort to extra-mathematical help is not, however, only a problem for him. What I would argue about *parerga* in general, and with particular force in the case of local testimony, is that in registering the discreteness of the subject, and in calling upon the discretion of the artist, they permit the artist, as does Alberti's indeterminate perspectival mathematics, to bid both for the absolute authority of liberal science, as common to all scholars, and for the more relative authority and specific agency which is the particular property of one suited to, experienced and licensed in his craft. Only the proper artist, such *parerga* imply, is capable of knowing how to find and express the form of particular native testimonies, and of each particular tract of ground, just as only the proper artist is capable of choosing the less-than-neutral signifier with which to design a perspectival painting or a geometric map. The conflict between these joint investments in the liberal and the proper is hidden in the indeterminacy of a supplementary logic which makes the discreteness of the subject and the discretion of the artist both part and yet not part of the 'work'.

7.1 John Smith, 'Map of Virginia' (1612)

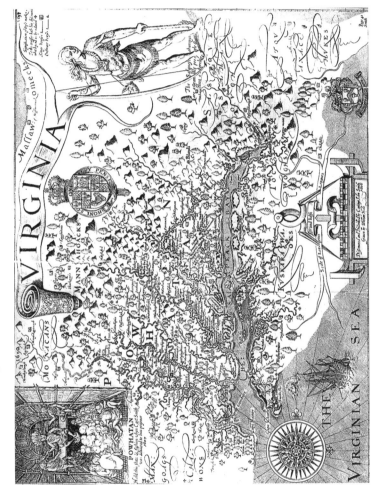

It should be clear by now that what I find at the margins of – though certainly not beyond – the modern map is history. History is what is missing from the truly punctual point which is first principle of the mathematical cartographic framework, and history is what is re-accommodated when such punctuality allows for a discrete art, a discrete subject, and thereby for a discrete difference between commemoration of the past and projection of the future. For the choices that the proper artist makes in such scenarios as Wood and Smith have found themselves – choices of information; choices of location – are nothing if not historically defined. It is a commonplace that geography, from the Renaissance to the present day, has defined itself as radically complementary to history. Speaking a mathematical 'language', and using mathematical methods, geography ostensibly looks to the horizon of a subject in which the historical has – in the terminology of mathematics itself – been 'reduced'. Naturally, as critics we look to avoid the rationalist geographer's mistake of 'reducing' history and discourse in such a way. My own argument suggests, however, that this reduction is in any case only one, perhaps the most overt aspect of the geographic project. Covertly, the map is not just a mechanism designed to exclude history, but, at the same time, one designed to allow history to subsist. In the paradoxical principle of this subsistence, I have argued, the cartographer, and in certain instances the colonialist, secures his own peculiar agency. But we have only understood this principle so far as indeterminacy: as the objective indeterminacy, the virtual materiality of design, and as the logical indeterminacy of the supplement – the dispensable presence of the physical, experience, locality and history. I want now to resolve these various aspects of mathematical-artistic indeterminacy into a unified point of origin, and to remove the false distinction separating the rhetorical nuts and bolts – the metonyms and metaphors – of Wood's anecdote from Smith's crude cartographic points and lines. To do this, I need to take a short detour through philosophy.

III

If philosophy needs an excuse, my excuse for turning briefly to Plato at this point is that I believe not just that the explicit epistemology of early modern cartography is always inextricably caught up in Platonism, but also that the less than rational mechanisms which I have argued are intrinsic to its operation are themselves indebted to post-Platonic discursive tradition. There is no need to say more of Platonism here than the obvious: that it presumes a category of ideal being radically different and indeed radically superior to material being, and a correspondent category of intellectual intuition radically different and superior to experience accumulated through the senses. True knowledge, for the Platonist philosopher, is to be looked for through 're-membering' that unified body of intellectual, soul-knowledge which his worldly birth and embodiment has caused him to dissipate and superficially to forget. The Italian Renaissance Platonist Pico della Mirandola expresses the Platonic doctrine of fundamental *an-amnesis*, or deep soul-knowledge in his faith that the truly intellectual being might engage himself in 'recollecting' the 'members' of ideal unities 'dismembered' in the world.[31] At the same time that it is a reversal of fragmentation, Platonist re-membering is also, characteristically, an 'escape'. Escape from the material, the sensory, the corporeal, the empirical, the local. Escape, in fact, from all which might seem most intimate to man, to that which in Platonic reality constitutes the essential core of his identity, and from which his intimacy with matter temporarily estranges him. The late-classical Neoplatonist Nicomachus describes the course of philosophical education as leading us 'from those material, physical things, our foster-brethren known to us from childhood, to the things with which we are unacquainted, foreign to our senses, but in their immateriality and eternity more akin to our souls.'[32]

It is important that Nicomachus does indeed speak here of e-ducation – of a leading out – and that he does not leave man to make his journey from the falsely familiar to the genuinely kin unguided.[33] There are, advises Proclus, another classical Neoplatonist, entities which, whilst they are certainly ideal, and not material, exist in the 'entrances or vestibules of primary forms'.[34] These entities, which, in Nicomachus's words again, 'serve as ladders or bridges' to lead us from 'things apprehended by sense and opinion' to 'things apprehended by the mind',[35] are the objects of mathematics – from individual numbers, through the geometric point and line, to particular kinds of triangle. Ideal, but only just, they offer man an Ariadne-thread – a 'clew' – through which to escape the labyrinth of empirical time and space and trace the better part of his Minotaurian humanity. If I seem to push the metaphor of the labyrinth, as plundered from Wood's colonial anecdote, a little far here, I find some justification in a rather explicitly Platonist alle-gory of e-ducation rehearsed in another seminal early modern mathematical treatise. This, William Cuningham's *Cosmographical Glasse*, published in 1559, was the first to introduce the method of geometric triangulation in surveying to an English readership. In the introduction to his mathematics, Cuningham tells the tale of 'Daedalus, that excellent Geometrician', who defied 'the monster of Ignorance', having seen her with 'the eyes of knowledge', and, with wings prepared '(through science aide)' flew 'oute of hir mooste filthy Prison', 'her lothsome Labyrinth', 'Ascending to the Sterrye Skie.'[36]

If such undiluted idealism as Nicomachus and Pico evince is uncommon in the philosophies of mathematics that succeed Plato, my argument must be that its departures never finally displace it. Of such departures – manifest in some of the early modern mathe-maticians already cited – Aristotle's is paradigmatic. Where Plato takes the separation of mathematics from the sensible realm, and thereby its universality to it, to be absolute, we know the Aristotelian mathematical object only through abstraction. If, as Aristotle suggests in one place, mathematicals are different from the physical bodies which they 'bound' or 'limit' in that the latter have other attributes *ek prostheseos* 'in addition',[37] such addition, together with the abstraction which precedes it, is a cognitive rather than an intellectual reality. Platonic re-membering of the materially dis-membered thereby becomes for Aristotle a piece of artificial intellectual surgery. Whilst we may think of the material as prosthetic to mathematics, he suggests, and of mathematics as the reality which remains when such inessential attributes have been unbuckled, or reduced; it is, in fact, a lively and integral limb. None the less, however, Aristotle considers the knowledge born of such reductions of mundane conditioning to be superior to knowledge that stays mired in the world. Whilst the conditioned mathematics that we come upon in everyday life may be relatively better known to us in the sense that it is more familiar, Aristotle suggests, that which we understand through abstraction is *absolutely* better known.[38] Aristotle's pseudo-Platonic adherence to at least the fiction of an unconditioned object of mathematical knowledge leaves the issue of actual ideality at the very least ambiguous. Any philosophy of mathematics which reproduced Aristotle's qualification of Plato without abandoning the Platonic hierarchy of absolute over familiar knowledge was thereby liable to misunderstand Aristotle, and in its turn to be misunderstood, as idealist, and so it was with several important medieval and early modern commentaries.[39]

To make a hierarchy depend on supplementary qualification is, it seems, to invite those who encounter this hierarchy to be mis-led: in much the same way, in fact, that – as Derrida has so vehemently pointed out – one may be mis-led by metaphor.[40] Such is the inescapably discursive nature of metaphysics. And such mis-leading makes more for the weaving of a heterogeneous unity in philosophical discourse than the clear definition of positions. Accordingly, whilst sixteenth- and seventeenth-century European mathematical thought manifests the often-remarked extreme poles of contemplative Platonism and of humanist pragmatism, of which contrary impulses John Dee and the Huguenot martyr Peter Ramus might serve respectively as examples, more common is a diffusion of these stances, and a bastardised epistemology which looks to find and apply mathematics in the world, but which yet leaves the Platonic horizon of mathematical ideality and intellectual transcendence at least implicitly intact.[41] The effects of such diffusion should, by now, be evident. Familiar, worldly manifestations of mathematics – embodiments and applications – can hereby function both as neutral references to the universal truths of which the mathematician enjoys absolute comprehension, and yet still seem to participate themselves, notwithstanding their exclusion from the Platonic domain of pure intellectual knowledge, in mathematics 'proper'. It does not matter, for the achievement of such effects, if the mathematician in question does not pledge explicit allegiance to the variant schools of Dee or Ramus individually, or indeed to both – though many do. Since this bid for both neutrality and participation is, as ever, paradoxical, the more naïvely practically-minded the mathematician – the more, in Vitruvius's words, he only 'dips' into, and practically disregards the metaphysics of his subject – the more effectively, in fact, he is able to maintain his tenuous ground. And the means by which he maintains this ground – beyond simple silence – leads us back again to Plato.

It is crucial to the Platonic philosophy of mathematics that the 'clew' of mathematical ideality in the labyrinth of human ignorance not be confused with any more familiar prompt, and that the clue of illustrative 'images' whether sensible, or indeed discursive, be treated as nothing more than props dispensable to ideal mathematical truth. To speak properly as a pure mathematician is, in Platonic terms, to mark of figuration as waste superfluity, and ultimately, is not to speak of art at all. However much the Platonist may believe in a private language of individual self-communication, and in an investiture of the empirical with ideality which exceeds rhetorical expression, none the less does he acquiesce in the employment of such rhetoric to communicate his metaphysics to others. Of course in a sense, since metaphor is dispensable in a Platonic epistemology to true meaning, it does not in theory matter how great such detours into discourse are, any more than it matters how clumsily the philosophical mathematician draws his triangle. Hence the shameless ladders, bridges, etc. of Neoplatonism. Where Platonism is not so rigorously asserted, however, and indeed where we cast a Derridean doubt on the possibility of a Platonic 'private' language – de-figurised, de-socialised, de-historicised – this metaphorical participation may be all there is. Of course it is crucial to the value of mathematics that such a descent into the abyss of nothing-more-than-rhetoric never be faced up to. The covert, discursive means by which the consciously philosophical mathematician familiarises his mathematics; by which he productively endangers it; lets it settle in the world; is only of use to him as a detour disavowed as anything *but* detour; a merely virtual dilation in the punctual relation of intellect and truth. But then the more naïve; the more pragmatic the mathematics, the more it can exercise such supplementary detours, without troubling the foundation of ideal, and extra-discursive certainty upon which they covertly may seem to rest. The less it knows its danger, the more courageously it may travel.

Accordingly, the 'naïve' mathematical text, which leaves its foundations more or less alone, is often crammed with metaphors, and the expanded metaphors of anecdote, which do the real work in maintaining vacillation between a neutral and a participatory mathematics in art, and thereby in assuring the mathematical artist both transcendence of and agency in the world. Alberti claims to speak 'not as a mathematician but as a painter', to express himself in 'cruder terms' than those of pure mathematics.[42] And it is precisely these crude, painterly, *metaphorical* terms – terms which figure the mathematical line, for instance, as a 'brim'; and as a 'fringe' – that allow Alberti 'the artist' to speak at all.[43] The meaninglessness of an objective indeterminacy – of a mathematics 'somehow' between concept and quantity – beyond rhetoric, whether it be the overt metaphoricity of ladders, bridges and so on, or simply the implicit metaphoricity of 'between-ness', cannot be over-emphasised.[44] It is then rhetoric, and only figuratively the silent objectivity it appears to constitute, that affords a domain of operation to the artist: a figure looking both to wield the authority of universal truths placed beyond material, historical contingency, and at the same time to wield this authority through particular interventions in particular geo-historical scenarios. It is rhetoric that thereby satisfies the artistic demand not only to speak (and draw) the truth, but also to speak (and draw) exclusively: for, not with, the educated patron, and to, not with, the illiterate craftsman. The post-Renaissance artist, it might be said, 'inhabits' the indeterminacy of mathematical metaphor – of what Michel Foucault, in a discussion of the exceptional function and exemplary linguistic problematic of the 'labyrinth' and the 'metamorphosis' in the literary work of Raymond Roussel, ironically calls the 'singular figure' – whether this indeterminacy is explicitly rhetorical, as in the labyrinthine anecdotes of Cuningham and Wood, or more silently embodied, as in the Albertian points embedded in John Smith's map.[45] He lives on the less-than-neutral frontier between intellect and Indian, and in the labyrinth that might – as it was for Daedalus, the geometrician who, let us not forget, built the very fortress that was one day to imprison him – be either wilderness or home.

Rather than the Platonic 'home' of utter 'escape', and self-presence in the realisation of divine humanity, we are left with a home somewhere between the absolute and the familiar. Such a home – as Derrida says of metaphor – is *'a borrowed dwelling'* in which – for the brief moment of virtual time in which metaphor detains,[46] or abducts final meaning – one 'wanders'[47], may be lost, and yet then still 'comes back to oneself, recognises oneself, reassembles oneself or resembles oneself.'[48] A home in which, in other words, the artist experiences a temporary metamorphosis which may be regarded as at once a brutal dis-membering at the hands of a Minotaurian host; the trying on of sensual, empirical, prosthetic limbs designed for and thereby proper if not integral to him; and a benign assumption of his natural humanity. The metaphor, the – finally – far from 'singular' figure, by constituting mathematical embodiment as ambiguous, and thereby important in itself, affords the artistic escapee-to-truth, and the colonialist whose aspect he so fittingly adopts, the desirable capacity to be detained in a labyrinth of less-than-neutral signifiers and accommodated – in Wood's words – as 'doubtful traveller', in his borrowed, proper home.

Notes

1. William Wood, *New England's Prospect* (London, 1634), p. 70.
2. Wood, *New England's Prospect*, p. 70.
3. Typical of such presumption is David Harvey's comment in *The Condition of Postmodernity: An Enquiry into the Origins of Cultural Change* (Oxford: Basil Blackwell, 1989), p. 246, that the geometric aesthetic of Ptolemaic cartography made the world in general seem 'conquerable and containable for the purposes of human occupancy and action'.
4. See, for instance, Homi K. Bhabha, 'The Other Question: Difference, Discrimination, and the Discourse of Colonialism', in Francis Barker *et al.* (eds), *Literature, Politics and Theory* (Colchester: University of Essex, 1986), p. 156: 'Colonial power produces the colonised as a fixed reality which is at once an "other" and yet entirely knowable and visible.' In insisting upon the inherence of human with environmental alterity, I take a similar approach to Paul Carter in his study of early European encounters with Australia, *The Road to Botany Bay: an Essay in Spatial History* (London: Faber and Faber, 1987).
5. In *The Body Emblazoned: Dissection and the Human Body in Renaissance Culture* (London: Routledge, 1995), Jonathan Sawday charts the emergence of a post-Cartesian language of the body as intellectually driven 'machine' – the 'other' of empiricism – displacing earlier modes of thinking of the body as the geographical unexplored, and at the same time as the grotesque condition of the soul/intellect's secular imprisonment – the 'other' of idealism. This essay will tend to suggest that this displacement is incomplete in seventeenth-century discourse bearing on the division of labour between intellectual government and corporeal executive in mathematical art, and that the two modes are capable of co-operation.
6. For a full account of Ptolemaic projection, attended by reflections on the epistemological implications of its placement of the geographic viewer, see Samuel Edgerton, *The Renaissance Rediscovery of Linear Perspective* (New York: Basic Books, 1975).
7. See A. W. Richeson, *English Land Measuring to 1800: Instruments and Practices* (London: The London Society for the History of Technology, 1966) for an account of the advent and dissemination of triangulation.
8. Quoted in Edgerton, *Rediscovery*, p. 111.
9. This is never more evidently so than with the mathematical enclosure of heterogeneous feudal field systems. There is an argument to be made, although not here, that mathematical art provides an aesthetic not just for Florentine Civic Humanism, but also for the private property rationale of a nascent English Republicanism.
10. See Spiro Kostof, 'The Architect in the Middle Ages, East and West', in Spiro Kostof (ed.), *The Architect: Chapters in the History of the Profession* (London: Thames and Hudson, 1991).
11. Marcus Pollio Vitruvius, *The Ten Books on Architecture*, translated by Morris Hicky Morgan (New York: Dover, 1960), pp. 11–12.

12. See Kostof, 'The Architect', p. 74.
13. See Edgerton, *Rediscovery* for a comprehensive account of the development of artificial linear perspective in Italian Renaissance painting. Edgerton explores the common ground of geometric optics shared by perspective painting and Ptolemaic cartography.
14. See Alfred Sohn-Rethel, *Intellectual and Manual Labour: A Critique of Epistemology*, trans. Martin Sohn-Rethel (London: Macmillan, 1978) for an exploration of the reductive metonymy 'head'/'hand', which can be traced from Plato, through Vitruvius, to Vitruvius's Renaissance disciples. Like me, Sohn-Rethel discovers the social/epistemological border between head and hand to be marked, typically, through mathematics.
15. Leonardo da Vinci, *The Notebooks of Leonardo da Vinci*, ed. Irma A. Richter, (Oxford: The World's Classics – Oxford University Press, 1980), p. 118.
16. Vitruvius, *Ten Books*, p. 5.
17. Vitruvius, *Ten Books*, p. 13.
18. See Catherine Wilkinson, 'The New Professionalism in the Renaissance', in Kostof (ed.), *The Architect*.
19. Leon Battista Alberti, *'On Painting' and 'On Sculpture'*, edited and translated by Cecil Grayson, (London: Phaidon, 1972).
20. John Dee, 'Mathematicall Preface', in Euclid, *Euclides Elementes of Geometry: The First VI Books*, trans. by Thomas Rudd (London: 1650), sig.B2^v. Rudd's is one of several recyclings of Dee's essay, which originally prefaced Sir Henry Billingsley's first English Euclid.
21. Dee, 'Mathematicall Preface', sig.B2^v.
22. Robert Recorde, *The Pathway to Knowledg* (London: 1551), sig.A1^r.
23. Jean Leurechon, *Mathematical Recreations*, translated by William Oughtred (London: 1633), sig.A2^r.
24. The notion of a common ground of facilitating indeterminacy sets aside, at least from my own concerns, a fairly long-running debate over the relative importance of the mystic-Platonist and the pragmatic, nascent empiricist currents in early modern science. The writers I identify unanimously refuse, at least implicitly, to choose between or dispense with either a conceptual, essentially Platonic-idealist mathematics, or a radically pragmatic, empiricist mathematics original in the full-blooded usefulness of craft and commerce.
25. For an exploration of supplementarity which makes particular reference to the spatial logic of the map, see Jacques Derrida, *The Truth in Painting*, translated by Geoff Bennington and Ian McLeod (Chicago: Chicago University Press, 1987).
26. R. A. Skelton, *Decorative Printed Maps of the Fifteenth to Eighteenth Centuries* (London: Staples Press, 1952), p. 18.
27. See, for instance, John Norden, *The Surveyor's Dialogue* (London: 1607), p. 24.
28. See, for instance, Leonard Digges, *Pantometria* (London: 1571), sig.K4^v – sig.L3^r.
29. John Smith, 'The Generall History of Virginia', in Philip L. Barbour (ed.), *The Complete Works of Captain John Smith 1580–1631) vol 2*, p. 52.

30. Smith, 'Generall History', *Complete Works*, vol. 2, p. 52.
31. Giovanni Pico della Mirandola, *Oration on the Dignity of Man*, trans. A. Robert Caponigri (Los Angeles: Gateway Editions, Inc., 1956), p. 9.
32. Nicomachus of Gerasa, 'Introduction to Arithmetic', in Robert Maynard Hutchins (ed.), *Euclid, Archimedes, Apollonius of Perga, Nicomachus*, Great Books of the Western World 2 (London: Encyclopaedia Britannica Inc., 1952), p. 812.
33. The Latin *educo* carries both the meaning which English draws directly from it, and the more physical one of drawing or leading out.
34. Proclus, *A Commentary on the first Book of Euclid's Elements*, translated by Glenn A. Morrow (Princeton, New Jersey: Princeton University Press, 1970), p. 4.
35. Nicomachus, 'Introduction', p. 812.
36. William Cuningham, *Cosmographical Glasse* (London: 1559), sig.A2^r.
37. Quoted in Edward W. Strong, *Procedures and Metaphysics: A Study in the Philosophy of Mathematical-Metaphysical Science in the Sixteenth and Seventeenth Centuries* (Hildesheim: Georg Olms, 1966), p. 11.
38. See Aristotle, 'Posterior Analytics', A.II.71b.33–72a.5, in W. D. Ross (ed.), *The Works of Aristotle* (Oxford: Oxford University Press, 1908–1952).
39. See Philip Merlan, *From Platonism to Neoplatonism* (The Hague: Nijhoff, 1960), pp. 62–83.
40. See, for instance, Jacques Derrida, 'White Mythology', *Margins of Philosophy*, translated by Alan Bass (Brighton: Harvester Press, 1982) for a discussion of the disavowed necessity of metaphor and the impossible horizon of a private language, in metaphysical discourse from Plato to Husserl. Derrida argues in this and other texts that the 'endangerment' of closed structures of denotation through the discursive and material embodiment of language is essential for meaning to 'settle down' into the world.
41. For the thesis that the ascendancy of 'empiricism' led in some cases to the 'codification' rather than the 'refutation' of Platonism, see Ernst Cassirer, *The Individual and the Cosmos in Renaissance Philosophy*, trans. Mario Domandi (Oxford: Basil Blackwell, 1963), p. 152. For a characterisation of the early seventeenth-century scientific community as 'protean' and 'heterogeneous', rather than divided into rigorously aligned camps, see Mordecai Feingold, *The Mathematician's Apprenticeship: Science, Universities and Society in England, 1560–1640* (London: Cambridge University Press, 1969).
42. Alberti, *'On Painting'*, p. 36.
43. See Edgerton, *Rediscovery*, p. 81.
44. It is for this reason that I do not prioritise an engagement with the problematic of vision in early modern art here (as, for instance, does Edgerton). Vision, I would suggest, is involved in the mechanisms I am already describing through functioning both as simply a discrete, sensual-empirical faculty, registering and participating in particular phenomena – the artist's own, hand-drawn geometric point; a given environmental subject – *and* as neutral metaphor for that intellectual vision which perceives the mathematical form *a priori*; universal to

such phenomena. This, rather than the unfettered scopic agency and possessiveness that some cultural historians have described, is – if not the Platonic philosopher's aesthetic of sensual blindness – at least an aesthetic of misrecognition. The perspectivist artist, for instance, must mistake what he sees for either/both its own particular self or/and a neutral metaphor for ideal form. Such misrecognition presumes an indeterminacy irreducibly linguistic, and I accordingly join with Derrida in setting aside the perceptual, in favour of the rhetorical inquiry.

45. Michel Foucault, *Death and the Labyrinth: The World of Raymond Roussel*, trans. Charles Ruas (London: Athlone Press, 1987).
46. Derrida, 'White Mythology', p. 253.
47. Derrida, 'White Mythology', p. 241.
48. Derrida, 'White Mythology', p. 253.

8
Seeing and Knowing: Science, Pornography and Early Modern Hermaphrodites

Ruth Gilbert

In *Paradise Lost* Milton's Satan confesses an 'unspeakable desire to see, and know'.[1] Satan's words, which anticipate his voyage into the New World, resonate with a particularly Renaissance excitement about specular exploration and the pursuit of knowledge. However, as St Augustine had already suggested these were potentially dangerous thrills. In the *Confessions* he meditated upon the temptations aroused by the 'lust of the eyes', arguing that such ocular desires were most dangerous when motivated by 'a relish for investigation and discovery'.[2]

This essay suggests that these epistemophilic urges proved to be irresistibly seductive to the early modern culture of heroic scientific 'discovery'.[3] It focuses on representations of so-called hermaphrodites in late seventeenth and early eighteenth century popular and scholarly texts to argue that they were the subjects of a particularly early modern gaze. Hermaphroditic individuals evoked a mixture of disgust and desire, fear and fascination, which positioned them at the borders of the human. As they occupied a vulnerable threshold between male and female, human and monstrous, fact and fantasy, hermaphrodites were in many ways the consummate objects of a scientific scrutiny which could not, however, be easily separated from the prurient curiosity of popular entertainments and erotic objectification. Hermaphroditic case-histories were reported in the *Philosophical Transactions* of the Royal Society as well as within more obviously popular and commercial paramedical and erotic literature. But rather than being distinct these differently motivated representations of hermaphrodites reveal that the discourses of science and erotica were inextricably entwined. This essay discusses these connections between the emerging discourses of the New Science and pornography and illustrates this discursive convergence through an analysis of a number of case histories from both popular and scientific accounts.

In conclusion, the essay demonstrates that beneath many enquiries into hermaphroditism was an implicit concern to construct and constrict what was seen as an excessive female sexuality. As sexual knowledge became disseminated in both scientific and pornographic texts, women were increasingly represented as being susceptible to carnal immoderation. Women were positioned as both the explicit subjects of the erotic adventures which were detailed within these narratives, and, it was repeatedly implied, the sexually susceptible readers who might easily slip into a dangerous hermaphroditic lasciviousness.

I   SEEING AND KNOWING

The seventeenth-century privileging of the visual was rooted in a Baconian paradigm of natural philosophy. In *The Great Instauration* (1620), Bacon outlined an intellectual programme which would be based on visual proof alone. He declared that he would admit nothing in his relentless pursuit of knowledge 'but on the faith of my eyes'.[4] As Abraham Cowley later styled it, in his celebration of the philosophical principles of the Royal Society, Bacon was a Moses-like figure who led science from the barren wilderness of superstition. In Cowley's rhetoric the New Science of the late seventeenth century had replaced illusive representations with empirical truths. Bacon, he declared, illuminated the expanding world of natural philosophy through his visionary message: he 'saw it himself, and shew'd us it.'[5]

The impulse 'to see and know' was both symbolised and actualised by Robert Hooke's development of the microscope, a device which visually probed and penetrated previously uninvestigated worlds. As Hooke announced in his Preface to *Micrographia* (1665), which was published two years before Cowley's 'Ode to the Royal Society' and Milton's *Paradise Lost*, technological developments in seeing the world represented a new confidence in knowing it:

By the means of *Telescopes*, there is nothing so *far distant* but may be represented to our view; and by the help of *Microscopes*, there is nothing so *small*, as to escape our inquiry; hence there is a new visible World discovered to understanding.[6]

The seventeenth-century scientist was thus cast as an heroic explorer of a newly discovered world. For Cowley, the purifying scientific endeavours which Bacon had instigated were equated with colonial possession. Knowledge was represented as undiscovered terrain which promised 'large and wealthy Regions to subdue'.[7] Although in *The History of the Royal Society* (1667) Thomas Sprat argued that the New Science was more effective than colonialism as a way in which 'to increase the Powers of all Mankind' contemporary images of 'discovery' and possession were evidently potent within the early modern scientific imagination.[8] In Hooke's words, the scientist was a conqueror of 'new Worlds and *Terra-Incognitas*'.[9]

The rhetoric of colonial exploration and scientific revelation was also a potentially erotically charged conjunction. As Thomas Laqueur has observed, when Renaldus Columbus claimed 'discovery' of the clitoris in 1559, he did so (like Christopher before him) with the confidence of a 'conquistador in an unknown land'.[10] Of course, like America, the clitoris had existed for a long time before it came into Columbus's view, but science had created in itself a new defining gaze. It was a gaze which was directed by an imperative towards the penetrative visual exploration of both the expanding geographical world and the equally compelling inner terrain of the human body.

II   THE SCIENCE OF PORNOGRAPHY/THE PORNOGRAPHY OF SCIENCE

Discussions of human biology and the reproductive body had, until the sixteenth century, traditionally been written in Latin and Greek and were thereby circulated primarily within an élite (and mainly male) culture. As these works were translated and adapted in vernacular versions throughout the sixteenth and seventeenth centuries, so the dilemma of how the sexed body could be represented objectively without exciting the reader to lustful thoughts had to be negotiated.[11] When, in St Augustine's words, 'the genital organs have become ... the private property of lust', how could they be represented without taint?[12] When, in other words, did a 'scientific' naming of the 'parts' become pornography?

For St Augustine, the pudenda etymologically and symbolically marked the genitals as 'parts of shame'.[13] However, these 'parts' were increasingly exposed as the classic works of Aristotle, Galen and Hippocrates which discussed sex and generation were returned to, translated and reiterated throughout the sixteenth and seventeenth centuries. Medical knowledge thus became more accessible and popularised as a new 'science' of sex began to emerge.[14] As William Harvey declared in his preface to *de Generatione* (1651), 'to Us the whole Theatre of the World is now open.'[15] But what did it mean to open up the world of the sexed body? Such imperial rhetorical flourishes evaded the ambivalent responses which were evoked by bringing these secrets to light.

In fact, many representations of genitalia in this period reinscribed metaphors of secrecy as they participated in discourses of disclosure. Helkiah Crooke's English anatomy text, *Microcosmographia: A Description of the Body of Man* (1615), had been typical of this tendency towards the veiled representation of female genitalia when it placed them under the heading of 'the Lap or Privities', and discussed them as 'too obscoene to look upon'.[16] In 1671, Jane Sharp included a chapter entitled 'Of the Secrets of the Female Sex' in her guide to midwifery. She noted that:

> The Lips, or Laps of the Privities are outwardly seen ... both are to keep the inward parts from cold, and that nothing get in to offend the womb, some call this the womans modesty, for they are a double door like Floodgates, to shut and open.[17]

These secret parts were interpreted as having a dual function. Like the bodily gates which framed Spenser's House of Alma, they were simultaneously both 'shut and open'.[18] The lips thus functioned to retain the secret interior of the female body but also to indicate its presence.

The entwinement of secrecy and disclosure, erotica and edification infuses many early modern studies of sex. The development of scientific studies of the sexed body could be described, in Foucault's terms, as a *scientia sexualis*, a series of discourses which attempted 'to tell the truth of sex'.[19] These early discourses of science, or natural philosophy, were always implicated in other forms of knowledge and interpretation. Foucault points out that the *ars erotica*, the knowledge of sexual pleasure which circulated as a secret between master and adept, was woven into the *scientia sexualis* as new pleasures were developed in the production of discourses about sex.

Many early modern authors of books about human reproduction were careful to emphasise the educational and scientific intention of their work by constructing it as a *scientia sexualis* in a self-conscious attempt to distance it from the *ars erotica*. But the erotic potential of the subject was difficult to dissipate. These texts were often prefaced by the author's or translator's disclaimer of any lewdness which might be read into their subject matter. This inevitably drew attention to the exact interpretation which they were ostensibly trying to suppress.

However, the question was not only one of authorial intention. With increasing levels of literacy and the emergence of print culture, the readership of a text was becoming unpredictable and potentially uncontrollable. Jane Sharp wrote *The Midwives Book* (1671) in English and addressed it explicitly to women who had hitherto been denied knowledge of classical texts. She frankly acknowledged the dangers (and implicit pleasures) of making this knowledge accessible when she advised readers of her text to:

> Use as much modesty in the perusal of it, as I have endeavoured to do in the writing of it, considering that such an Art as this cannot be set forth, but that young men and maids will have much just cause to blush sometimes.[20]

In spite of such protestations many supposedly medical advice manuals were often close to the developing genre of pornography. As Lynn Hunt has pointed out, 'pornography was not a given' but had a history in which it almost always intersected with other discourses.[21] Rather than constituting a genre in itself it often figured as part of political commentary, social satire and scientific enquiries.[22] In early modern medical and erotic works the discourses which, to a twentieth-century reader, might be classified as science and pornography often drew upon exactly the same material and presented it in a remarkably similar style.

In practice a great deal of erotic material was disseminated through the vast amounts of sensational paramedical literature which was produced for profit.[23] These texts could often inform as well as arouse the reader.[24] Popular and enduring works such as

Aristotles Master-Piece, for example, contained some practical information about sex and generation as well as more explicitly titillating material.[25] However, it remained a convention for the author of these studies to deny, perhaps with a certain amount of irony, the book's erotic content. This was held to be entirely in the eye of its reader. As the anonymous writer of the 1684 edition of *Aristotlés Master-Piece* explained, the work was scientific in intention and not meant for the eyes of any 'obscene person':

> I shall proceed to unravel the mystery of Generation, and divers other Mysteries, as I well hope, to the satisfaction of the learned and ingenious of the Age, whose discretion, past doubt, will wrest it to no other than what it was designed; viz. for the benefit and advantage of the modesty of either Sex;[26]

The subtext of these works was clear: by uncovering the secrets of generation, in a penetration of *scientia sexualis*, the mysteries of *ars erotica* would also be revealed.

In 1657 Richard Head, under the pseudonym of 'Erotodidascalus', translated *Geneanthropeiae*, an erotic Latin text which was written by Joannes Benedictus Sinibaldus in 1642. The title of Head's text, *Rare Verities: the Cabinet of Venus Unlocked, and Her Secrets Laid Open*, played on familiar tropes of secrecy and revelation in erotic discourse. Head confronted potential accusations of obscenity by admitting that: 'It may be some seemingly modest, will hold me for a Capitall offender for Transcribing those things into English, which should have remained still in the obscurity of an unknown tongue.'[27] He argued, on the contrary, that he was performing a valuable service by transmitting such knowledge. In the spirit of the New Science, he cast himself as the heroic explorer of Nature's secrets:

> Either commend or pity me for the pains I have taken, to make you and others more intelligent in these occult mysteries. I am content to be the pick-lock of Venus her Cabinet, to let you with more ease enter and rifle and despoile her inestimable treasure.[28]

The language of erotica and science coincided as Head echoed Cowley's characterisation of Harvey as the penetrator of 'coy nature'.[29] Harvey's entry into Nature's (as he termed it) 'Closet-secrets' through scientific knowledge is supplemented by the language of sexual pleasure as the scientist and pornographer explore similar terrain.[30] In Head's metaphor, however, he is only the lock-picker, not the agent of penetration. He merely clears the way for the reader, the erotic explorer, 'to enter and rifle' within.

III   NAMING THE PARTS: THE HERMAPHRODITE AS OBJECT OF ENQUIRY

Studies of hermaphrodites routinely combined an interest in physical anomalies, human biology, scientific taxonomies and sexual excitement. The hermaphrodite had been popularised as a subject of scientific enquiry in the studies of Jacques Duval (1612), Gaspard Bauhin (1614), and Jean Riolan (1614) as well as in the medical works of Jacob Rueff (1554) and Ambroise Paré (1573).[31] Apart from Bauhin's each of these works was published in the French vernacular and was either translated into English or transmitted into English texts. Such works often straddled an unclear boundary between science and sensation, and writers of medical and paramedical enquiries into hermaphrodites skilfully manipulated the slippage between these unstable terms. As Lorraine Daston and Katharine Park have observed, the authors of vernacular works which discussed hermaphrodites exploited the commercial possibilities attached to the erotic nature of their subject matter.[32]

Duval's introduction to his study of hermaphrodites (which was seized by the Rouen authorities shortly after its publication) constituted a frank admission of the pornographic implications of his material. It amounted to an effective advertisement for the rest of his text:

> Powerful Nature, that excellent artisan, desiring to encourage men to the propagation of their species, was not content to produce great enjoyment when we actually use our genitals, but also – moved by what instinct I do not know – arranged that we would experience such pleasurable titillation and lustful attraction when they are but named or indicated, that even if I were to use hieroglyphics borrowed from the Egyptians ... to designate them ... I could not eliminate the simple wantonness with which Nature has ornamented and decorated their commemoration.[33]

Duval thus articulated a definition of pornography, and the hermaphrodite had a special place within that discourse. In scientific

studies the hermaphrodite was determined by its genital organisation. His/her representation consequently necessitated a detailed
and repeated naming of the parts. In this way the hermaphrodite
was an ideal subject of the sort of 'pleasurable titillation' which
Duval described as inextricably linked to the depiction (however
codified) of sexual parts.

The hermaphroditic body could be seen therefore as the paradigmatic focus of a pornographic gaze. To describe it was to engage in
the language of genitalia. Antonio Beccadelli, the author of the noto-
rious fifteenth-century pornographic Latin poem, *Hermaphroditus*,
made this point succinctly. 'In effect', he wrote, 'my book has both a
penis and a vagina.'[34] Its title thereby entirely described its subject.
Beccadelli had bluntly recognised the hermaphrodite as a symbol for
sexuality, a codification which would remain current throughout
later treatments of similar material.

Giles Jacob's *A Treatise of Hermaphrodites* (1718) secured the place
of the hermaphrodite within eighteenth-century erotica. The treatise was printed by Edmund Curll with the blatantly pornographic
work, *A Treatise of the Use of Flogging at Venereal Affairs*. Jacob's text
coupled a well-worn account of the causes and manifestations of
hermaphroditism with a long textual excursion into lesbian adventures. Whereas Beccadelli's poem had drawn on the explicit
pornography of classical priapi, Jacob embedded his subject in the
language of curiosity and exploration. In his preface he argued
that:

> The Secrets of Nature have in all Ages been particularly examin'd
> by Anatomists and others, and this of *Hermaphrodites* is so very
> wonderful, that I am perfectly assur'd my present Enquiry will
> be entirely acceptable to all Lovers of curious Discoveries, and as
> it is my immediate Business to trace every Particular for an ample
> Dissertation on the Nature of *Hermaphrodites*, (which obliges me
> to a frequent Repetition of the Names of the Parts employ'd in
> the Business of Generation) so, I hope, I shall not be charg'd with
> obscenity, since in all Treatises of this kind it is impossible to
> finish any one Head compleatly, without pursuing the Methods
> of Anatomical Writings.[35]

For Jacob, the imperative to 'trace every Particular' marks the
confluence between the methodologies of early modern science,
and the techniques of pornography.

Jacob's process of erotic discovery and Head's lock-picking pursuit of the secrets of sex, thus echoed the explicitly heroic principles of the New Science. In 1667 Thomas Sprat had described the aims of the Royal Society as a quest for truth based on a rigorous process of naming. The scientific mission, he proclaimed, was:

> To make faithful *records*, of all the Works of *Nature*, or *Art*, which come within their reach ... to restore the truths, that have lain neglected: to push on those, which are already known ... and to make the way more passable, to what remains unreveal'd.[36]

Sprat argued that a detailed and accurate recording of observable facts would direct natural philosophy towards the fulfilment of its valiant quest. The explorers of both scientific and sexual knowledge shared a manifestly similar impulse as they each sought to penetrate and reveal the 'secrets of nature'.

IV   CASE HISTORIES, CURIOSITIES AND DISPLAY

The anomalous and confusing spectacle of hermaphroditic bodies focused the seventeenth-century New Scientific desire 'to see and know'. Potentially, hermaphrodites were both intellectually intriguing and erotically stimulating sights. Many earlier representations of hermaphrodites, such as those depicted in Ambroise Paré's sixteenth-century study, were presented as anonymous bodies without social or cultural history. Duval's detailed account of the case of Marie/Marin le Marcis in 1612 marked a shift in the representation of hermaphrodites. Throughout the seventeenth century hermaphrodites were increasingly depicted as specific and distinctive cases rather than as universalised examples of God's wonder, or as the abstract signs of political, social or religious corruption. By the late-seventeenth century the New Science demanded names, locations, histories and most importantly ever more probing anatomical details.

Two particular cases of hermaphroditism which were related in letters published in the *Philosophical Transactions* of 1667 and 1686 characterised the ways in which the hermaphrodite became the focus of a developing scientific gaze in this period. Significantly, neither were published in English. The use of Latin in one letter and French in the other identified hermaphroditism as a fitting subject of scientific detachment in one case and cultural distance in the other.

'An Exact Narrative of an Hermaphrodite now in London' (1667) was written in Latin by Thomas Allen, a physician and a member of the Royal Society. It concerned the case of Anna Wilde, an hermaphrodite who had been born in 1647 in Ringwood, Hampshire.[37] This account is characteristic of the mid-seventeenth-century scientific representation of hermaphrodites. Its preface in the *Philosophical Transactions* declared it to be fit 'for the view of the Learned'. It was clearly marked as *scientia sexualis*, an object to be placed under the inquiring gaze of the educated spectator. Accordingly, this case of hermaphroditism was presented as an unfolding development of sexual ambiguity rather than as a depiction of a static moment of abnormality.

The story that Allen related was marked by dramatic moments of transformation in a narrative structured by the visible signs of changed sex. Anna Wilde had been classified as female at birth, but at the age of six, whilst wrestling with boys of her/his own age, testicles apparently were seen. Allen explained that the scrotum developed from the labia of her/his vulva. However, Anna Wilde was still regarded as a girl until s/he was thirteen. At this time a penis suddenly emerged, which Allen described as being capable of erection but not ejaculation. The ejaculate was instead issued (apparently with considerable force) from the vagina. From the age of sixteen, Anna Wilde began to menstruate but s/he also developed a beard and other secondary male characteristics which made sexual classification problematic. Allen thus presented her/him to the Royal Society as one of nature's rare occurrences: a case of physical hermaphroditism.

Allen's report was presented as the authoritative observations of a member of the Royal Society. But evidence suggests that his account was largely compiled from the stories of Anna Wilde's 'owner' who displayed her/him as freak in a travelling show. In his diary entry for 22 August 1667, John Evelyn mentioned that this popular spectacle was currently being shown in London:

There was also now an *Hermaphrodite* shew'd both *Sexes* very perfectly, the *Penis* onely not perforated, went for a woman, but was more a man, of about 21 years of Age: divers curious persons went to see her, but I would not.[38]

Evelyn did not elaborate on why he would not view this show, although it was clearly something of considerable contemporary interest. S/he was viewed for entertainment by 'divers curious persons' and the 'facts' of her/his history were mediated through the stories told in this commercial context.

The early modern scientist was part of a viewing public who paid to look at curiosities. An advertisement from the early-eighteenth century, for example, announced that for one shilling an hermaphrodite could be viewed:

> Compleat Male and Female, perfect in both Parts, and does give a general Satisfaction to all Quality, Gentry, Physicians, Surgeons and Others, that have seen it, constant Attendance is given from One a Clock in the Afternoon 'till Nine at Night ... There is a paper Lantern over the Door, with these Words upon it, *The Hermaphrodite is to be seen here without a Moments loss of Time*.[39]

Allen's description of his viewing of Anna Wilde for the *Philosophical Transactions* was drawn from this culture of curiosity and display. James Parsons in his later, more sceptical study of hermaphrodites, *A Mechanical and Critical Enquiry into the Nature of Hermaphrodites* (1741), reviewed the case. He dismissively referred to Allen's account as a clear sign of 'how little credit ought to be given to the Tales of Shew-men, by the Learned'.[40]

The Dutch physician Isbrand de Diemerbroeck, whose *Anatomy of Human Bodies* was translated by William Salmon in 1689, reported viewing an hermaphrodite in Utrecht in 1668 (the year after Anna Wilde had been shown in London). Although s/he is unnamed in this account the evidence suggests that Diemerbroeck was also describing Anna Wilde.[41] Before he related the details of the case, Diemerbroeck signalled how hermaphrodites were presented as popular spectacles in street shows as well as in specifically learned contexts. He recalled that he had previously seen a similar hermaphrodite in Anjou, who 'for a small matter turn'd up her Coats to any one that had a mind to satisfy Curiosity.'[42] However, the curious passer-by might also be the enquiring scientist. His anecdote demonstrated that the desire to fulfil the epistemophilic urge 'to see and know' could be easily exploited as a money-spinning show and tell.

Diemerbroeck's account of viewing Anna Wilde in 1668 was again predicated on the history given by the hermaphrodite's

'Governour'. This verbal history was supplemented by a visual examination of the hermaphrodite's anatomy and Diemerbroeck reported that, 'We saw the Yard hanging forth about half a Finger long'. According to 'his Governour' the hermaphrodite menstruated every month, and also ejaculated semen at orgasm, but Diemerbroeck noted that 'the *Hermaphrodite* himself could not tell whether it flow'd through his Yard, or from his Female Privities.'[43]

As Parsons later observed, there were several inconsistencies between Allen's and Diemerbroeck's versions of the case. For example, in Utrecht the 'owner' claimed that the hermaphrodite menstruated regularly, in London he had reported that s/he had stopped menstruating at eighteen. Parsons wrote disdainfully about Allen's account that:

> The inconsistencies that appear thro' this whole Narration from first to last, should promise no great credit, for it is entirely taken from the Owner of the Girl, and securely presented ... without the Author's considering that no one Part of his History can be reconciled to the known structure of the human Body.[44]

The integrity of the report was derided because it was based on second-hand information. Allen had neglected Bacon's maxim to trust nothing 'but on the faith of my eyes'. But, for Parsons, looking through the lens of 'enlightenment' rationality, the real weakness of Allen's muddled narrative was that it contradicted the known facts of the body.

In December 1686, Monsieur Veay, a French physician, wrote a letter to the *Philosophical Transactions* about another sensational case of hermaphroditism which he had seen in Toulouse.[45] A note in the *Philosophical Transactions* underscored the special nature of this account when it explained that 'this communication is reprinted in the original French, it being judged improper to appear in English'. But in 1687, Edmond Halley commented that:

> There is some difficulty to believe this story, tho it seems well attested, being from a noted physitian of the place; but the bantring ridiculing humour of that light nation makes one suspect all that comes from thence.[46]

Halley's suspicion, based on a mistrust of the French, suggests a particular doubt about French scientific integrity. This was, perhaps because although 'that light nation' had produced all the significant contemporary studies of hermaphrodites, it was also associated with the production of pornography.[47]

The case of Marguerite Malause which Veay related in his letter was widely discussed in early modern medical, paramedical and pornographic literature. Veay's account gives a detailed description of the history and anatomy of Marguerite Malause. S/he was born in Pourdiac, near Toulouse, where s/he lived as a woman until s/he became ill in 1686 and was examined by Veay. He declared that s/he was an hermaphrodite, 'une chose fort extraordinaire'. S/he was, according to his account, in all superficial respects an attractive young woman of about twenty-one, but on closer examination it was discovered that, although she appeared to be female, she could only be penetrated to about two finger widths deep. Moreover, s/he was found to have a penis ('un membre viril d'une grosseur fort considérable') which could erect to about eight inches. According to Veay both urine and semen, as well as menstrual blood, flowed through this penis. Veay stressed that he would not have believed this possible if he had not seen it with his own eyes. He showed this extraordinary figure to several other doctors, who, in consultation with the governors of the hospital declared her/him to be predominantly male and ordered her/him to change her/his name to the masculine Arnaud and adopt the clothes and life-style of a man. The testimony of Marguerite her/himself was not considered to be credible. Veay noted that there was no hesitation over the verdict because 'notre hermaphrodite' was able to perform the functions of a man and not a woman.

Later anecdotal evidence suggests that Marguerite/Arnaud did not live happily with this new male persona. S/he was the subject of considerable local curiosity and scandal and eventually left Toulouse and reverted back to a female identity. In 1691 s/he was arrested for transgressing the boundaries of the sex and gender which had been attributed to her and was ordered again to live as a man. In 1693 s/he came to Paris where her case was considered by the famous physicians Helvétius and Saviard who concluded finally that s/he was in fact a woman.

In Saviard's account of the case, which was published in 1702, he described how Marguerite/Arnaud had arrived in Paris:

in the guise of a boy, sword at his side, with his hair nonetheless hanging like a girl, and tied behind with a ribbon in the manner of the Spaniards and Neapolitans. She used to appear at public assemblies and allow herself to be examined for a small tip by those who were curious.[48]

Marguerite/Arnaud may have participated in presenting her/himself as a spectacle for the view of 'those who were curious'. One anonymous pornographic work, which shifted the emphasis of the case from medical curiosity to erotic titillation, also suggested that 'she got Mony by shewing herself.'[49] In contrast to the situation of Anna Wilde, there is no evidence that Marguerite/Arnaud had a master who controlled this commercial display.

Saviard's account of the case represented the hermaphrodite without compassion. He described her/him in purely scientific terms, declaring that he 'examined her in each part with exactitude.'[50] Marguerite/Arnaud's body was thus fragmented into a series of pieces which were thoroughly objectified by this scientific/pornographic examination. For the hermaphrodite nothing could be hidden from the scientist's probing gaze. Saviard reported the physical demonstration which Marguerite/Arnaud was obliged to perform to himself and the gathered assembly in the hospital, Hotel Dieu:

I made her urinate before the gathered assembly, upon her claiming that urine did issue from two separate places; and in order to make apparent the contrary, while she urinated I did spread apart the lips of her vulva, by which means I did make the spectators see the urinary meatus from whence the flow did proceed exclusively.[51]

On this evidence, couched in the language and methodology of scientific objectivity, the hermaphrodite was presented as a public experiment, as the proof of 'true' sex was viewed, witnessed and recorded.

V   UNSPEAKABLE DESIRES: THE HERMAPHRODITE AS EROTIC ENTERTAINMENT

In a collection of advertisements dated between 1680 and 1700 which are held in the British Library there is a handbill reporting the case of 'An HERMAPHRODITE (Lately brought over from ANGOLA)'.[52] The general description of this hermaphroditic woman was written in English, and was followed by a Latin section which provided the details of genital organisation that were presumably intended to attract the educated 'curious examiner'. Again Latin was used as an exclusive language which encoded sexual knowledge for the learned whilst signalling the special (and sensational) nature of that knowledge to the unlearned. This spectacle could be viewed near Charing Cross, for the price of 2s 6d.

The background to this show demonstrates how the early modern European plunder of the world was not only an economic enterprise. It was also motivated by a colonial desire to posess the bodies of racially encoded others. The Angolan woman had been taken from Africa to America as part of the slave-trade and was later brought to Bristol and exhibited as a freak. In 1741 James Parsons claimed that his study of hermaphroditism had been motivated by what he considered to have been the misinterpretation of this case. His aim was to present the case objectively to 'all Lovers of Truth in Natural History'.[53] However, the large fold-out engraving of the vulva of the Angolan woman, which Parsons meticulously detailed and reproduced in his medical text, is a graphic illustration of the eroticisation of the colonial gaze within a scientific context. Such displays drew from a pornographic and scientific requirement to represent the genitals in explicit detail but was intensified by the frisson of fear and desire aroused by the idea of 'foreign parts'.

The exhibition of the Angolan woman as an hermaphroditic spectacle also, however, suggested an anxiety about prodigious female sexuality closer to home.[54] François de Chavigny de la Bretonnière's *The Gallant Hermaphrodite* (1688) typified the interplay between erotic 'discovery', hermaphroditic anatomy, and female same sex desire that characterised the development of the pornographic novel. The body of the text, which described itself as 'An Amorous Novel', comprised a complicated plot of sexual intrigue and disguised identity. The story's dénouement comes when the Princess heroine makes love to a character called Iphigenia, believing her to be a woman, 'who instructed her of what she was ignorant of till then', and discovers that she is an hermaphrodite.[55] This scene of lesbian seduction, and the revelation of hermaphroditism, is representative of much contemporary erotic literature.[56] However, the narrator in this story, with a self-conscious display of modesty, does not relate details about what exactly occurred between the lovers. He pauses tactfully, and intimates that 'the curtains have robb'd us of the rest.'[57]

The preface to this text provides a striking insight into the strategies of veiled representation which formed a motif of these texts. The hermaphrodite is clearly placed within the context of early modern popular entertainment but the audience for this spectacle is not here the implied masculine viewer of scientific demonstration. The author declares:

> As to those Ladies who delight in the sight of the Elephants, Hairy Maids, Turks, &c. I hope our Gallant Hermaphrodite will be kindly entertain'd by them, since they may, without scandal, even in their Alcoves, freely view and converse with this — what shall we call it?
>
> Sir, or Madam, chuse you whether;
> Nature twists them both together.[58]

The word left blank, 'what shall we call it?', and the couplet, quoted from John Cleveland's 'Upon an Hermophrodite' (1640), create a discursive openness. The playful suggestion of an interaction between the gallant hermaphrodite and the reader, the object of observation and the observer, points to a realm of textual reception within domestic, and in this case implicitly female, spaces. The consumption of such erotic literature was presented therefore as a particularly private viewing pleasure of an emerging, and increasingly female, bourgeois readership. However, the textual construction of this implied female reader as being intimately absorbed by the gallant hermaphrodite's erotic adventures whilst alone (and 'without scandal') in their alcoves, also allowed the male reader to fantasise the imagined pleasures of this scene.

In Jacob's *Treatise of Hermaphrodites* (1718) the woman reader was again made a focus of prefatory attention. He teasingly disclaimed the possibility that women could be incited to imitate the seductive behaviour which his text related:

> My Design in the following sheets is meerly as an innocent Entertainment for all curious Persons, without any Views of inciting Masculine-Females to Amorous Tryals with their own Sex; and I am perswaded there will not be one single *HERMAPHRODITE* the more in the World, on account of the publishing this TREATISE.[59]

Jacob's denial that the 'innocent Entertainment' of his text could possibly transform the female reader into an hermaphrodite implied that such a corruption was perhaps possible.[60] Seeing was indeed the prelude to knowing. Hermaphrodites were, in other words, created not born. They were defined by their sexuality as well as their sexual anatomy. For Jacob, hermaphrodites were, in effect, lustful women whose enlarged clitorises reflected their equally enlarged sexual appetites. His textual revelations about hermaphrodites thus brought to light the possibly disconcerting but potentially thrilling realm of female sexual desires.

Jacob continued by light-heartedly bringing into focus the dialectic between the hidden and the revealed which infused such erotic explorations of hermaphroditism:

It may be expected by some faithless Persons, that I should produce an *HERMAPHRODITE* to publick view, as an incontestable Justification of there being Humane Creatures of this kind; but as I have no Authority to take up the Petticoats of any Female without her Consent, I hope to be excus'd from making such demonstrable Proofs;[61]

The presentation of this potentially salacious material in print was part of the prevailing cultural appetite for curiosities and display. Like the New Scientific physical examinations of hermaphroditic individuals Jacob's treatise engaged in a textual exploration of hermaphroditic anatomy and sexual activity. However, unlike the New Scientists Jacob does not authenticate his text with the spectacle of an hermaphroditic body.

The New Scientific principles of the seventeenth century imbued observers such as Allen, Veay, and Saviard with the authority to scrutinise the bodies of supposedly hermaphroditic subjects such as Anna Wilde and Marguerite/Arnaud Malause in a relentless search for 'demonstrable proofs'. But Jacob's ironic admission of his own lack of such authority highlighted how both the scientific and pornographic gaze continually probed into forbidden places in order to unpick the secrets of Venus.

By relating the scientific 'proof' of hermaphroditism to the indecent explorations beneath the petticoats of women, Jacob exemplified the paradox of early modern scientific display. The earnest medical accounts written about Anna Wilde and Marguerite Malause were derived as much from a culture of commercialised shows and sensationalised anecdotes as 'scientific' observation. Such narratives were easily absorbed into salacious or erotic discourse as the epistemophilic imperatives of *scientia sexualis* and *ars erotica* converged. The New Science had found a way in which to articulate its imperative 'to see and know', but that discourse could not easily be distanced from the pornographic impulse to speak the 'unspeakable desires' of the erotic imagination.

Notes

1. John Milton, *Paradise Lost*, in John Carey and Alastair Fowler (eds),*The Poems of John Milton* (London: Longman, 1968), III.662.
2. St Augustine, *Confessions*, trans. R. S. Pine-Coffin (Harmondsworth: Penguin, 1961), p. 242.
3. For a discussion of the epistemophilic drive see Toril Moi, 'Patriarchal Thought and the Drive for Knowledge', Teresa Brennan (ed.), in *Between Feminism and Psychoanalysis* (London: Routledge, 1989), pp. 189–205.
4. Francis Bacon, *The Great Instauration*, in James Spedding, Robert Leslie Ellis and Douglas Denon Heath (eds), *The Works of Francis Bacon*, 14 vols (London: Longman, 1857–1874), IV, p. 30.
5. Abraham Cowley, 'To The Royal Society', in A. R. Waller (ed.), *Poems*, (Cambridge: Cambridge University Press, 1973), p. 448. Cowley's ode was originally published with Thomas Sprat's *History of the Royal Society* (London, 1667).
6. Robert Hooke, *Micrographia: Or some Physiological Descriptions of Minute Bodies made by Magnifying Glasses with Observations and Inquiries thereupon* (London, 1665), sig.A[v].
7. Cowley, 'To The Royal Society', 6.
8. Thomas Sprat, *The History of the Royal-Society of London, for the Improving of Natural Knowledge* (London, 1667), 'Epistle Dedicatory', n.p.
9. Hooke, *Micrographia*, sig.D[v].
10. Thomas Laqueur, *Making Sex: Body and Gender from the Greeks to Freud* (Cambridge MA: Harvard University Press, 1990), p. 64.
11. For an analysis of some of the issues surrounding the translation of medical texts into the vernacular in the early part of the seventeenth century see H.S. Bennett, *English Books and Readers 1475–1640*, 3 vols (1970), (Reprinted, Cambridge: Cambridge University Press, 1989), III, pp. 140–3.
12. St Augustine, *City of God*, translated and edited by Henry Bettenson (1972), (Reprinted, Harmondsworth: Penguin, 1984), p. 581.
13. Augustine, *City of God*, p. 578. The English definition of the Latin 'pudendus' is, 'of which one ought to be ashamed, shameful, scandalous'. Freud also noted the uncanny function of the '*heimlich*' parts

of the human body, *pudenda'*. See Freud, 'The Uncanny' (1919), in *Art And Literature*, Penguin Freud Library, 15 vols (Harmondsworth: Penguin, 1985), XIV p. 346.

14. Patricia Crawford notes that 'from the early to the mid-seventeenth century, especially during the Civil Wars and Interregnum, there was a movement to popularise medical knowledge.' See 'Sexual Knowledge in England, 1500–1750', in Roy Porter and Mikulàs Teich (eds), *Sexual Knowledge, Sexual Science: the History of Attitudes to Sexuality* (Cambridge: Cambridge University Press, 1994), pp. 82–106, quotation, p. 86.

15. William Harvey, *Anatomical Exercitations Concerning the Generation of Living Creatures* (London, 1653), sig. A3.

16. Helkiah Crooke, *Microcosmographia: A Description of the Body of Man* (London, 1615), p. 293.

17. Jane Sharp, *The Midwives Book* (London, 1671), pp. 41–2.

18. Edmund Spenser, *The Faerie Queene*, ed. A. C. Hamilton, (London: Longman, 1977), II.23.

19. Michel Foucault, *The History of Sexuality: an Introduction*, trans. Robert Hurley (1976), (Reprinted, Harmondsworth: Penguin, 1978), p. 57.

20. Sharp, *Midwives Book*, p. 5.

21. Lynn Hunt, 'Introduction: Obscenity and the Origins of Modernity, 1500–1800', in *The Invention of Pornography: Obscenity and the Origins of Modernity, 1500–1800*, Lynn Hunt (ed.), (New York: Zone, 1993), pp. 9–45, quotation, p. 11.

22. For discussions of early modern pornography, see Roger Thompson, *Unfit for Modest Ears: a Study of Pornographic, Obscene and Bawdy Works Written or Published in England in the Second Half of the Seventeenth Century* (London: Macmillan, 1979); David Foxon, *Libertine Literature in England 1660–1745* (Reprinted with revisions from *The Book Collector*, 1964); and Peter Wagner, *Eros Revived: Erotica of the Enlightenment in England and America* (London: Paladin Grafton Books, 1990).

23. See, Peter Wagner, 'The Discourse on Sex – or Sex as Discourse: Eighteenth-Century Medical and Paramedical Literature', in G. S. Rousseau and Roy Porter (eds), *Sexual Underworlds of the Enlightenment* (Manchester: Manchester University Press, 1987), pp. 46–68.

24. See Roy Porter, 'The Literature of Sexual Advice before 1800', in *Sexual Knowledge, Sexual Science*, pp. 134–157.

25. *Aristotlés Master-Piece* was first published in 1684 was reprinted regularly throughout the eighteenth century. See Roy Porter, '"The Secrets of Generation Display'd": *Aristotle's Masterpiece* in Eighteenth-Century England', in R. F. Macubbin (ed.), *Unauthorized Sexual Behaviour During the Enlightenment*, (special issue of *Eighteenth-Century Life*, 1985), pp. 1–21.

26. Anon, *Aristotlés Master-Piece or the Secrets of Generation Displayed in all the Parts Thereof* (London, 1684), p. 4.

27. Richard Head, *Rare Verities: the Cabinet of Venus Unlocked, and Her Secrets Laid Open* (London, 1657), sig.A5.

28. Head, *Rare Verities*, sig.B^v.

29. Cowley, 'Upon Dr. Harvey', I.
30. William Harvey, 'Preface', *Anatomical Exercitations, Concerning the Generation of Living Creatures* (London, 1653), sig.A2ᵛ.
31. Jacques Duval, *Traité des hermaphrodits, parties génitales, accouchemens des femmes, etc* (Rouen, 1612); Gaspard Bauhin, *De hermaphroditorum monstrorumque partum natura ex theologorum, jureconsultorum medicorum, philosophorum et rabbinorum sententia libri duo* (Oppenheim, 1614); Jean Riolan, *Discours sur les hermaphrodits. Ou il est demonstré contre l'opinion commune, qu'il n'y a pont de vrays Hermaphrodits* (Paris, 1614).
32. Lorraine Daston and Katharine Park, 'The Hermaphrodite and the Orders of Nature: Sexual Ambiguity in Early Modern France', *Gay and Lesbian Quarterly*, 1 (1995), 419–38, quotation, 422.
33. Quoted from Daston and Park, 'The Hermaphrodite and the Orders of Nature', 428.
34. Antonio Beccadelli, *Antonio Beccadelli and the Hermaphrodite*, ed. Michael de Cassant , (Liverpool: Janus Press, 1984), I, p. iii.
35. Giles Jacob, *Tractatus de Hermaphroditis: Or, A Treatise of Hermaphrodites* (London, 1718), sig.B.
36. Sprat, *History of the Royal Society*, p. 61.
37. Thomas Allen, 'An Exact Narrative of an Hermaphrodite now in London', *Philosophical Transactions of the Royal Society of London* (1667), no. 32, p. 624. I am grateful to Anthony Archdeacon for his advice on the translation of this letter.
38. John Evelyn, *The Diary of John Evelyn*, ed. E. S. de Beer, (Oxford: Oxford University Press, 1959), 22 August, 1667, p. 513.
39. *A Collection of 77 Advertisements relating to Dwarfs, Giants, and Other Monsters and Curiosities exhibited for Public Inspection* (London, 1680–1700), n.p.
40. James Parsons, *A Mechanical and Critical Enquiry into the Nature of Hermaphrodites* (London, 1741), p. 21.
41. Diemerbroeck describes the hermaphrodite as being English and aged approximately twenty-two in 1668. Isbrand de Diemerbroeck, *The Anatomy of Human Bodies*, translated by William Salmon (London, 1689), p. 183.
42. Diemerbroeck, *Anatomy of Human Bodies*, p. 183.
43. Diemerbroeck, *Anatomy of Human Bodies*, p. 183.
44. Parsons, *Mechanical and Critical Enquiry*, pp. 20–1.
45. Mr Veay, 'An Extract of a Letter written by Mr. Veay Physician at Toulouse to Mr. de St. Ussans, concerning a very extraordinary Hermaphrodite in that City', *Philosophical Transactions of the Royal Society of London* (1687), no. 282, pp. 282–3. I am grateful to Jonathan Sawday and Bill Marshall for their advice on the translation of this letter.
46. Edmond Halley, *Correspondence and Papers of Edmond Halley*, E. F. MacPike (ed.), (Oxford: Clarendon Press, 1932), 9 April 1687, p. 81.
47. In general the Continent was inextricably linked with erotic representation. As Peter Wagner claims, by the eighteenth century it was 'an English myth that everything perverse or "unnatural" could only have had its origin in such immoral and sexually corrupt countries as

Bulgaria, France, Italy and other Mediterranean localities', 'The Discourse on Sex – or Sex as Discourse', p. 57.

48. Barthélemy Saviard, (Paris, 1702). Quoted in Pierre Darmon, *Trial by Impotence: Virility and Marriage in Pre-Revolutionary France*, translated by Paul Keegan (Paris, 1979; London: Chatto and Windus, the Hogarth Press, 1985), p. 50. For a discussion of this and several other case histories of hermaphrodites, see F. Gonzalez-Crussi, 'Sexual Undifferentiation', in *Three Forms of Sudden Death and Other Reflections on the Grandeur and Misery of the Body* (London: Picador, 1986), pp. 43–64.

49. Anon, *An Apology for a Latin Verse in Commendation of Mr. MARTEN'S Gonosologium Novum* (London, 1709), p. 17. This was written (possibly by John Marten) as a defence of John Marten's *Gonosologium Novum, or a New System of all the Secret Infirmities and Diseases Natural Accidental and Venereal in Men and Women* (London, 1708) which had been published as an appendix to his treatise on venereal disease, and was prosecuted for obscenity.

50. Saviard, in Darmon, *Trial by Impotence*, p. 51.

51. Saviard, in Darmon, *Trial by Impotence*, p. 51.

52. *A Collection of 77 Advertisements* (London, 1680–1700), n.p.

53. Parsons, *Mechanical and Critical Enquiry*, p. liv.

54. For discussions of this issue see Emma Donoghue, *Passions Between Women: British Lesbian Culture 1668–1801* (London: Scarlet Press, 1993), pp. 25–53 and Cath Sharrock, 'Hermaphroditism; or, "the Erection of a New Doctrine": Theories of Female Sexuality in Eighteenth Century England', *Paragraph*, 17 (1994), 38–48.

55. François de Chavigny de la Bretonnière, *The Gallant Hermaphrodite, An Amorous Novel* (London, 1688), p. 122. The use of the word 'gallant' in this context contains the sense of a 'ladies man' thus punning on the gender ambiguity of the hermaphrodite.

56. See for example, Anon, *The Supplement to the Onania* (1724); Giles Jacob, *Treatise of Hermaphrodites* (1718); and Nicholas Venette, *Le Tableau de L'Amour Conjugal* (1696), translated as, *The Mysteries of Conjugal love Reaveal'd* (1707).

57. Chavigny de la Bretonnière, *Gallant Hermaphrodite*, p. 122.

58. Chavigny de la Bretonnière, *Gallant Hermaphrodite*, sig.A2.

59. Jacob, *Treatise*, p. ii.

60. Jacob's suggestion recalls Francis Beaumont's address to his reader in *Salmacis and Hermaphroditus* (1602): 'I hope my Poeme is so lively writ, / That thou wilt turne halfe-mayd with reading it'. Francis Beaumont, *Salmacis and Hermaphroditus*, in Nigel Alexander (ed.), *Elizabethan Erotic Narrative Verse* (London: Edward Arnold, 1967), p. 168.

61. Jacob, *Treatise*, p. iii.

9

'Forms Such as Never Were in Nature': the Renaissance Cyborg

Jonathan Sawday

When he walks, he moves like an engine, and the ground shrinks before his treading. He is able to pierce a corslet with his eye, talks like a knell, and his 'hmh!' is a battery. He sits in his state like a thing made for Alexander. What he bids be done is finished with his bidding. He wants nothing of a god but eternity and a heaven to throne in.

William Shakespeare, *The Tragedy of Coriolanus* V.iv.15-20[1]

I INTRODUCTION: FROM BODIES TO MACHINES

Standing two metres tall, with arms and legs splayed in the familiar Vitruvian posture, 'Clear Man' is a resin model of the human form which can be seen at the Science Museum in London. Embedded within his transparent body are over fifty different 'devices' ranging from the banal to the very edge of science fiction.[2] Dentures and glass eyes have an ancient history, but the anterior cervical plate – a device which fuses the head and the neck bones – or the artificial larynx used to replace damaged or diseased vocal cords, hint at cyber-fictional fantasies as much as they represent the advances of medical technology. Prosthetic surgery – the replacement of damaged body parts by artificial features – has a long history. But 'Clear Man' shows us how prosthesis has now reached deep into the human interior. Of course, 'Clear Man' does not represent a mechanical or robotic figure: the organic body still predominates. Neither do the supplementary parts enhance the basic design specification of the human being. The individual fitted with a carbon fibre bone plate cannot run faster or further than someone who has not been so modified. Rather, damaged or worn-out organic features – hips, knee joints, blood vessels, heart valves – can now be made to function once more, at least after a fashion. The flesh, it is true, is still heir to Hamlet's 'thousand natural shocks'. But some of those shocks – the harbingers of disease, infirmity, and death – may be cushioned by the skills of the medical technologist.

'Clear Man' represents an accepted aspect of what has come to be known as 'Body Modification' – the practice of modifying the human form in pursuit of either health or fashion. 'Body Modification', however, is not only the preserve of Western science and technology. The practice is as old as human culture itself; perhaps, even, it is one of the defining characteristics of human culture. Enhancing or altering the body form artificially, whether through adornment – tattoos, cosmetics, padded shoulders, bustles, cod-pieces, wigs – or through more invasive procedures – silicone implants, surgical modification, scarification, the piercing of ears, lips, and other features – may be traced through a bewildering variety of cultural and historical moments.[3] In the late twentieth century, however, the alliance between technology and art has allowed body modification to reach a new level of plasticity. But what is natural? 'Clear Man', just as much as the 'art' of body modification, may *appear* to challenge our sense of the body as the defining limit to our own sense of selfhood, but artificial implants and surgical modification perhaps only serve to underline what the body is not.[4] It cannot be casually re-arranged. Though many non-western cultures practise different forms of body modification, these practices are manifestations of deep-rooted belief and social systems. In such societies, as Bryan S. Turner writes: 'the body is an important surface on which the marks of social status, family position, tribal affiliation, age, gender, and religious condition can easily and publicly be displayed.'[5] But to Westerners, body modification is shocking because it appears to transgress a series of cultural norms: that 'art' and 'science' should not be confused, that tampering with one's 'given' body for frivolous reasons should not be encouraged, above all, that *who* we are is a function of *what* we are, and what we are (hitherto) has not been a matter of negotiation. Until very recently, only sickness or accident forced us to transcend this prohibition. Thus, it is argued, body modification together with its variants (body play, body art, body customising, body contouring) may challenge our sense of identity or even our sense of self. Is the body modifier an artist or a surgeon, a fashion designer or a psychic healer? 'What these practices share' writes Susan Benson, in a review of some of the recent literature of postmodernism and the body is 'a way of refashioning the self, often by means of an active and aggressive appropriation of technology'. The body, she speculates, may be 'the only thing – "that you really own"' and, as such, 'customising' it is to stamp on the outward form the mark of inward 'ownership'. But this speculation may, in turn, prompt the question: if bodies really do 'belong' to us in this proprietal fashion, why bother to go to such lengths to tag each body with the mark of individuality? Or is individuality itself a much more fragile entity than we normally care to admit?[6]

For Donna Haraway, the (con)fusion of the organic and the cybernetic, or between the human and the animal, is a feature of the late twentieth century 'our time, a mythic time' in which 'we are all chimeras, theorised and fabricated hybrids of machine and organism.'In short' she writes 'we are cyborgs.'[7] In Haraway's 'ironic political myth', the Cyborg stands for fluidity, a de-coupling of those modes of dualistic thought we have inherited from Descartes and earlier. The cyborg has 'no origin story in the western sense', it cannot 'dream of returning to dust', and nor is it 'structured by the polarity of public and private'. Above all, the cyborg teaches us how to undo that familiar construction of the European Renaissance: 'Man'. 'From our fusion with animals and machines' Haraway observes we can learn 'how not to be Man, the embodiment of western logos'.[8] But what of Shakespeare's Coriolanus as described by Menenius, in the quotation which prefaces this essay? Is he a forerunner of the cyborg as described by Haraway? Surely not, for cyborgs *have* no forerunners. 'Pre cybernetic machines' Haraway explains:

> could be haunted; there was always the spectre of the ghost in the machine. This dualism structured the dialogue between materialism and idealism … . But basically machines were not self-moving, self-designing, autonomous. They could not achieve man's dream, only mock it. They were not man, an author of himself, but only a caricature of that masculinist reproductive dream. To think they were otherwise was paranoid. Now we are not so sure.[9]

II 'A THING MADE FOR ALEXANDER': THE RENAISSANCE CYBORG

'But out affection!/All bond and privilege of nature break!' cries Shakespeare's Coriolanus, confronted by the evidence of his origins – his mother. His resolve is to enter the machine-world fantasised on his behalf by Menenius. Ironically, in terms of the impossible history of the cyborg which Haraway has sketched for us, to enter that world is to become, precisely, an 'author of himself':

> I'll never
> Be such a gosling as to obey instinct, but stand
> As if a man were author of himself
> And knew no other kin.
>
> (V.iii.34–7)

Here, then, is an early seventeenth-century text in which we may glimpse an alternative (though not contradictory) manifesto for the cyborg. In Shakespeare's pre-Cartesian creation of the 'engine' which is Coriolanus, we encounter a denial of reciprocity, of kinship, of origin, of filial affection, which is neither a caricature of humanity, and nor is it paranoid delusion. Rather, the machine is a refuge, a place of sanctuary, a hardened carapace into which the battered psyche might flee. To be human, on the other hand, is to be a mere 'gosling' – a slave to instinct. Better, then, to be a 'noble thing', which is how Coriolanus's enemy and admirer, Aufidius, addresses him when he has finally turned on his country and his family. To become an 'engine', or a 'thing', is to achieve, paradoxically, a dream of autonomy. True machines, in the alternative world of *Coriolanus* (where war is the norm, and where treachery and duplicity are civic virtues) are those humans who rely on human affection. To be human, as Coriolanus discovers when he surrenders himself, once more, to the 'bond and privilege of nature' is to lose oneself. Only to be an engine is to be free.

When Menenius describes Coriolanus as being 'like a thing made for Alexander', he is evoking a specific technological history which appears to have escaped most commentators on Shakespeare's play. Both the Riverside and the Norton editors have assumed that Menenius's simile is comparing Coriolanus to a statue of Alexander the Great, a comparison which seems to puzzle the Norton editors since they point out that Alexander 'actually postdated Coriolanus.'

Shakespeare, of course, is famous for such lapses of attention, particularly when it comes to chronology. But perhaps latter-day Shakespeareans have been a little too hasty at this point, since a more literal reading of the simile opens up an alternative vista of humans and machines which lies buried in the art and technology of the European Renaissance. When Coriolanus is described, then, as a 'thing made for Alexander', the conclusion that he is being metaphorically transformed into a statue sits oddly with the drift of the rest of Menenius's description: that Coriolanus is an automaton, a vehicle of destruction and death, rather than a sentient human being. 'These are the ushers of Martius', exclaims Coriolanus's mother, Volumnia, as she awaits her son's return from the wars:

> Before him he carries noise, and
> behind him he leaves tears.
> Death, that dark spirit, in's nervy arm doth lie,
> Which being advanced, declines, and then men die.
>
> (2. i.144–7).

Resistless, premeditated, and sequential, Coriolanus is a robotic engine of war, designed by his mother, Volumnia: 'Thou art my warrior. I holp to frame thee' (5. iii.63) she claims. To 'frame' Coriolanus is to transform him into something more than human, and yet lacking in humanity.

So, like a machine made for Alexander, Coriolanus has been 'framed' for just one purpose. And it was Alexander, or rather Alexander's engineers and designers who, according to Brian Cotterell and Johan Kamminga, effected a 'revolution in warfare' through the deployment of ever more deadly mechanical weaponry. The torsion catapults, for example, which began to appear in the armies of Alexander's father, Philip of Macedonia, about 340 BC, were capable of hurling boulders of up to 40 kg in weight over distances of hundreds of metres. The great ship-born catapults which were used by Alexander at the siege of Tyre (332 BC) battered harbour defences into submission which, some 250 years earlier, had resisted the artilleryless armies of Nebuchadnezzar in a siege lasting thirteen years.[10] Such engines of destruction reached an apogee of technical efficiency in the ancient world, though they were still being constructed in the medieval period.

With the coming of 'modern' gunpowder-powered artillery, it might be supposed that such engines would have become objects of only antiquarian interest to the engineers and technologists of the European Renaissance; but such was not the case. Detailed instructions for building these machines were to be found in Vitruvius, and it was perhaps as part of the general veneration for classical architectural ideals that Renaissance engineers and designers devoted considerable time and energy to devising ever-more baroque variations on this ancient form of mechanical warfare.[11] Thus, the final sections of Agostino Ramelli's magnificent treatise on machinery *Le diverse et artificiose machine* published in a dual French and Italian text at Paris in 1588, were devoted to military engines whose fundamental principles of design would have been familiar to the Roman armies which, according to Josephus, deployed machines capable of hurling 26 kg of stone 400 metres at the siege of Jerusalem (AD 69).[12] Ramelli's interest in such ancient machines is unsurprising, given his career as a military engineer. But Ramelli was not content merely to describe such engines. Rather, as he explains, his machines are 'taken from the ancients but better devised' so that they are 'still useful in modern times'.[13]

Whether, however, a machine such as the mechanical monster to be found in Fig. 9.1. was ever constructed or used in anger is doubtful. But that, perhaps, is not the point. Ramelli's gigantic multiple catapult dwarfs its human operators who busy themselves within its enormous wooden skeleton, turning the system of cranks, worm-gears, screws, and pulleys, which serve to 'cock' the engine. 'Death in's nervy arm doth lie', Volumnia had exclaimed of her son, Coriolanus. Looking at Ramelli's machine, with its straining ropes under tension, its five mechanical feet which bite into the ground when it has been manoeuvered into firing position, and the simple release mechanism operated by a single individual, we may wonder if Coriolanus is, in some fashion, a symbolic portrait of such a machine: a half-human or supra-human being who 'when he walks, moves like an engine' and before whose tread the ground itself 'shrinks'.

III   FROM MACHINES TO BODIES

The machine-books of the Renaissance were replete with fabulous and fantastic machines, of a kind similar to that which Ramelli described. We tend to assume that Leonardo da Vinci's now familiar sketches of various mechanical devices – hoists, cranes, screw-jacks,

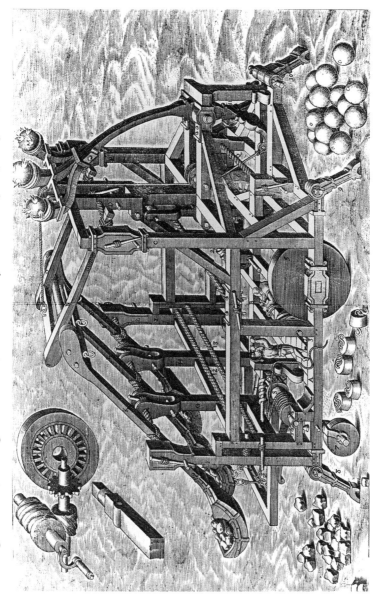

9.1 Engine of War, from Agostino Ramelli, *Le diverse et artificiose machine* (Paris, 1588)

rotary bearings, worm-gears, barrel springs, and, above all, the so-called 'flying machine' – were the first sustained exploration of the mechanical world. But, in common with his anatomical studies, much of Leonardo's impressive oeuvre was unknown to his contemporaries. His drawings and descriptions remained unpublished, existing as potential designs in the various notebooks. Far more influential was the work of engineers and designers of the next generation: figures such as Ramelli, Georgius Agricola, Jacques Besson, and Vittorio Zonca. These engineers and designers circulated their ideas through the production of beautiful (and costly) 'machine books', dedicated to aristocratic patrons as (in the words of Kenneth J. Knoespel) 'advertisements for their inventors'.[14] These machine books – which included Ramelli's designs, as well as Book VI of Agricola's *De re metallica* (1556), Besson's *Livre des instruments mathematiques et mechaniques* (1569), and Zonca's *Teatro Nuovo di Machine et Edificii* (1607) – opened up a world of *interior* mechanical invention which was analogous to the interior world which the magnificent Vesalian and post-Vesalian books of anatomy laid before their wealthy readers.[15] In the words of Elizabeth L. Eisenstein:

> Readers who turned the pages of Jacques Besson's appropriately named *Theatre of Machines* were witnessing a dramatic spectacle that previous scholars had not seen, just as readers of Agricola and Vesalius had their eyes opened to 'veins and vessels' that had been less visible before.[16]

Indeed, the visual rhetoric with which the illustrators of both the machine books and anatomy texts worked was a shared system. Text and image were combined with one another through the new 'invention' of keying systems – a device which seems to have been first deployed by anatomical illustrators, and then appropriated by the machine-artists.[17] Showing a machine *in situ*, with a human or animal operator providing motive force, was only one part of this convention. Revelation, or the bringing into the light of the reader's understanding otherwise hidden sequential relations of parts to whole, was also crucial to the understanding of these illustrations. 'In effect' says Knoespel of Ramelli's machine illustrations, the reader is led 'to expect that machinery exists behind a scene ... the emphasis [is] on concealed pumps, pipework, pulleys, and gearworks – often exhibited through superimposed and cutaway drawings.'[18] This, of course, was exactly the visual language which had been pioneered by the illustrators of anatomical texts in the period.

In such a world of visual communication, the questions which a modern designer might ask of a given machine-design – will it work? Will it perform to its design specification? Is this the most efficient means of executing the task in hand? – are, if not irrelevant, then, at least secondary. In modern terms, Fig. 9.2 (which shows a device with which 'one man alone can easily draw water from a well'), incorporates double interrupted crown gears and lantern gear (the structure H S), with a horizontal tread mill (F) as prime mover, powered by a human operator. A spur gear and lantern (R) in turn operate a pair of piston rods, encased within the cylinders (P T). These 'force pumps' push water up the vertical pipes (Z X), to ground level. The crucial structure within the machine is, however, not shown. In order to operate, the pistons and vertical pipes need to be connected to one another with a system of opening and closing valves. This element of the machine is explained in the text. So, as illustrated, a crucial component appears to be missing. But, to a modern engineer, such an omission is only half the story. The elaborate gearing system placed above the head of the human operator, a system which can be found in arabic works of the thirteenth century, as well as in Leonardo's notebooks is, in the words of Ramelli's modern commentators, 'ingenious' but it was perceived to be 'an eventual loser'. Such a machine simply would not 'work' in the modern sense of that term.[19]

But to appeal to modern design criteria in assessing these illustrations is, inevitably, to miss the rhetorical point of the images. One might as well object that Ramelli's water-lifting device is conceptually redundant, given not only the immense friction the human operator has to be overcome within the system, but the fact that the whole operation might be performed more easily (though not as swiftly) using a simple winch and bucket. But these illustrations are not designers' blueprints. Rather, as Knoespel explains, they exist in the same intellectual framework as emblem books, calling upon the reader to 'puzzle out hidden mechanical relations' in the same way that Alciati's *Emblemata* (1531) 'requires the reader to puzzle out hidden morals.'[20] Again, the mechanical relations which Ramelli explores are, quite literally *explorations* – visual exercises in combining and re-combining different mechanical structures. What Ramelli gives us, then, are hybrid machines which are not necessarily

9.2   Water-lifting Device, from Agostino Ramelli, *Le diverse et artificiose machine* (Paris, 1588)

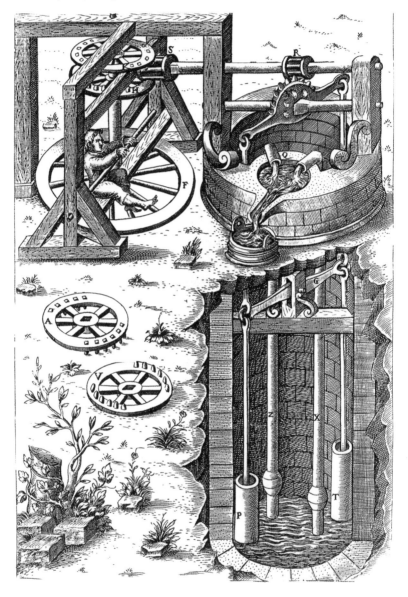

defined by the task for which they have ostensibly been designed. Instead, the Renaissance reader is being educated in underlying mechanical principles, discovering the possibility of re-combining the structures into new, and unforseen, patterns. In this way, the reader turned the pages of a work such as Ramelli's, 'reading' the pages sequentially as a series of pictorial essays. The reader's task was not to construct the precise machine which was to be found in the pages of Ramelli's text, but to participate in the creation of other machines, incorporating the grammar and vocabulary learned from scanning the pages. The result would be something entirely new, something which never existed 'in nature'.

To the modern designer, looking back with the advantage of four hundred years of hindsight, the complexity of these designs is troubling. As Martha Teach Gnudi observes, the designs are 'unnecessarily encumbered by complex linkages and redundant – sometimes self-defeating – gear trains ... it was not until the eighteenth century that the advantages of simplifying rather than complicating a machine began to be understood.'[21] In this respect, however, the mechanists were merely imitating the complexity to be found in the design of God's own most admired piece of machinery – the human form. Hence, as Bert S. Hall has pointed out, the title of Ramelli's treatise – *Artificiose machine* or 'artificial machines' – seems 'pleonastic to the modern ear'.[22] What other kinds of machines are there, other than artificial kinds? But the distinction between the 'natural' and the 'artificial' was breaking down in the sixteenth century. Or rather, the ever-more complex fabrications of the technologists threatened to ape the supreme artificer – a source of both pride and theologically-driven anxiety.[23] As the anatomists' explorations revealed ever more intimate relationships between different structures hitherto perceived as discrete, so they began to find themselves dismantling what gradually began to appear as an enormously complex mechanism. The chains and gear-linkages, the sinewy ropes and pulley systems with which Ramelli and his contemporaries invested their machines, should be understood, then, as informed by a desire to imitate the mastery over sequential action and re-action to be found within the human frame. The two nascent 'sciences', in other words – the science of technology and the science of anatomy – found themselves conspiring together to offer a complete 'mechanical' image of the world and the creatures which inhabited that world.

In other respects, too, the machine book can be compared to an anatomical text such as Vesalius's 'epitome' to the *De humani corporis fabrica* of 1543, where readers were encouraged to cut out structures from the printed sheets before them, in order to construct their own anatomised bodies in two dimensions. The stress was on the reader's participation in the undertaking through replicating the anatomist's researches. If no corpse was to hand, then Vesalius has conveniently supplied a replica – a paper or (in the modern sense) 'virtual' body – with which the reader could begin their own researches.[24] Though Ramelli, in the preface to his work (addressed 'To the Kindly Reader') protested against the practice by which his drawings were 'taken from me, transformed, and completely altered from their true meaning' the very fact that he was moved to complain at such appropriation of his designs hints at the reality of how such machine books were 'used'.[25] Just as the poets who, trained in rhetoric, plundered the works of classical authors, 'digesting' their images and ideas, and incorporating metaphors and similes into new combinations of meaning, so Renaissance designers, unencumbered by any system of patents (in much the same way that the poets and playwrights were unprotected by any law of copyright), worked with the material of other designers to achieve their objectives. In this respect, Ramelli's over-elaborate designs represent (in Hall's words) 'pure' or 'absolute' machinery, a lexicon of design rather than a design manual.[26]

More than this, the machine images relied on an oscillation between surface and depth, or between the hidden and the revealed, which was very similar to the visual language of anatomy. Turning back to figure 9.2, for example, we can see how the complete machine is shown to exist in two complementary dimensions. That which is open to exploration exists on the surface of the earth. But below ground level is a hidden mechanical structure. The ground is cut away to reveal this structure, in much the same way that the anatomist peeled back the skin to display the corporeal interior. In physiological terms, the 'heart' of Ramelli's machine is the human operator, forcing the horizontal treadmill to rotate. But the hidden 'soul' of the machine, its true mystery, lies beneath the ground. And, as we have already seen, the vital mechanical component – an implied system of double valves – is not opened to us for inspection. The machine, in other words, promises far more than it can deliver.

Ramelli and his late sixteenth-century readers had begun to explore a mechanical world which, as is well known, had formed the object of study of Leonardo many years earlier. But, for all that

Leonardo's designs circulated only amongst the privileged few who had access to his manuscripts, the principles with which he was working were, essentially, to become a commonplace of Renaissance thought. Under the influence of Copernicus and Kepler, all of nature was, in essence, to be understood as organised according to mechanical principles. 'Sure, the sky is as the great wheel of a clock' wrote Philip de Mornay in 1581, a sentiment which was to echo throughout the seventeenth century as the 'mechanic philosophy' seized the imagination of European natural philosophers.[27] For Leonardo, writing in the early sixteenth century, 'The instrumental or mechanical science is the noblest and useful above all others, since by means of it all animated bodies which have movement perform all their actions ...'[28] By harnessing the power of the true prime movers inhabiting all of nature – weight, force, motion, and percussion – the human intellect might be able to replicate the divine act of creation itself:

Weight and force together with the motion of bodies and percussion are the four powers of nature by which the human race in its marvellous and various works seems to create a second nature in this world; for by the use of such powers all the visible works of mortals have their being and their death.[29]

Leonardo's evocation of the possibility of human re-creation (or rather mechanical imitation) of a 'second nature in this world' might remind the student of literature of Sir Philip Sidney's defence of the poet in *An Apologie for Poetry* (1595). For Sidney, the poet was, above all, a 'maker' whose task surpassed mere imitation to create 'things either better than nature ... or, quite anew, forms such as never were in nature.' There is even a hint of mechanical principles in Sidney's depiction of poetry itself as a 'force' manipulated by the poet in imitation of the force of the divine breath with which the world was created.[30] To create 'forms such as never were in nature' was the goal of the Renaissance engineer or designer, as much as the poet. For Sidney, such forms were creatures of the imagination – 'Heroes, Demigods, Cyclops, Chimeras, Furies and such like' – but for Leonardo the prospect of creating such creatures, so that they existed in reality, was the work of human intellect mediated through the principles of mechanics and mathematics. Indeed, in describing his famous 'flying machine' Leonardo seems to have prefigured Descartes's exploration of the mechanics of organic life:

A bird is an instrument working according to mathematical law, which instrument it is in the capacity of man to reproduce .... We may therefore say that such an instrument constructed by man is lacking in nothing except the life of the bird, and this life must needs be imitated by the life of man.[31]

Here is a statement with which Descartes, writing some 150 years later, would have found little to disagree.[32] Indeed, For Leonardo, as much as for Descartes, the claim that the creature is an 'instrument' opens up the possibility that all that is required for motion is a sufficient vital force to guide its flight. In modern terms, of course, we would explore this problem as a difficulty associated with the power-to-weight ratio of the machine. But these were not the terms familiar to either Leonardo at the beginning of the sixteenth century, nor Descartes in the first half of the seventeenth century. Rather, the problem was one of 'substitution'. If the vitality of the bird is replaced by the reasoning faculty of man, then, in theory what will take to the air is neither man nor bird, but a fusion of the two: an 'artificial' bird-man, operating according to the shared laws of mathematics. The bird-like body is the product of human ingenuity, an ingenuity capable of grafting a mechanical structure with human volition. Just as the poet, according to Sidney's formulation, is able to create something, via the 'force' of imagination, which never was in nature, so the designer, drawing on human intellect and the laws of mathematics, and substituting human life for the bird's life, will have succeeded in 'fusing' two 'machines' so that they have become one: an Ovidian fantasy of transformation has become a reality.

IV   THE AUTOMATON

In other words, (*pace* Cartesian 'dualism' and the modern cyborg) machines and humans, or bodies and engines, have a long history of intersection with one another. To Ramelli, as much as to Leonardo, machines had to be understood in terms of bodies, since it was via the exploration of a new 'grammar' of the body, devised by the anatomists, that they were able to explore the ever more complex nature of mechanical devices. For Leonardo, the understanding of mechanics rested on an understanding of the operation of human and animal bodies. 'Arrange that the book of the

Elements of mechanics' he reminded himself in his *Notebooks* 'shall precede the movement and force of man and other animals and by means of these you will be able to prove all your propositions.'[33]

Over a hundred years later, this theoretical model for the understanding had been translated into what, for many twentieth-century readers, was to become the cruel heart of Cartesian philosophy: Descartes's apparent 'reduction' of the human being to little more than an automaton. This, certainly, was the conclusion offered by Julian de LaMettrie when he published his Cartesian manifesto *L'homme machine* in 1747. But Descartes himself, perhaps aware of the fate of Galileo, was always circumspect in challenging theological orthodoxy in this way. Instead, he understood organic life as operating in a machine-like way – which is a different proposition to that which concludes that human beings *are* machines. 'Since art copies nature', he wrote in a long and important letter (5 February 1649) to the English Neoplatonist philosopher Henry More:

> and people can make various automatons which move without thought, it seems reasonable that nature should even produce its own automatons, which are much more splendid than artificial ones – namely the animals.[34]

Observing that 'worms, flies, caterpillars and other animals move like machines', and that, in both human and animal bodies, the 'mechanism of the body moves despite the mind', Descartes was confirmed in his view that nature was constructed according to the same mechanical principles with which automata were constructed.[35]

The 'imitation' of life by artificial means is a theme which reaches back into legend and classical antiquity: Daedalus, Pygmalion, and Prometheus were all held to be creators of 'artificial' life, whilst functioning, mechanical figures are mentioned in the works of Homer, Archyas of Tarentum, Hero of Alexandria, and Philostratus. But in the Renaissance, the desire to produce such imitations gave rise to what Roy Strong has described as a fantastic 'cult of automata', to an extent that we might even speak of the emergence of a proto-Robotic industry in certain urban centres of Europe.[36] Like a forerunner of Silicon Valley in late twentieth-century California, clock-manufacturing centres such as Blois, Paris, Augsberg, Nuremburg, Geneva, and London welcomed a new industry, where some of the earliest examples of the division of labour were to be encountered. The creation of automata is, then, contemporaneous with the appearance of a phenomenon we more usually associate with the nineteenth century – the specialisation of labour into discrete tasks. In the manufacturing of mechanical devices, human industry itself had begun to be reconstituted as a mechanical process, an ordered sequence of functions.[37]

Renaissance automata may be categorised into two distinct classes. First there were the hydraulic 'machines' which were to be found in increasing numbers in the gardens of the nobility. These water-powered machines – moving human and animal forms, giants, speaking statues, and mobile sculptures – were constructed according to ancient principles associated with the mechanics of the School of Alexandria (3rd century BC).[38] In the Renaissance, the works of Ctesibius, Philo of Byzantium, and Hero of Alexandria were transmitted through latin and arabic translations, the most important of which was Aleotti's 1589 translation of Hero's *Pneumatics*. But the true translation of this body of classical knowledge took place when the abstract theorems on the behaviour of pressurised gas, steam, air, and water were transformed into moving figures. One Elizabethan traveller, Fynes Moryson, writing in the mid-1590s, recorded his impression of the moving figures to be found in the most famous gardens of the age, those designed between 1569 and 1584 by Bernardo Buontalenti for the Grand Duke Francesco de Medici at Pratolino. In the grottos Moryson saw:

> a head of marble distilleth water; and two trees by the turning of a cocke shed waters abundantly, and a little globe is turned about by Cupid, where the Images of Duckes dabble in the water, and then look around about them ...[39]

According to Roy Strong, what impressed Moryson most was the *tableau vivant* in which 'the Image of Fame doth loudly sound a Trumpet, while the image of a Clowne putteth a dish into the water, and taking up water, presents it to an image of a Tyger, which drinketh the same up, and then moves his head and lookes around with his eyes.'[40]

This class of 'hydraulic' automata, then, promised to re-create a mythical world, ushering the images, characters, stories, and fables of Ovid and classical antiquity into the present. In some sense, to the imagination of Spenser's contemporaries, the mechanical world might appear better, more pleasing, more regulated, than the world in which they lived. When, for example, Thomas Nashe in *The Unfortunate Traveller* (1594) evoked the gardens which he had seen in Italy during his foreign travels of the 1580s, the artificial world of 'bodies without souls ... substances without sense' appeared to be a recreation of Eden, a theatre of 'soul-exalting objects'.[41]

The creation of 'soul-exalting' objects introduces the second class of automata developed by Renaissance designers and craftsmen. These were the fantastic clockwork human and animal figures which, initially, adorned the monumental clocks which began to appear in Europe in the fourteenth century. The 'culmination and grandest fulfilment' of this class of mechanical marvels was the second Strasbourg Cathedral clock, finished in 1574 and replacing its equally admired 14th-century predecessor.[42] The Strasbourg clock (Fig. 9. 3), with its celestial globe, its astrolabe, and its moving figures – an angel turning a sandglass, the four ages of life, and the figure of Christ – represented much more than a timepiece, no matter how elaborate. Rather, the clock linked human temporality to the supra-temporal plan of scriptural salvation. It demonstrated how the unravelling of the wonders of the 'mechanical' universe on the part of the natural philosophers did not challenge or de-throne God's universe. Instead the clock was a mechanical hymn of praise offered to the supreme mechanic: 'Oh divine inventions of the human hand! What work does either God or Nature do anywhere which we do not imitate with our thumb ...'[43] Thus the humanist Nicodemus Frischlin celebrated the Strasbourg clock, and its makers who had undertaken to 'imitate' God's own work of creation.

The skills which were developed in the manufacture of such grandiose public expressions of the craftsman's power to 'imitate' both God and nature were also developed on a more intimate scale. In the late sixteenth and seventeenth centuries a craze for minia-ture automata developed. Such objects were vastly expensive, the gift-tokens of emperors and kings. More often than not these automata represented figures and scenes from the scriptures: Adam and Eve, the Virgin Mary, the flagellation, and the crucifixion, all could be represented in motion. But alongside such 'soul-exalting' marvels, were to be found moving ships, horsemen, eagles, cocks, griffins, parrots, unicorns, camels, lions, and elephants: rarities of nature, or objects not to be discovered outside the texts and descrip-tions of the mythographers. To this bestiary of fabulous and exotic artificial creatures were added mythological figures: a Bacchus

9.3   The Strasbourg Clock, from Nicodemus Frischlin, *Carment de astronomico horologio Argentoratensi* (1575)

whose eyes rolled, whose arms moved, and whose mouth opened; a drinking vessel in the figure of Diana on a stag which could propel itself over the table; a centaur, able to fire an arrow and roll its eyes, bearing a swivel-headed Diana and accompanied by hounds with moving heads and opening mouths; moving carriages bearing Minerva or Cupid; a fort manned by miniature trumpeters, and so on. Strangest of all, perhaps, were the stuffed animals, their organic interiors replaced by clockwork, which danced, or flapped their wings, or raised their heads in imitation of their former movements in life.[44] To term such devices 'Cartesian' seems appropriate when it is recalled that Descartes himself, in his youth, had 'planned mechanical models to simulate animal activity.'[45] In some measure, the makers of such automata and figurative clocks traced the footsteps of the mythological artificers. But the ability to 'replicate' life was also held to be a branch of magic. The tradition of the artificial fly and eagle, said to have been built by Regiomantanus in 1436 and which flew at the visit of the emperor to Nuremburg, may have seemed benign. But what of the figure of a woman supposedly made by Albertus Magnus, and smashed as the invention of the devil by Thomas Aquinas? Like the latter-day cyborg or robot, encountered in science fiction books and films, the Renaissance automaton represented a fusion of fantasy and technology. As a fantasy, however, the automaton was not morally neutral – within its mechanical heart, there seemed to stir a darker purpose.

V CONCLUSION: TALOS/TALUS

Perhaps the most famous automaton of legend was that recorded in the *Argonautica* of Apollonius of Rhodes – Talos, the man of bronze said to have been forged by Hephaestus in Sardinia. Though the precise origins of Talos are confusing, his twofold task was clear: protecting the island of Crete from invasion, he was also charged with the task of progressing around the island, displaying the law inscribed on brazen tablets. But Talos, for all his superhuman power, also possessed (almost literally) an Achilles' heel. Running from his neck to his ankles was a single vein, stoppered by a bronze pin. By pulling on this pin, the life-blood of the artificial creature could be drained away.[46]

The association of the law with this artificial creature, forged by human ingenuity was to become one of the key images of the fifth

book of Edmund Spenser's *The Faerie Queene* (1596): the legend of
Artegall or Justice. In Book V, Talos reappears as Talus, bestowed on
Artegall as a companion by Astraea at the point where the goddess
of justice leaves the world behind her:

> But when she parted hence, she left her groome
> An yron man, which did on her attend
> Alwayes, to execute her steadfast doome,
> And willed him with *Artegall* to wend,
> And doe what euer thing he did intend.
> His name was *Talus*, made of yron mould,
> Immoueable, resistlesse, without end.
> Who in his hand an yron flale did hould,
> With which he thresht out falsehood, and did truth vnfold.
>
> (*FQ* V.i.12)[47]

Within the allegory of Book V of *The Faerie Queene*, with its terrible
vision of retributory 'justice', Talus is the Law as Spenser imagined it
should be exercised by the Elizabethan imperium at the expense of
Ireland. As Michael O'Connell observes, Talus is: 'an Elizabethan's
dream of an as-yet-nonexistent police force; he looks more sinister in
a world where he actually exists.'[48] But Talus is also a fantasy figure
derived from the machine-world inhabited by Coriolanus, rather
than the world of garden designers, or precision engineers. Just as
Coriolanus – that 'thing made for Alexander' – seems to be a fore-
taste of the dystopic cyber-world of twentieth-century machine
fantasy, so Spenser's Talus looks forward to a moment when human
and machine have merged to become one. Possessing no will of his
own, or any aura of human sensibility, Talus is nevertheless an agent
of human invention. Created to achieve a single task – to thresh out
'falsehood' and unfold 'truth' – Talus is imagined (rather as
Shakespeare had imagined Coriolanus) as a kind of perpetual motion
machine 'Immoueable, resistlesse, without end'.

When did we first begin to fear our machines? Spenser's Talus is
a figure of horror, but did he appear so to the first readers of *The
Faerie Queene*? Certainly, by the end of the seventeenth century, the
dominance of the mechanistic model within European modes of
understanding had become unassailable. The world, human society,
the human and animal body, all could be analysed in terms of the
functioning of machinery. 'My subject' wrote the English anatomist
Walter Charleton in his *Enquiries into Human Nature* (1680) is:

the most abstruse oeconomy of nature in the body of man; a system of innumerable smaller engines, by infinite wisdom fram'd and compacted into one most beautiful, greater automaton.[49]

This 'greater automaton' was, for a scientist such as Charleton, a thing of beauty and admiration. But the 'greater automaton' of Charleton (just as for Hobbes) was also a fantasy expression of power and domination. If human beings could be understood in terms of the rational operation of machines, then human behaviour itself might be less unpredictable, more open to analysis and, even, control. When Hobbes, in the opening sentences of *Leviathan* (1651) asked 'why may we not say that all *Automata* (Engines that move themselves by springs and wheeles as doth a watch) have an artificial life?' his question was not merely rhetorical.[50] The modern human relationship with machines, from its emergence in the earlier part of the sixteenth century down to the present, has always been tinged with a measure of unease. 'They' have always been nearer kin to 'us' than we have cared to admit; and in that lies their fascination, as well as their potential horror. It is an uncomfortable prospect, that what it is to be human may be defined by 'forms such as never were in nature'.

Notes

1. All references to the works of Shakespeare are to Stephen Greenblatt *et al.* (eds), *The Norton Shakespeare* (New York and London: W. W. Norton and Company, 1997).
2. 'Clear Man' is part of 'The Challenge of Materials' exhibition at the Science Museum in London. For a description, see: Charles Arthur, 'Man of Many Parts', *Independent on Sunday* (11 May 1997) pp. 44–5. Clear Man is, technologically speaking, male. Amongst his many add-on or replacement parts is a penile prosthesis, an internal support helpful in maintaining an erection.
3. Some of the literature on 'cross-cultural body decoration' (ranging from tattoo practices in ancient Egypt to the latest work of self-confessed 'urban primitives') is surveyed in Raven Rowanchilde 'Cross Cultural Body Decoration: a Literature Review' (1993) to be found on the web pages of the *Body Modification Ezine*: http://www.bme. freeq.com/culture/ cc/crosscult.html
4. In referring to the 'art' of body modification, I have in mind, in particular, the French conceptual artist, Orlan. See Barbara Rose, 'Is it Art? Orlan and the Transgressive Act' *Art in America* 81 (1993), 85; Philip

Auslander, *From Acting to Performance* (London and New York: Routledge, 1997), pp. 128–140.

5. Bryan S. Turner, 'Recent Developments in the Theory of the Body' in Mike Featherstone *et al.* (eds), *The Body: Social Process and Cultural Theory* (London: Sage Publications, 1991), pp. 5–6. See also R. Brain, *The Decorated Body* (London: Hutchinson, 1979); T. Polhemus, *Social Aspects of the Human Body* (Harmondsworth: Penguin Books, 1978).

6. Susan Benson, 'Bodies to Call our Own' *Times Literary Supplement* 4922 (1 August 1997), p. 24. See also Andrew Kimbrell, *The Human Body Shop: The Engineering and Marketing of Life* (London: HarperCollins, 1993). On a possible history of 'selfhood' and the body see: Jonathan Sawday, 'Self and Selfhood in the Seventeenth Century' in Roy Porter (ed.), *Rewriting the Self Histories from the Renaissance to the Present* (London and New York: Routledge, 1997), pp. 29–48.

7. Donna Haraway, 'A Manifesto for Cyborgs: Science, Technology, and Socialist Feminism in the late 1980s' in Linda J. Nicholson (ed.), *Feminism/Postmodernism* (New York and London: Routledge, 1990), p. 191.

8. Haraway, 'Manifesto for Cyborgs', pp. 190–3.

9. Haraway, 'Manifesto for Cyborgs', p. 193.

10. Brian Cotterell and Johan Kamminga, *Mechanics of Pre-industrial Technology* (Cambridge and New York: Cambridge University Press, 1990), pp. 188–9. See also E. W. Marsden, *Greek and Roman Artillery – Historical Development* (Oxford: Clarendon Press, 1969).

11. Marcus Vitruvius Pollio, *The Ten Books of Architecture* translated by Maurice Hickey Morgan and A. A. Howard (1914 reprint, New York: Dover Publications, 1960), pp. 303–9.

12. Cotterell and Kaminga, p. 192. See also Flavius Josephus, *Bellum Judaicum* translated by W. Whiston (London: Pickering and Inglis, 1960), V. p. 240.

13. Agostino Ramelli, *The Various and Ingenious Machines* (1588) ed. and trans. Martha Teach Gnudi and Eugene S. Ferguson (London and Baltimore: The Scolar Press/The Johns Hopkins University Press, 1976), p. 516.

14. Kenneth J. Knoespel, 'Gazing on Technology: *Theatrum Mechanorum* and the Assimilation of Renaissance Machinery' in Mark L. Greenberg and Lance Schachterle (eds.), *Literature and Technology* Research in Technology Studies 5 (London and Toronto: Associated University Presses, 1992), p. 99. On Renaissance machinery in general, see: Silvio A. Bedini, 'The role of automata in the history of technology' *Technology and Culture* 5 (1964), 24–42; Bertrand Gille, *Engineers of the Renaissance* (Cambridge, Mass.: MIT Press, 1966); Alex G. Keller, *A Theatre of Machines* (London: Chapman and Hall, 1964); Ladislao Reti, 'Leonardo on Bearings and Gears' *Scientific American* 224 (February 1971), pp. 100–10; Ladislao Reti, 'Leonardo and Ramelli' *Technology and Culture* 13 (1972), pp. 577–605; Charles Singer *et al.* (eds), *A History of Technology*, 5 vols (Oxford: Oxford University Press, 1954–8).

15. To the works of Ramelli, Besson, Agricola, and Zonca may be added the following 'machine-books' of the period: Georg Andreas Böckler,

Theatrum machinarium novum (Nuremburg, 1661); Jean Errard, *Le premier livre des instruments mathematiques mechaniques* (Nancy, 1584); Guidobaldo del Monte, *Mechanicorum liber* (Pesaro, 1577); Niccolò Tartaglia, *La nova scientia* (Venice, 1537); Fausto Veranzio, *Machinae novae* (Florence, 1615); Heinrich Zeising, *Theatri machinarum* (Leipzig, 1613). Machine designs were also disseminated in treatises on subjects as disparate as architecture, music, fortification, ship-construction, and gardening.

16. Elizabeth L. Eisenstein, *The Printing Press as an Agent of Change*, 2 vols (Cambridge: Cambridge University Press, 1979), II. p. 556.

17. See Jonathan Sawday, *The Body Emblazoned: Dissection and the Human Body in Renaissance Culture* (London: Routledge, 1995), p. 133.

18. Knoespel, 'Gazing on Technology', p. 111.

19. Too much load was placed on a single gear tooth in absorbing the 'shock of halting and reversing the movement of a machine'; see Ramelli, *Various and Ingenious Machines* (commentary), p. 576.

20. Knoespel, 'Gazing on Technology', p. 110.

21. Ramelli, *Various and Ingenious machines* (Introduction), p. 26.

22. Bert S. Hall, 'The Didactic and the Elegant: some Thoughts on Scientific and Technological Illustrations in the Middle Ages and the Renaissance' in Brian S. Baigrie (ed), *Picturing Knowledge: Historical and Philosophical Problems Concerning the Use of Art in Science* (Toronto and London: The University of Toronto Press, 1996), p. 35.

23. See John Hedley Brooke, *Science and Religion: Some Historical Perspectives* (Cambridge: Cambridge University Press, 1991) particularly chapter 4 'Divine Activity in a Mechanical Universe', pp. 117–151.

24. A similar stress on the reader's 'participation' in the investigation lies behind the emergence, in the mid-fourteenth century' of 'flap' anatomies: illustrations in which anatomical structures were depicted on flaps of parchment, glued to the main illustration, which could then be opened for inspection by the reader. This sense of 'participation' perhaps echoes the shift in anatomical understanding which took place when the anatomist's task became that of interpreting the body itself, rather than the texts of Galen and the classical medical corpus. For some sample 'flap' anatomies, see Hall, 'The Didactic and the Elegant', pp. 14–15.

25. Ramelli, *Various and Ingenious Machines*, p. 55.

26. Hall, 'The Didactic and the Elegant', 36. Or as Ramelli himself wrote: 'these drawings of mine … will be definitive and perfect', unlike those, he claims, of his rivals who 'after adding or subtracting some useless details … printed them thus mutilated as their own' (Ramelli, *Various and Ingenious Machines*, p. 55).

27. Philipe de Mornay, *A Worke concerning the Truenesse of the Christian Religion* translated by Arthur Golding and Philip Sidney (London, 1617), p. 95. On the triumph of the 'mechanic philosophy', see E. J. Dijksterhuis, *The Mechanisation of the World Picture*, trans. C. Dikshoorn (Oxford: Clarendon Press, 1961).

28. Irma A. Richter (ed.), *The Notebooks of Leonardo da Vinci* (Oxford: Oxford University Press, 1980), p. 88.

29. *Notebooks of Leonardo*, p. 61.
30. Sir Philip Sidney, *An Apology for Poetry* (ed.) Geoffrey Shepherd ed., (Manchester: Manchester University Press, 1973), pp. 100–1.
31. *Notebooks of Leonardo*, p. 104.
32. Substitution of the term 'soul' (anima) for the term life ('vita') in this translation from a passage in the *Codex Atlanticus* (161ʳ) was proposed by the authors of the section on Leonardo's flying machine in the catalogue to the Leonardo exhibition at the Hayward Gallery in London (1989), where a beech wood model of the flying machine was exhibited. See *Leonardo da Vinci* (exhibition catalogue) (London: The South Bank Centre, 1989), p. 236. Such a substitution does not, however, make theological sense. In sixteenth-century terms, birds may be held to possess vitality, but only human beings possess 'souls'.
33. *Notebooks of Leonardo*, p. 56.
34. René Descartes, *Philosophical Writings* edited and translated by John Cottingham *et al.*, 3 vols (Cambridge: Cambridge University Press, 1991), III. p. 366.
35. Descartes, *Philosophical Writings*, p. 366.
36. Roy Strong, *The Renaissance Garden in England* (London: Thames and Hudson, 1979), pp. 75–8.
37. See Silvio A. Bedini, 'The Mechanical Clock and the Scientific Revolution' in Klaus Maurice and Otto Mayr (eds), *The Clockwork Universe German Clocks and Automata 1550–1650* (Washington, DC, and New York: Smithsonian Institution and Neale Watson Academic Publications Inc., 1980), p. 20.
38. It should be noted that some of the most complex hydraulic automata had a non-European origin. On this topic see Joseph Needham, Wang Ling, Derek de Solla Price, *Heavenly Clockwork: The great Astronomical Clocks of Medieval China* (Cambridge: Cambridge University Press, 1960), pp. 179–99. Of equal importance were the many hydraulic automata to be found in the early thirteenthth century work of Al-Jazari; see Ibn al-Razzaz al-Jazari, *The Book of Knowledge of Ingenious Mechanical Devices* translated and annotated by Donald R. Hill (Dordrecht / Boston, MA: D. Reidel Publishing Co., 1974).
39. Fynes Moryson, *An Itinery*, quoted in Strong, p. 79.
40. Moryson, *An Itinery*, quoted in Strong, p. 79.
41. Thomas Nashe, *The Unfortunate Traveller and Other Works*, ed. J. B. Steane, (Harmondsworth: Penguin Books, 1972), pp. 328, 330.
42. Francis C. Haber, 'The Clock as Intellectual Artifact' in Maurice and Mayr, *The Clockwork Universe*, p. 16.
43. Nicodemus Frischlin, *Carmen de astonomico horologio Argentoratensi* (1575) quoted (and translated) in Haber, 'The Clock as Intellectual Artifact' in Maurice and Mayr, *The Clockwork Universe*, p. 18.
44. Such clockwork creatures were common, but since the materials out of which they were composed were so fragile, very few have survived. Illustrations of all the automata I have described above may be found in Maurice and Mayr, *The Clockwork Universe*, pp. 234–88. The English term for a clockwork automaton was the 'jack', a word

perhaps coined from the French description of the figure which struck the bell on a clock: *jacquemart*. Whatever the etymology of the term, the 'Jack' was an ambiguous figure, a puppet which acted without volition, a body whose 'soul' had been enslaved to another. In the penultimate scene of Shakespeare's *Richard II*, the defeated Richard compares himself to a clockwork figure, robbed by Bolingbroke of both will and purpose: 'I stand fooling here' exclaims Richard 'his Jack of the clock' (V v 60).

45. Brooke, *Science and Religion*, p. 128.

46. See Robert Graves, *The Greek Myths* (Harmondsworth: Penguin Books, 1955), I, pp. 314–15.

47. Edmund Spenser, *The Faerie Queene*, ed. A. C. Hamilton (London and New York: Longman, 1977).

48. Michael O'Connel '*The Faerie Queene*, Book V' in A. C. Hamilton *et al.* (eds), *The Spenser Encyclopedia* (London: Routledge, 1990), p. 280.

49. Walter Charleton, *Enquiries into Human Nature in VI Anatomic Praelections* (London, 1680), sig. B^r.

50. Thomas Hobbes, *Leviathan*, ed. Richard Tuck, (Cambridge: Cambridge University Press, 1991), p. 9.

10

Bodies without Souls: the Case of Peter the Wild Boy

Michael Newton

Peter the Wild Boy was discovered in the woods near Hamelen in Germany either in July 1725, or around Christmas of the same year.[1] The case of Peter the Wild Boy represents the first major account of an actual feral child, a key symbolic figure in Enlightenment culture.[2] Such children exist as images of 'essential' humanity, human beings living in a realised and unique state of nature. Although the possibilities inherent in the subject are not fully explored in the writings on this case, Peter's story does employ a number of themes that would become central in the representation of the feral child, including: the understanding of silence; the relation between nature and culture; the differences between animals and human beings; and the political image of the institution of society.

As is the case with most accounts of feral children, the facts of the boy's history are enmeshed in a web of contradictions. The December dating for instance might well be a mythic interpolation, linking the boy to the infancy of Christ. The boy was either found sucking milk from a cow in the fields, or roaming wild in the forests. He was naked, tanned, black-haired, and apparently between twelve and fifteen years of age. It was said at first that the boy lived purely on a diet of herbs and nuts (in some accounts, grass and moss), lacked the power of speech, and could climb trees as swiftly, and with as much skill, as a four-footed animal. He was taken in by the House of Correction at Zell, and brought from there by the Intendant to the court of George I at Hanover, where he was presented to the king at Herenhausen.

In the spring of 1726 Peter was brought to England at the request of the future Queen Caroline, then the Princess of Wales, and placed according to her wishes under the care of Dr John

Arbuthnot, the Scottish physician and friend of Jonathan Swift, John Gay and Alexander Pope. For a while, the boy was a London celebrity. He lived at court, and was visited by numerous notables, including Jonathan Swift. After less than a year Arbuthnot abandoned his education, and as fashionable interest in the boy waned, he was given to the care of a Mrs Titchbourn, a member of the Queen's household. Mrs Titchbourn, being used to spend her summer holidays at the house of James Fenn, a yeoman farmer, entrusted the boy to the Fenns at Haxter's End Farm, Broadway, near Berkhamstead. A sizeable pension was awarded to the family to provide for Peter's upkeep. Peter died in February 1785 and was buried at Northchurch. He never acquired language.

There are at least seven pamphlets written about Peter the Wild Boy in the two years 1726–7, of which by far the most substantial is Daniel Defoe's *Mere Nature Delineated*.[3] A series of preoccupations emerge from these pamphlets, illuminating the pre-Rousseauist idea of the feral child. Firstly, it appears that these pamphlets took the place of the direct exhibition of the wild boy – an exhibition which was limited to those granted access to the Princess of Wales's court. The texts operate as a means of displaying the boy to the curious, thereby imitating the usual means by which curiosities of nature were exhibited at fairs or other public entertainments. In the same way, a waxwork effigy of the wild boy was exhibited in the Strand, and a half-length model was displayed for many years at the house of Mrs Salmon in Fleet Street.[4] In Defoe's text in particular, this image of exhibition becomes enmeshed with satire on the court and a self-consciousness about the text's own commodifying of the boy. In this way, there enters into the Defoe's pamphlet the sense that the wild boy is a commodity whose value exists in his own appearance.

Further, in the pamphlets Peter the Wild Boy becomes a focus for a series of interconnected debates concerning a human condition in which surface appearances exist deprived of any ratifying interiority. In this way, Peter is seen as an animal, a human in bestial form, and also as a human-machine, having a human shape but lacking the essential guarantee of the human: that is, the possession of a soul. The rest of this essay concentrates on the significance of the absence of soul in Defoe's text, and implicitly in the wider culture of early eighteenth-century England. Defoe's reflections on the absolute materiality that such a condition embodies prepare us for the later understanding of the feral child, an understanding which begins with, and returns to, the puzzling nature of silence. This silence limits Peter to existence at the surface of the body; this surface itself therefore comes to signify the idea of pure materiality and appearance. Further, Defoe demonstrates that the essential nature of the human soul reveals itself within another kind of material existence: that is, the economic movements of the marketplace. The soul becomes another kind of commodity, appearing within the system of exchange.

I

Defoe's pamphlet was published on 23 July 1726, and sold, relatively cheaply, at the price of one shilling and sixpence. The title-page reads as follows: '*Mere NATURE Delineated: or, A BODY without a SOUL. Being OBSERVATIONS Upon the Young FORESTER Lately Brought to Town from GERMANY. With Suitable APPLICA-TIONS. Also, A Brief Dissertation upon the Usefulness and Necessity of FOOLS, whether Political or Natural.*'

Before he is anything, Peter is to Defoe a human being apparently without a soul:

> The World has, for some Time, been entertained, or amused rather, with a strange Appearance of a Thing in human Shape; but, for ought that yet appears, very little else, and in some sense, *as it were*, without a Soul; for *Idem est non esse, & non apparere*; Not to be, and not to be in Exercise, is much the same to him; as Not to be, and not to appear by its Operation, is much the same to us.[5]

Peter embodies 'mere nature'. He is entirely, supremely, and exclusively natural – as it were, the quintessence of the natural. If Peter is putatively without a soul, he must be defined in terms of what he lacks, and, conversely, some definition of the soul itself must also be attempted – a definition which remains problematic within Defoe's book. The text is thus concerned with the gap between two intertwined objects of comprehension: between Peter himself, in his mere nature, and that which defines our humanity, the invisible essence of the soul.

Debates on the nature and existence of the soul had existed in England at least since the late sixteenth century.[6] By the early eighteenth century the most influential models of the soul derived from

Aristotle, Decartes, or Christian doctrines. In *De Anima*, Aristotle described the soul as a principle of life found in an individual, soul and body being inseparable, though the soul itself is immaterial. The soul is expressed within the process of the realisation of the self, the natural end of that process being its 'entelechy'. There are three kinds of soul: the nutritive, common to vegetables, animals, and men; the sensitive, common to animals and men; and the rational soul which is uniquely and definitively human. Each develops towards God, moving through a hierarchy gradated between Formless Matter and Matterless Form (God).[7]

In *The Dumb Philosopher* (1719), an anonymous writer (previously thought to be Defoe) presents the orthodox Christian idea of the soul through the words of Dickory Cronke, the mute philosopher of the book's title:

> I most firmly believe that it was the eternal Will of God, and the Result of his infinite Wisdom, to create a World, and for the Glory of his Majesty to make several sorts of Creatures in Order and Degree one after another: That is to say, *Angels* or *pure immortal Spirits*: Men consisting of immortal Spirits and Matter, having rational and sensitive Souls. Brutes having mortal and sensitive Souls, and mere Vegetatives, such as Trees, Plants, *&c.* And these Creatures, so made, do (as it were) clasp the higher and lower World together.[8]

Humanity's place in the universe is here defined through the nature of its soul. The Augustinian concept of the soul follows both Plato and Aristotle, while re-formulating their concepts in terms of a narrative. The soul becomes the intrinsic self bound up within a story of its own corruption and potential for salvation: it represents a self revealed in, and dependent upon, the actions of the person within the world of appearances, though it remains hidden from that world. Once again, only human beings have rational souls: it is the possession of such a soul that defines us as human.

By the middle of the seventeenth century, the Aristotelian definitions and Christian doctrines were being challenged by the formulations of Descartes, and by a new materialism. Descartes, of course, begins with the questioning of what is real, doubting all until drawn down to the irreducible reality of consciousness. Cartesians maintained that the material body was simply a type of machine, within which is a consciousness identified with the concept of the self and of the soul. Matter, the *res extenso*, the appearing surface of the body, is dead, whereas mind, the *res cogitans*, (or the soul) is living. Descartes's dualistic distinction between an animal body of pure matter likened to a machine and a human soul of an incorporeal nature was partly a product of Christian apologetics. Yet this distinction split the Christian unity of body and soul. The external world now could be seen as dead and mechanistic, its living meaning concealed and internal.[9]

One natural end of Descartes's line of thought can be witnessed in La Mettrie's *L'Homme Machine* (1748). La Mettrie moves towards concluding that the division in Descartes is a false one, and that it is probable that consciousness is not distinct from the machine of the body, but is rather a product of its mechanics, and so is itself material in origin.[10] Defoe's representation of Peter hesitates before this final step, yet it nonetheless imagines Peter as though he were a Cartesian animal. Like the deaf, the blind, the mad, the melancholic, and the idiotic in La Mettrie's account, Peter embodies an animal and mechanistic materiality. He manifests a behaviouristic model of humankind, though with this proviso: unlike other animals, humanity exhibits no behaviour which is natural to it. Peter exists like a discarded puppet, a broken machine, or a clockwork toy. Defoe's writing on Peter forms part of this debate on the nature of the soul, and is significant therefore as much for its assumptions as for its uncertainties. However, that the definition of the soul required defence and reformulation is apparent from Defoe's tract. Defoe argues that it is necessary to believe in the soul's existence:

> We are not easily able to conceive of a Human Body, without any such Thing as a reasonable Soul infused at its first being form'd, unless we had ever seen or read of such a Creature in the World before, or unless we had a Method in Science, to obtain a Mathematical, or Anatomical System or Description of the Soul itself; that it was a Substance capable of Measurement, and having a Locality of Dimensions and Parts ascribed to it; but, as we define Soul by Rational Powers, Understanding, and Will, Affection, Desires, Imagining, and reflecting Operations, and the like, we are, *I say*, at some Difficulty in suggesting a human Body in Life, without those Operations.[11]

The immateriality of the soul renders it impenetrable to scientific inquiry since its existence can only be inferred from visible manifestations of interior actions. Hence, the child's apparent mere physicality would seem to deny this immaterial soul. Yet the child's physical presence undermines the idea of the non-existence of the soul within it, as it is so difficult to imagine a human being living without the 'operations' of a soul. The body, in its apparent identity with the human, provides evidence of the invisible soul, since the soul's existence only appears through actions without which it is impossible to imagine a specifically human life. Peter's visible humanity therefore acts against the assertion of the text that he is without a soul, and in fact Defoe, at times, has to concede him a human soul:

> This, I think then, is the Sum of what we may say of this Creature, *viz.* That he has a Soul, though we see very little of the ordinary Powers of a Soul acting in him, any more than are to be discerned in the more sagacious Brutes; Now we deny the Capacities of a Soul, such as Reflection and Retention, Understanding, Inquiring, Reasoning, and the like, to the Brute Creatures; and we say, That to allow it them, would tend to destroy the Principles of natural Religion, and to overturn the Foundation of the Divine Sovereignty and Government in the World: On the contrary, we see him, as I observed before, in a State of MERE NATURE, acting below the Brutes, and yet we must grant him a Soul: He has a Body, in its Shape Human, the Organick Parts Anatomically, we believe, the same as Human; he acts the Powers and Motions of sensitive Life, and of rational Life, alike, as if they were confused and huddled together undistinguished, and just as Nature directs in other Creatures; but he is a Ship without a Rudder, not steer'd or managed, or directed by any Pilot; no, hardly by that faithful Pilot called Sense, the Guide of Beasts.[12]

The soul that resides in Peter (and here Defoe's text reveals a distinct Aristotelian influence) is therefore immanent, locked up within him and unable to develop into a fully human soul. This is not the only point at which Defoe reveals that his concept of the soul relies on the definitions of Aristotle. At the beginning of the text, he remarks that Peter 'lived a vegetative Life ... that he acted below Brutal Life, hardly a Sensitive, and not at all a Rational.'[13] The natural progresses into the human through a series of gradations inspired by 'the Laws of Nature'. Peter represents the human being stuck at the level of the natural due to an inability to pass through the necessary stages.[14]

It is possible that Defoe's discussion of Peter's lack of a soul in fact aims to preserve the idea of the soul as the defining essence of the human, an invisible ground of being from which human life assumes coherence and meaning. Defoe's analysis implies that if there was no such thing as a soul, then all humans would be like Peter: mute, ignorant, isolated, and bestial. Our humanity in that case would not emerge from the metaphysical origin of the spirit, but from the materialistic and bestial ground of the natural. In this sense our (the reader's) very difference from Peter is itself one strong argument for the soul being that which defines the human. Defoe's description of Peter as the exemplar of 'mere nature', of human life deprived of that soul which differentiates it from the natural, can therefore be understood as an attempt to argue for the existence of the human soul. The alternative reading it fends off was to become the staple in considerations of the feral child: that is, the human is exactly the merely natural, who must be acculturated into becoming a realised human being. This idea was to be central in later representations of the feral child, most particularly in Jean-Marc Gaspard Itard's *De l'Education d'un Homme Sauvage* (1801).[15] For Defoe, Peter's distinction from humanity is constituted as a fact of his being: he even looks at his body with surprise when it does not reveal actual physical differences from civilised humanity.[16]

At other times in his pamphlet on Peter, Defoe explores the mechanistic product that results from removing the soul, itself an idea bound up with Descartes's notion of the animal as machine:

His Want of Speech, assists very much to keep him just in the same State of Nature, that he was in when brought first among us; and I do not find that he makes much Improvement in any thing, nor can his Teachers, as I understand, give much Account yet, whether they think he is capable of any Instructions or no: This shews us, what a strange Machine the Body of a Man is, that any little Breach in the whole Contexture, interrupts the whole Motion; nay, which is really a miserable Testimony of our Infelicity, it goes farther, and the least Disorder of the Parts, even of the mere *Apparatus*, as it may be called, made by Nature for the Reception of a Soul, renders that Soul unhappily useless to itself, unable to act, unfurnished with Tools to work with, imprisoned and chained, and, in a Word, fit for nothing.[17]

Here Defoe plays upon the Cartesian notion of the body as machine in order to show that machine acting against the soul. The materiality of the body becomes supreme, overcoming that incorporeal essence which might have humanised it.

In the metaphors of the human as beast and machine, implying vulnerability and weakness, Defoe offers us an image of human origins as unregenerate and despicable when conceived of in terms not of the soul, but of the soul's absence or incarceration. The human becomes a non sequitur, a thing deprived of those qualities which constitute its essence. The knowledge of this soul-less 'self' is fraught and contradictory. At times this bestial origin is privileged: like many later observers of the feral child, Defoe imagined that observation would reveal characteristics of the truly human, whether in discovering primal modes of thought (prior to language) or in the operation of the senses.[18] So the human without a soul exhibits both an 'essential' and an incomplete human nature. It represents one defining point of what it is to be human, but is still an origin from which the truly human, the metaphysically human, cannot emerge.

Through its concentration upon the soul as the incorporeal site of the human, Defoe's text becomes a quest for the evidences of such a soul. Each piece of evidence leans upon other definitions of the human, so that Peter may be said to have a soul in so far as he is seen to be capable of laughter, or rational thought, or social life. However, the evidence appears on closer scrutiny to be insufficient: the proof appears to recede as it is more closely examined. For instance, Peter's humanity is briefly posited in terms of his ability to laugh. However, after a brief digression noting that this would allow monkeys to be counted as human, Defoe rescinds this temporary elevation to the fully human: Peter's laughter is seen as unmeaning and hollow. His laughter is then linked to that of the aristocrats' who self-consciously imitate him. Rather than establishing his humanity, the kinship of this kind of laughter draws the aristocrats down to the level of '*Meer Nature*'.[19]

II

The question of the evidence for the soul shades subtly into an elucidation of how the soul might be formed. Curiously, this question of the formation of the soul takes us back to the theme of exhibition.

Peter as an exhibited curiosity is the object of the gaze of others. However, while being observed, Peter himself is not observing: the sense is of a person watched without reciprocating the gaze of the watcher:

> And, indeed, to take him as he appears to be, he is a Subject of Observation, and affords more Speculation to us that look on him, than, I believe, all the World, with the infinite Variety of Objects which it presents to his Eye, affords to him. Nature seems to be *to him*, like a fine Picture to a blind Man, ONE UNIVERSAL BLANK, as Mr. *Milton* very beautifully expresses it; he sees the Surface of it, but seems to receive no Impression from it of one Kind, or of another: He looks on the infinite Variety, with a kind of equal Unconcernedness, as if every Object were alike, or that he knew not how to distinguish between Good or Evil, Pleasant or Unpleasant.[20]

Peter's 'blindness' is of a peculiar kind. He sees the world of appearances without being able to discriminate among them. This flattening out of the world leads to indifference. Peter exists in a state of perceptual detachment, the result of standing outside the frame of the human artifice and therefore seeing things deprived of the idea of formalised presence which ascribes to them individuality, interest, and beauty. Defoe conceives of this viewpoint as not privileged but disadvantaged, for its unreciprocating gaze looks blankly at a world without criteria by which it may be valued.

Later in the text this indifference to the world is equated unequivocally with the soul's immanence, locked up in itself, and requiring the process of education to draw it into the world of appearances. Without this education the world is a blank:

> He has Eyes, but knows not what he sees; knows not what to call any thing he looks on, or what Uses any thing he sees are appropriated to: When he sees it Rain, he does not know that it is Water, *much less* that this Water cools, refreshes, and fructifies the Earth; *still less*, that the Plants and Fruits would not grow without it ... a compleat Ignorance possesses his Mind, he knows not the Use of his own Passions; he knows not the proper Objects of Grief or Joy, Fear or Anger, much less the Meaning of them; he has no Taste of Knowledge, and, with *Solomon's* Fool, has no Delight in Understanding ...[21]

Here Defoe links the lack in Peter's perception of the world, its blankness, to a cognitive deficiency established in the absence of knowledge itself, so that Defoe is forced into manifest absurdities, such as declaring the boy would not know that rain is water. Moreover, and this is typical of the texts representing Peter, there is no sense here that an understanding independent of words might be valuable or enviable. Instead, Defoe conceives of Peter's ignorance in terms of emptiness, absence, and the deadness of the unemotional.

Defoe goes on to link this perceptual detachment with a type of moral defect. Just as Peter cannot distinguish among the appearances of the world, so he seems unable to distinguish among human actions: 'had he seen the late Mrs *Hayes* burnt alive at a Stake, it would not have been at all any Surprize to him, or have given him any Ideas differing from a Dance on the *Theatre*.'[22] Lacking the ability to comprehend people as other subjects, Peter is seen as unable to imagine objective consequences for them. Human life appears to him as insubstantial and artificial as a play, albeit a play in which the stimulation of sympathy has been denied. Peter sees and hears in the same way that he laughs, that is, without being conscious of what he perceives. This lack of inward reflection denudes the world of appearance, which remains (in a Lockean sense) at the level of pure unmediated sensation.[23]

In the absence of a reciprocating interest in others, Peter is reduced to the status of a mirror. Denied a subjectivity – or a soul – of his own, Peter exists as the other wherein his observers project themselves and constitute a sense of their own identity, through the formulation of Peter's difference. Peter remains a screen since the answering gaze which would designate an independent and reciprocal self fails to exist. He remains waiting to be called into being, 'a Life wanting a Name to distinguish it ...'[24]

Stuck in the recurrent newness of the state of nature, Peter remains purely a surface, since his body does not openly display a hidden interiority, but exhibits rather the condition of secrecy. Defoe's text displays an unsettled perplexity in being obliged to remain at this surface:

If he has the ordinary Affections of human Soul, they must be seen at Nature's Leisure, and as she pleases to admit them to exert themselves; for at present we are able to make almost as little Judgment of him, as he can of us: This, in my opinion, is one of the most curious Things that belong to him; I mean, as he now appears, that we can give no Account how, and by what secret Power the Faculties of his Soul are restrained, or withheld and lock'd up from Action, while yet they are, perhaps, in Being within, and reserved for a proper Season, when he shall be restored to himself.[25]

The surface is exposed but remains meaningless:

> As we see him in his ordinary Appearance, his Figure is, indeed, a little differing from what it was represented to be before; but he is still a naked Creature; though he has Cloaths on, his Soul is naked; he is but the Appearance or Shadow of a rational Creature, a kind of Spectre or Apparition; he is a great Boy in Breeches, that seems likely to be a Boy all his Days, and rather fit to have been dress'd in a Hanging-sleev'd Coat; and, if he is not a Fool, or Natural, or *Idiot*, or a Something that we generally understand by those Terms of Nature, we may be still at a Loss about him.[26]

Defoe's text enacts a dispute between knowledge and doubt, a dispute in which the only evidence is the paltry and unmeaning nature of a surface unguaranteed by interiority. The text seeks the certainty of rational knowledge, but finds itself continually cast into doubts, or led up paths of argument which lead to the impossibility of knowledge. The end is only unverifiable conjecture: one recurrent word used in Defoe's text is 'perhaps', and on closer examination Defoe's statements of belief in certain ideas about Peter prove shifty and uncertain. The only certainty is his being brought to England as 'a Curiosity in Nature, for the Rareness of it worth enquiring into.'[27] Peter is human externally: internally he may be lacking the essentially human, 'Guesses therefore at Outsides, will not reach the Case, *Fronti nulla fides*, The Face is not always an Index of the Mind ...'[28]

So, although the surface is the only site at which Peter can be apprehended, because that site exists in insufficiency, doubt, and mystification, the incorporeal and invisible soul that he seems to lack in fact becomes the key to understanding the boy. Peter exists in terms of the thing which he does not fully possess. This soul becomes the invisible barrier between the human and the animal: Peter exists on that boundary, in both having and not having a soul.[29] He must possess a soul in order to reinstate again the essential difference of human beings from animals ('That to allow it [i.e. a soul] them, would tend to destroy the Principles of natural Religion, and to overturn the Foundation of the Divine Sovereignty and Government in the World'[30]); but the counterpart to this is that his soul must actually be locked up, useless and unapparent, in order to maintain our difference from him.

Peter both resembles and does not resemble an animal. He is first seen 'creeping on Hands and Knees, climbing Trees like a Cat, sitting on the Boughs like a Monkey', yet Defoe asserts that in fact he would seem to stand upright 'as the Soul-in-formed Part of Mankind do'.[31] Here Peter's bodily posture manifests that he does possess a soul, *in potentia* at least, and that the nature of his body acts as a distinguishing fact separating his being from those of the four-legged animals. The body resists the loss of the soul by reason of its very shape:

> How much might be said here by Way of Excursion upon the happy Disposition of Man's Body? that, in Spight of a sullen Degeneracy in some Men, shewing their strong Inclination to turn Brutes, they are not really qualify'd for that great Accomplishment; that they can't throw off the Soul, or its Faculties, and that even the Body itself will not comply with it; when an obstinate Brutality seems to remain, the very Shape and Situation of their Microcosm rebels against the sordid Tyranny, forbids the stupid Attempt, and denies them the Honour of being Beasts in Form, and in the ordinary Functions of sensitive Life, whatever they will be in Practice. In a Word, they can't tread upon all Four; they can't run, gallop, leap, trot, &c. like the more sagacious and superior Brutes, the Horse, or the Ass …[32]

That the difference suggested here resides in the observable materiality of the body would appear to give it extra strength. Defoe appears at times to move away from the single distinguishing fact of the soul to reasons less fraught with ambiguity. He argues that without the rational soul the human body would prove insufficient to guarantee survival in the wilderness, 'his Carcass left utterly destitute, is unqualified to live …'[33] Human inadequacy compares unfavorably with the animals' ability to deal with the rigours of nature:

> he cannot Burrow like the Rabbit, or earth himself in a Den like the Badger: They are warm and secure from the Weather, safe and preserved from their Enemies, in their Holes and Hollows

under Ground; but the poor naked, tender-skin'd Brute of Human Kind, must have a House to keep him dry, Cloaths to keep him warm, and a Door to shut him in, or he is lost ...[34]

However, Peter's very survival of his exposure manifests a human body which, despite its inherent weakness, manages to deny this characterisation of the human as being in a state of natural inadequacy.

In these ways the observable surface reality of the boy refutes the single defining condition of his humanity – that is, the incorporeal soul – and yet also depends upon it. It can at times suggest the ineradicable presence of the soul (as in the fact of uprightness), or alternatively show that without the soul the human is in fact less than the animal (though this is *because* he is human). For the surface is of course the substantial reality in which belief in Peter's humanity, and indeed his physical existence, resides: 'for that there is such a Person, is visible, and he is to be seen every Day, all wild, brutal, and as Soul-less as he was said to be; acting MERE NATURE .... This, I say, is evedent [*sic*], He is himself so far the miserable Evidence of the Fact.'[35]

III

Thrust back upon the evidence of the body as self, Defoe's text becomes an exploration of solitude. Peter's isolation is in itself one proof of the absence, or the dormancy, of a soul. His aversion to humankind,[36] and his desire to flee from company, is palpably strange to Defoe, who depicts Peter's solitariness as an all but stubborn refusal to participate in the life of society:

It would indeed be a terrible Satyr upon the present inspir'd Age, first to allow this Creature to have a Soul, and to have Power of thinking, qualify'd to make a right Judgment of Things, and then to see that under the Operation and Influence of that regular and well-order'd Judgment, he should see it reasonable to chuse to continue silent and mute, to live and converse with the Quadrupeds of the Forest, and retire again from human Society, rather than dwell among the inform'd Part of Mankind; for it must be confess'd he takes a *Leap in the Light*, if he has Eyes to see it, to leap from the Woods to the Court; from the Forest among Beasts, to the Assembly among the Beauties; from the Correction House at *Zell*, (where, at best, he had convers'd among the meanest of the Creation, *viz* the Alms-taking Poor, or the Vagabond Poor) to the Society of all the Wits and Beaus of the Age: The only Way that I see we have to come off of this Part, is to grant this Creature to be Soul-less, his Judgement and Sense to be in a State of Non-Entity, and that he has no rational Faculties to make the Distinction: But even that remains upon our Hands to prove.[37]

Defoe's text manifests here and elsewhere both satire directed against the Court and a radical ambivalence about the nature of isolation – a loneliness presented as a condition made in the interstices of fear and desire. As in Defoe's fictions, especially *Robinson Crusoe* (1719), *Moll Flanders* (1722), and *The Fortunate Mistress* (1724), the subject of this text is a character existing in a state of isolation. Moll and Roxana's loneliness is a product of their social and economic existence: their isolation is the background against which the necessity for survival operates. In all three novels, this condition of solitude is played out against the encroachment upon the self of the other: in this way *Robinson Crusoe* acts out a dialectic of solipsism and relationship. A fear of the other acts against the terrible isolation of the individual. This receives its most dramatic treatment in the closing pages of *The Fortunate Mistress* as Roxana is pursued and plagued by Amy, the only person who might end Roxana's alienation. Woven into the processes of Defoe's fictions is the idea that the two greatest horrors of life are to be alone and not to be alone.

It may then be the nature of Peter's essential isolation which attracts Defoe to his story. Unlike Defoe's fictional heroes, he remains trapped in the condition of his solitude, and so embodies more clearly than any other of Defoe's characters the cost involved in such a perpetual isolation. What Defoe demonstrates is that this cost is the inability to be human; that humanity as such belongs within the framework of social relationships. Moreover, it renders the self lost within a radical alterity, precisely because it cannot conceive the otherness of others. This alterity manifests itself in the absence of the soul. Defoe's works have sometimes been seen in terms influenced by Tawney and Weber. We have grown used to connecting the Protestant image of the solitary self before God with the capitalist concept of society as composed of atomised individuals motivated by self-interest and responsible for their own survival.[38] The text of *Mere Nature*, without contradicting this reading of Defoe, nonetheless does complicate this view of his works.

Defoe's writing on Peter embodies the conjunction of the idea of the self as commodity and of the self as individual soul. Peter, denied the status of full humanity through the absence or non-appearance of a soul, yet possesses the selfhood of commodity, 'the extraordinary intrinsick Value of him ...'[39] As described above, this value resides in the fact of his own existence, and the price that can be extracted for the exhibition of his person in the public realm. Defoe's texts display the rise of economic man: an individual alive in a world of loosened hierarchical bonds – a world in fact where the only distinction viable is between the human and the non-human. The 'savage' and the feral child are objects of ambivalence in this opposition, being both human and yet inferior to the 'more human' civilised individual. Their closeness to, or actual belonging in the merely natural, mark them out as separate and equivocally human. In terms of the commodity value of the self, the feral child and the 'savage' exemplify a state of nature which is opposed to the social realm, and yet, through the disintegration of that realm in the atomisation of the market, uncannily like its most modern manifestation. However, the feral child is outside the bonds constituted by money, and though his person is a commodity (a commodity established in exhibition) he is therefore outside the realm in which such social and economic relations acquire the ability to appear in semi-permanence.

The self becomes an index against which humanity may be discerned, and this self in turn is found to exist in the dual and interconnected realms of the soul and of the market. Peter's isolation becomes the dark opposite and realisation of this self, delimiting its outline and exemplifying the fearful consequences of the end of its tyranny. In Defoe's pamphlet on Peter we can see that the isolation brought about by the operations of the market reduces the human to the state of nature in which the materiality of the body is all. Yet the market allows, or parodies, the means by which the self becomes human at all: that is, the formation of the self through contact with others. It is in the lonely flux of economic exchange that the materiality of the body is invested with the interiority of the soul.

The economic realm is therefore not to be opposed to the domain of the soul, or that which establishes the human, but is rather the fulfilment of that domain, the place in which the soul may appear. It is in the marketplace that the human soul constitutes itself. In *An Essay Upon the Public Credit* (1710), Robert Harley compares the soul to the workings of credit in the market:

Like the soul in the body, it actuates all substance, yet, it is itself immaterial; it gives motion, yet, itself cannot be said to exist; it creates forms, yet, has itself no form; it is neither quantity nor quality, it has no *whereness*, or *whenness*, *site* or *habit*. If I should say it is *the essential shadow of something that is not*, should I not puzzle the thing, rather than explain it, and leave you and myself more in the dark than we were before?[40]

In this apologia for the new economic system, Harley brings to the subject of money the mystifying definitions of theology. What is most revealing here is the lack of embarrassment at the incongruity of the two subjects. The workings of the soul and the workings of money share the identity of being the productive forces which define the human.

In this way, Defoe places in his pamphlet on Peter an idea counter to that which operates through the majority of the text. If Defoe's central worry is that of the difficulty of locating a human essence, then this worry is implicitly replaced by a contrary system which is uninterested in essence except as intrinsic value. What matters instead is the positioning of the person in systems of exchange.

The radical loneliness of Defoe's Crusoe is a dual loneliness, being that of the sinner before God, and also of the self within the structures of competition. The two coalesce: one is the merely worldly counterpart of the other. However, the loneliness of Peter is that of the human deprived of these constitutive forces, exiled from their humanising realms. The loneliness which Defoe's characters exhibit is primarily an economic and social loneliness, one in which all ties and bonds have been broken except those of money (that is, an artificial means of exchange) and the assumed presence of shared humanity. Peter belongs in a state in which even this shared fact of humanness cannot be said to exist: he lives on the boundary of such shared belonging, entitled on this borderline to the consideration of charity, but still alien, strange, and other.

Notes

1. Biographical information relating to the case of Peter the Wild Boy is drawn primarily from contemporary pamphlets. These will be described fully in endnote 3. Other sources of information are: Robert Zingg, *Wolf-Children and Feral Man* (New York: Harper Row, 1942)

and Johann Friedrich Blumenbach, *The Anthropological Treatises of Johann Friedrich Blumenbach* (London: Longman, Green, Longman, Roberts, & Green, 1865). Some details are drawn from James Burnet, Lord Monboddo, *Antient Metaphysics* (Edinburgh: W. Creech, 1779–99). Some additional information derives from the periodical press of the period, in particular Dodsley's *Annual Register* (London: J. Dodsley, 1787).

2. Excluding mythic or purely fictional accounts, there are, in fact several cases of feral children written about in the two centuries prior to Peter's discovery. These include: Phillipus Camerarius, *Operæ Horarum Subcisivarum, sive Meditationes Historicæ* (Frankfurt: Petri Kopffij, 1609) and Nicolaus Tulpius, *Observationes Medicæ* (Amsterdam: Daniel Elzevir, 1671). However, these stories are limited in size and ambition, and always form part of work primarily devoted to other subjects.

3. Aside from Defoe's *Mere Nature Delineated*, the pamphlets are: *It Cannot Rain but it Pours: or London Strow'd with Rarities* (London: J. Roberts, 1726); *The Most Wonderful Wonder that ever Appear'd to the Wonder of the British Nation* (London: A. Moore, 1726); *The Manifesto of Lord Peter* (London: J. Roberts, 1726); *Vivitur Ingenio* (London: J. Roberts, 1726); *An Enquiry How the Wild Youth, Lately taken in the Woods near Hanover (and now brought over to England) could there be left, and by what Creature he could be suckled, nursed, and brought up* (London: H. Parker, 1726) (this exists in two versions); *The Devil to Pay at St. James's* (London: A. Moore, 1727). All these pamphlets are anonymous, though *It Cannot Rain* and *The Most Wonderful Wonder* have been at various times ascribed to Swift or Arbuthnot, and *The Devil to Pay* has been ascribed (in a notoriously bad eighteenth-century edition) to Arbuthnot.

4. See Sylvanus Urban, *The Gentleman's Magazine: and Historical Chronicle*, (1785) Vol. 55, p. 236.

5. Daniel Defoe, *Mere Nature Delineated* (London: T. Warner, 1726), p. 1.

6. Ideas of the soul among Socinians, Arians, and 'Mortalists' obviously focus on one area of debate. The existence of a number of philosophical treatises is also of importance here: Kenelm Digby, *Two Treatises: In the one of which, The Nature of Bodies, In the other, The Nature of Mans Soule, Is Looked Into* (1644); Henry More, *The Immortality of the Soul* (1659); Matthew Smith, *Philosophical Discourse of the Nature of Rational and Irrational Souls* (1695); Henry Dodwell, *The Natural Mortality of Human Souls clearly demonstrated from the Holy Scriptures* (1708); John Norris, *A Letter Concerning the Soul and Knowledge of Brutes* (1721). In one way or another, each of these works is responding to the writings of Descartes, although Aristotle and Plato continue to exercise a profound influence in the period, as does orthodox Christian theology.

7. See Aristotle, *De Anima*, trans. R. D. Hicks, Loeb Edition (Cambridge: University Press, 1907).

8. Quoted from *The Dumb Philosopher* (pp. 32–3). In *The Canonisation of Daniel Defoe* (New Haven and London: Yale University Press, 1988:

p. 192), P. N. Furbank and W. R. Owens point out that the attribution of this text to Defoe has been disputed by Rodney Baine in his *Daniel Defoe and the Supernatural* (1968).

9. See René Descartes, *Philosophical Writings*, trans. Elizabeth Anscombe and Peter Thomas Geach (London: Thomas Nelson and Sons, 1970).

10. See the second edition of Julien Jan, Offray de La Mettrie's *Man A Machine* (London: G. Smith, 1750).

11. Defoe, *Mere Nature Delineated*, p. 23.

12. Defoe, *Mere Nature Delineated*, pp. 23–4.

13. Defoe, *Mere Nature Delineated*, pp. 2–3.

14. Defoe, *Mere Nature Delineated*, p. 58.

15. See Jean Marc Gaspard Itard, *De l'Education d'un Homme Sauvage, ou des Premiers Développemens Physiques et Moraux du Jeune Sauvage de l'Aveyron* (Paris: Gouyon, 1801). Itard's case history refers to the story of a boy discovered living wild in the woods near Aveyron in 1798.

16. Defoe, *Mere Nature Delineated*, pp. 23–4.

17. Defoe, *Mere Nature Delineated*, p. 59.

18. Defoe, *Mere Nature Delineated*, pp. 39 and 34. James Burnet, Lord Monboddo, for example, often uses the behaviour of feral children as a means of ascertaining the essential characteristics of human beings.

19. Defoe, *Mere Nature Delineated*, pp. 19–20. This relates to the pamphlet's exploration of the ways in which Peter can be understood as both a kind of fool and an aristocrat. This theme also appears in a number of the other pamphlets about Peter the Wild Boy, in particular *The Manifesto of Lord Peter*.

20. Defoe, *Mere Nature Delineated*, p. 27.

21. Defoe, *Mere Nature Delineated*, p. 64.

22. Defoe, *Mere Nature Delineated*, pp. 33–4.

23. See Chapter 1, Book 2, of John Locke's *An Essay Concerning Human Understanding*, ed. Peter H. Nidditch (Oxford: University Press, 1975).

24. Defoe, *Mere Nature Delineated*, p. 5.

25. Defoe, *Mere Nature Delineated*, p. 28.

26. Defoe, *Mere Nature Delineated*, p. 28. The idea of a feral child as bound forever to a perpetual infancy was to prove central to later case histories. By the end of the eighteenth century it was already taking on an evolutionary slant, in which the child is cast as a 'savage', and the savage is imagined as a child.

27. Defoe, *Mere Nature Delineated*, p. 16.

28. Defoe, *Mere Nature Delineated*, p. 57.

29. Defoe, *Mere Nature Delineated*, pp. 23–4.

30. Defoe, *Mere Nature Delineated*, p. 23.

31. Defoe, *Mere Nature Delineated*, p. 3.

32. Defoe, *Mere Nature Delineated*, p. 12.

33. Defoe, *Mere Nature Delineated*, p. 7.

34. Defoe, *Mere Nature Delineated*, p. 7.

35. Defoe, *Mere Nature Delineated*, p. 3.

36. Defoe, *Mere Nature Delineated*, p. 21.

37. Defoe, *Mere Nature Delineated*, p. 22.

38.   Carol Houlihan Flynn, *The Body in Swift and Defoe* (Cambridge: University Press, 1990) offers a revealing account of the uses of the body in the writings of Swift and Defoe. Although her work does not mention Peter the Wild Boy, some of her conclusions are suggestive in connection to my own.

39.   Defoe, *Mere Nature Delineated*, p. 35.

40.   Robert Harley, *An Essay upon the Public Credit* (1710), p. 8. Harley's text is available in a later edition published in London in 1797 by W. Baynes.

11

Monstrous Perfectibility: Ape–Human Transformations in Hobbes, Bulwer, Tyson

Susan Wiseman

I THE PHILOSOPHER

And if the *Pygmies* were only *Apes*, then in all probability our *Ape* may be a *Pygmie*; a sort of *Animal* so much resembling *Man*, that both the Ancients and the Moderns have reputed it to be a *Puny Race* of Mankind.[1]

What is an ape? This question troubled the natural philosophers of the Enlightenment just as much as the early modern mythographers because the ape was where the border between the human and its others was both maintained and dissolved. The work of Edward Tyson, the late seventeenth-century anatomist, in dissecting and analysing a '*Pygmie* ... much resembling *Man*' enables us to investigate the qualities attributed to the ape – qualities which brought it, despite empiricism's best efforts, dangerously close to the human. These include the ape's mythic dimensions, and its perceived transformability. In the epochs before the 'taxonomic and *therefore* political ... ordering [of] differences' – what Donna Haraway calls 'simian orientalism' – fantasies around the ape informed both scientific and socio-political writing.[2] What – if anything – held apart ape and human?

The distinguishing of social and political uses of the body (usually regarded as highly metaphorical, symbolic, analagous) from the recording and detail produced by 'scientific' and empirical logics of the body is habitually ascribed to the moment of the early modern and Enlightenment scientific revolution.[3] Yet in Tyson's anatomy of a 'pygmie' *Orang-Outang, sive Homo Sylvestris* (1699) and later writings the relationship between the empirical and the social, even political, continues to be intimate. Although current writings on the history of science acknowledge that the discourses and emergent genres of natural science – empiricism – were inhabited by other languages, including those of myth and politics, the interrelationships between the two are less often traced in detail.[4] This essay takes the subject of the ape – human border, one which exercised contemporary anatomists and political theorists, to explore the intimate connections of political and anatomical, empiricist discourses in the late seventeenth and eighteenth centuries. In this period, I shall argue, ape myth is used in conjunction with anatomy and empiricism to open up new possibilities in the reshaping of the 'human' as a social and cultural being. Those who examine the ape find contradictions; cast as the 'natural', contemporary, animal, the ape nevertheless antithetically figures the social, historical, and human.[5]

II   THE APE IMAGINARY

A 'creature of the brain, produced by a warm and wanton imagination'; so Tyson described the ape after his 1699 dissection.[6] As Tyson's attention to fantasy suggests, his understanding of ape-human relations drew on mythic ideas. Within the early modern understanding of a chain of being, the conceptualisation of ape-human relations changed as the cultural and material field which generated images and fantasies of the ape shifted. In 1607 Topsell 'proved' the distinctness of man and ape using both new discoveries about ape physiology – '*Vesalius* sheweth, that their proportion differeth from mans in moe things than *Galen* observed' – and myth – the 'body of an Ape is Ridiculous, by reason of an indecent likeness and imitation of man, so is his soule or spirit.'[7] What seems to a modern reader to be discursive hybridity was characteristic of the dual observational and narrative modes used to describe the ape as an unusual, even extraordinary, creature.[8]

H. W. Janson's iconographic study indicates that fetishised details of the ape and monkey body and imagined behaviour inscribed it as troubling to the sacred hierarchy.[9] For example, whilst the presence of a tail on a man consigns him (or even more problematically, her) not to the realm of the animal but to the place between human and animal culture, where the perceived deviation from 'true' humanity produces an excess of meaning, the *lack* of tails in some apes was one of the earliest features foregrounding the problematic relationship between ape and human. Without a tail the ape was linked to Satan.[10] As in Bruegel's image of the ape as antichrist, in early Renaissance Europe the ape seems to have epitomised the disturbing nature of that which exceeds the human, interrupting appropriate relations amongst beast, man, god. The ape, supposedly signalling the divide between man and beast, underwrote heaven's given hierarchy. Yet – as when in Bruegel's image the figure of the ape-antichrist fused the unreconcilable roles of beast, devil, human – it also disturbed the pattern.

In the Renaissance it seems that the ape disturbed by mimicking the qualities of man (as the devil might mimic those of God) and thereby suggested manifestations of supernatural evil. Thus Bruegel painted the archangel Michael with the features of virtuous masculine beauty, figuring the angel as a distillation of human perfection – and with his foot on a creature whose human features mixed those of ape and devil.[11]

The dominant Renaissance articulation of the ape–human problem (is the ape similar or different? nature or culture? ground or metaphor?) is itself inhabited by complex inversions and composite images which tend to confound opposition. The pun on simian and simia, ape and imitation, naturalised in ape nomenclature suggests the way in which the ape generated implications. The use of a pun to produce similarity suggests the troubled way in which apes and humans were found comparable in a dynamic of similarity and difference. Perhaps the clearest acknowledgment of the problem of resemblance and differentiation between human and ape can be found in the medieval bestiaries which consigned apes to the realm of the monstrous *because* they looked too like men.[12]

If in Renaissance eyes apes and humans coincided disconcertingly, Vesalian anatomy's trenchant attack on Galen's use of apes rather than humans might be expected to give a decisive impetus towards *difference* as the dominant characteristic of the ape–human relationship. At the end of his *Observationum* Nicholas Tulp, the anatomist, published an illustration of the orang-outang emphasising animal qualities. Mythic implications remain, however, in its captioning as '*Homo sylvestris, Orang-outang*' (see Fig. 11.1. Tyson quotes the figure from Tulp's text). Indeed, Tulp's discussion of the

11.1 Versions of the Ape, from Edward Tyson, *Orang-Outang, Sive Homo Sylvestris* (1699). The figure bottom right is taken from Tulp.

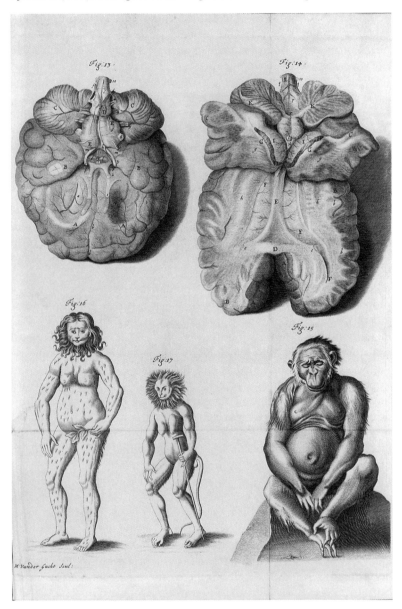

orang-outang, which also ends the book, concludes, *'Omnibus placere, difficile.'*[13]

Edward Tyson's 1699 anatomy of an orang-outang, pygmie or wild man of the woods (in fact a chimpanzee) follows Tulp and, as one of the acknowledged founders of comparative anatomy, we might expect Tyson to banish fantasy, pun, myth, in order to place the ape very firmly as animal rather than human. Indeed, when translating Joseph Swammerdam's account of the ephemeron (a fly 'that lives but five hours'), while acknowledging that science increases respect for the marvels of God's creation, Tyson trimmed the 'Pious Meditations, and Poetry', reducing the book from 420 pages to 44.[14] The *Orang-Outang* indicates clearly Tyson's interest in the nature of the 'human' and its others, also a focus in his work with the mad at Bedlam, who had 'nothing left but their outward shape to distinguish them from the Creatures below them.'[15] However, whilst when translating Swammerdam Tyson easily makes a separation of 'pious' and 'dissective' material, empirical methodology and historico-anthropological narrative coexist in his study of the *Orang-Outang*. Tyson's dissection, officially committed to maintaining the God-given gap between apes and men nevertheless occurred in a scientific as well as a general culture in which the ape already occupied a central place in iconographic, folkloric, moral and dream life and his text is accordingly is marked by generic diversity. Tyson's publication was taken up as a classic text in comparative anatomy, understood as successfully placing the ape as all animal (it was reprinted in 1966 as an example of the 'excellence' of his empirical and anatomical precision; as a scientific case study).[16] It is also, as I show, marked by juxtaposed understandings of the social as much as the 'natural' qualities of its object.

Tyson's *Orang-Outang* consisted of a dedication, preface, and 'Anatomy' followed by *A Philological Essay Concerning the Pygmies*. Tyson complicates the discourses of natural science by following it with what Robert Wokler has called 'conjectural history' reinterpreting classical myth.[17] Even as it appears to eschew an Ovidian sense of metamorphosis the very title is inhabited by Pigmies as well as orang-outangs; beings at an undefined border between 'human' and 'animal' and as a whole the text offers a sample of the late seventeenth-century languages enunciating the problem of the human and its others.

Tyson's introductory comment, that he plans to examine *'Nature's Gradation* in the Formation of *Animal* Bodies, and the Transitions made from one to another', a 'transition ... so gradual, that there appears a very great similitude ... between the lowest Rank of Men, and the highest of kind of Animals', makes clear the project's social as well as natural emphasis.[18] The term 'gradation' is – for a modern reader – tantalisingly suspended between separation and connection: the term 'gradual' seems to suggest change over time, but are the 'transitions' taking place in time, or in some other dimension? And Tyson uses another ambiguous analogue:

> The Animal of which I have given the Anatomy, coming nearest to Mankind; seems the nexus of the Animal and the Rational, as your Lordship, and those of your High Rank and Order for Knowledge and Wisdom, approaching nearest to that kind of Being which is next above us; Connect the Visible and Invisible world.

This comparison of human – animal distinctions to social status, ideally stable but in fact mutable, returns the reader's attention to the potential for ape transformation, and to its troubling power within the hierarchy of animal-human-superhuman.

In the dedication's hierarchy the ape is both forensic-anatomical and human-social and this is a key to Tyson's analytical mode. Existing at the nexus of 'animal and rational' bodies are in communication with the states above and below them, and Tyson has an acute sense of the potential of bodies to undergo exterior and psychic transformations as social situations change. Although extended discussion of the imaginative history of the ape is confined to the appended *Philological Essay*, ostensibly reading mythic creatures through the naturalising image of the ape as animal rather than monster, the project itself repeatedly poses the problem of the ape's similarity and difference in terms supplied by ape-myth. Indeed, the choice of the 'orang-outang' itself as an object of study, is generated and informed by the mythic status of the ape discussed earlier.

Even in the anatomical section of the text the distinguishing of ape and human remains potentially problematic. When Tyson notes that the orang-outang has 'viscera' *like* a human does this emphasise difference or similarity? Does the listing of similarities and differences adequately reinforce Tyson's position that the ape is animal, given that both can be found? In what he describes as a 'digression' Tyson discusses the problem of similarity between organs in man and monkey, suggesting initially that since 'the *Brain* of our *Pygmie* does so exactly resemble a Man's' that similarity might mean that 'our *Pygmie* might really be a *Man*', Tyson goes on to follow recent discussion in anatomy to locate the difference as follows:

> those *Nobler Faculties* in the *Mind* of *Man*, must certainly have a *higher Priciple*; and *Matter organized* could never produce them; for why else, where the *Organ* is the same, should not the *Actions* be the same too? If all depended on the *Organ* not only our *Pygmie*, but other *Brutes* likewise, would be too near akin to us. This Difference I cannot but remark, that the *Ancients* were fond of making *Brutes* to be *Men*: on the contrary now, most unphilosophically, the *Humour* is, to make *Men* but meer *Brutes* and *Matter*. Whereas in truth *Man* is part a *Brute*, part an *Angel*; and is that *Link* in the *Creation*, that joyns them both together.[19]

As Robert Wokler's brilliant analysis of Tyson's anatomy indicates, the use – not form – of organs, such as speech organs, becomes central in indicating an essential difference between ape and man.[20] However, in mounting the defence of the *use* of the body being different Tyson raises the spectre of the transformational relationship between *learning* and the body – the ape might learn language.

The illustrations to Tyson's text reproduce, even foreground, the problem of similarity. Tyson uses a copy of the figure from Tulp's *Observationum* as well as the 'figure that *Jacob Bontius* gives us of the *Orang-Outang* in Piso' and a figure 'taken out of *Gesner* which he tells us, he met with in a *German* Book, wrote about the *Holy Land*' (see Fig. 11.1).[21] The illustrations of the orang-outang alone show both carefully sketched organs and a monkey-person, walking upright with the aid of a stick (Fig. 11.1, 11.2). Indeed, the images Tyson offers of the beast are markedly more anthropomorphic than that offered by Tulp in his *Observationum* (Fig. 11.1). Tyson, in looking for the ape as animal found repeatedly the ape as human, and illustrations reiterate this problem.

The spectre of similarity, mediated through the discovery of the ape as social and compared to people, is emphasised further in the 'Philological' essay where apes and men are once again seen in close relationship. He writes:

> This great Agreement, which I have observed between the *Orang-Outang*, and a *Man*, put me upon considering, whether it might

11.2   Ape with Stick, from Edward Tyson, *Orang-Outang, Sive Homo Sylvestris* (1699)

not afford the Occasion to the Ancients, of inventing the many Relations, which they have given us of several *sorts* of *Men*, which are no where to be met with but in their Writings. For I could not but think, there might be some Real Foundation for their *Mythology*.[22]

Here, too, the question of ape – human transformability and closeness can be read into his analysis. Myths make their return in his very insistence on placing them in a 'real' foundation, for in discussion of myth he enters the realm of conjectural history and fantasy from which the figural cannot be wholly banished.

In the placing of the man-monkey myths on a rational and 'real' foundation Tyson finds that 'what created the greatest difficulty, was their calling them *Men*, but yet with an Epithet for distinction sake; as the … *Wild Men*, the *Little Men*, the *Pygmean Men*, the *Black Men*, the *Men* with *Dogs Faces*, &c'.[23] In trying to adequately separate physical types he finds disturbance to the order of separation built in to the very nomenclature. Moreover, the 'many *Romances*' existing about them and usually dismissed as 'meer Fictions of the *Poets*' he wishes to recuperate by binding to an underlying truth, presumably a truth of empirical observation, in the ancients who can thereby be rendered relatively usable within an empirical frame:

> *Homer's Geranomachia* therefore, or *Fight* of the *Cranes* and *Pigmies*, I have rendered a probable Story. *Aristotle's* assertion of the being of *Pigmies*, I have vindicated from the false Glosses of others.[24]

Tyson's essay reverses the order of signification – rather than looking for the creatures described by the ancients he translates the ancient signifiers into the vocabulary of contemporary science: 'I have fully proved, that there were such *Animals* as the ancients called *Pigmies, Cynocephali, Satyrs*, and *Sphinges*; and that they were only *Apes* and *Monkeys*.' Paradoxically, in disproving myths Tyson finds himself in the business of proving them. Moreover, the ape-as-human returns when he embarks on a discussion of the *Savage Man'* – the 'wild man of Borneo'. He comments, 'one should have much ado not to reckon them equally men with Certaine Barbarians in Africa' and barbarians here are obviously another inbetween category, their implicit lack of language situating them, despite human appearance, at the border of the human. The undecidability of animal and human returns and, yet again, it is focused around the social versus the natural body: neither the animal nor the human body 'speaks for itself' to tell whether it is culture or nature, wild or political.

In sum, the genres used in the *Anatomy* articulate the problem of whether the body is 'social' or 'natural' by offering multiple views of the 'same' thing, understood differently. In the text Tyson tells us that the 'pigmie' is an 'orang-outang, or wild man of the woods' recasting classical and other figures: 'the *Pigmies* of the Antients were a sort of *Apes*, and not of *Humane Race*.' Tyson allocates the ape to the animal realm yet repeatedly uses comparisons, myths, narratives which acknowledge the wonderful aspect of the ape – the aspect which repeatedly both invites and frustrates comparison with the human. In Tyson's text, ape-myth exists in an implicit refusal to split nature and culture.

However, the point is not simply that Tyson is subject to the myths his work imagines it has banished. Indeed, it seems to be later commentators rather than Tyson himself who insist on detatching the imaginary organisation in which the tailless ape troubled sacred and human hierarchy – at least a factor in causing Tyson to select this subject – from the world of organs, viscera and comparative anatomy. The emphasis on Tyson as a comparative anatomist has to an extent obscured the way in which he used the descriptive languages available to him not as antithetical but as complementary, augmenting an apparently spatial understanding of the human/non-human border expressed in anatomy with philological speculation and setting traveller's drawings alongside organs.

On the one hand the ape-imaginary returns uninvited even within the very empirical language of the anatomy; on the other hand the text is clearly juxtaposing the different insights generated by different discourses. The dualities marking the anatomy are not solely the oft-staged 'competition' between the old and new science in which the highly empirical text is marked by traces of residual discourses of ape-fantasy, but at points suggest the coexistence of ways of understanding or symbolising the body. The body of the orang–outang is understood as 'nature', a 'ground' on which social meaning might be built but which still, for the moment, precedes it; yet the body, woven about with assumptions about the ape, is always produced as figural, within the sphere of the 'social' and, if not symbolic, potentially political.

The apparently value-free empirical project, by comparing man and monkey, tends to 'discover' the ape in language imbued with ideas about socialisation, even politics and the ape's figurality and potential humanness is revealed in the anatomical processes which ostensibly render it animal. The record of the anatomy suggests that the border cannot be reliably drawn by the visual sense, by a judgement about whether the specimen 'looks' human or animal, but is organised by the imaginary lineaments of its connection to a social world. In the combined act of consigning the orang-outang to the realm of the animal *and* publishing a range of mythic material including the 'Philological' essay Tyson's discussion of the ape reaches towards a way of writing that can articulate its ambiguous significances, and these are most sharply focused by the problematic, and therefore fascinating, ape – human border. Tyson's text articulates the transformable, socialisable, ape even as it places it as animal, thereby re-posing rather than repressing or abolishing the problem of ape–human similarity, or indeed, of ape–human transformability – the fantasy of ape – human transformation.

III   ART, ORGANS, AND POLITICS

Tyson's essay is only one example of mixed-genre writing of social/natural science. However, the *Anatomy* invites close attention because of the linguistic and generic hybridity it displays. It juxtaposes understandings of the body as socio-political and natural, is informed by the seventeenth-century political vocabularies, and was taken up in the eighteenth century in terms which challenge the purity of Tyson's empiricism. This last aspect of the influence of Tyson's *Anatomy* involves his work being used to describe the ape-human relation as a *social* problem.

Hobbes's *Leviathan* opens with an insistence on the natural as art:

Nature, the art whereby God hath made and governs the world, is by the *art* of man, as in many other things, so in this also imitated, that it can make an artificial animal. For seeing life is but a motion of limbs, the beginning whereof is in some principal part within; why may we not say, that all *automata* ... have an artificial life? For what is the heart but a spring ...? *Art* goes yet further, imitating that rational and most excellent work of nature, *man*. For by art is created that great *Leviathan* called a *Commonwealth*, or *State*, in Latin *Civitas*, which is but an artificial man.[25]

In the Hobbesian Commonwealth 'art' – fusing mechanicity and organicity – seems to extend to all acts of creation; 'Nature' is the first word of the text but once present is transformed; it may be God's art, but in *Leviathan* nothing is outside the realm of art which, in its godly aspect and dimension transcends and subsumes 'nature'.

Hobbes, then, puts this perception before us: if the body is a machine, someone made it (that can be God) but if it is made, it is artificed, crafted and *articifical*. *Leviathan* argues on from the createdness of man to the createdness of the state. Even though Hobbes does not explicitly extend the model of artificiality to God's art in creating, the logic is there. He writes, 'The *Pacts* and *Covenants*, by which the parts of the Body Politique werre at first made, set together, and united resemble that *Fiat*, or *let us make man*, pronounced by God in the Creation.'[26] As Howard Caygill notes, the prototype or paradigm for the creation of the state is the 'production of a work of art', visualised in unity.[27] Hobbes's emphasis on the body as a machine echoes Descartes who also calls the heart a 'great spring,' but what is significant is the inflection of the mechanical as 'art', embracing divine and human creation at the start of *Leviathan*; this clearly links body and state in terms of art.

That such ideas found currency in less wholly élite discourses than political theory is indicated by the writings of John Bulwer in the 1640s and 1650s.[28] *Anthropometamorphosis*, 'Man Transformed; or, the Artificial Changeling' challenges generic classification but includes comparative anthropological observations as Bulwer ambivalently analyses the significances of bodily adaptation, adding, he claims, a 'Vindication of the Regular Beauty and Honesty of NATURE'.[29] Published in several editions throughout the 1650s, in *Anthropometamorphosis* the successful placing of the body as natural or artificial, and the ethical implications of each category, is an abiding difficulty. Bulwer notes that alteration is virtually universal, perhaps inevitable, and a register of cultural difference. Even before birth the body, for Bulwer, is being made, for the infant is 'curiously wrought in his Mother's womb as a piece of Embroidery or Needle-work, as the Hebrew word (rukkanthi) signifies'.[30] He finds it hard, ultimately, to sustain the ethical contrast between God's good art and 'altering the humane figure.'[31] For as he notes such alterations are all pervasive as the body is acculturated to become a 'figure':

almost every Nation having a particular whimzey as touching corporall fashions of their own invention. In which kind of mutations, they do schematize or change the organicall parts of their bodies into diverse depraved figures.[32]

The term 'figure' is one that moves between the body and language, natural and social.[33] And the question of the ground and starting place of such artificiality returns Bulwer to Hobbes, as follows:

> in discourse I have heard to fall, somewhat in earnest, from the mouth of a philosopher (one in points of common beliefe (indeed) too scepticall) That man was a meer Artificiall creature, and was at first but a kind of Ape or Baboon, who through his industry (by degrees) in time had improved his Figures and his Reason up to the perfection of man. It is (indeed) an old observation of Pliny that all the Race and kind of Apes resemble the proportions of men perfectly in the Face, Nose, Eares and Eye-lids.[34]

If people can adapt the edges and centres of their body to an extraordinary degree, why might not apes have managed to do the same? Bulwer is referring to Hobbes, and his use the ape to figure a way of thinking about 'art' and the 'artificial' as spanning nature and culture, albeit framed as a rejection, indicates that thought's dissemination in populist writing that exists between anthropology and social theory. The figure of the artificing ape, developed by its own tailstraps from 'nature' to 'culture', 'animal' to 'human' suggests the dissolution of the categories of good art (God's) and bad art (man's) in the adaptation of the body. Even as he refuses it, the logic of the transforming ape animates Bulwer's text in his echo of Hobbes's understanding of art as all pervasive.

This strand of thinking – in which not only are the natural and the social seen as interwoven but also the human and human institutions are understood as artificed (and, implicitly, within which ape-human transformation *is* at least conceivable) is central in the use of narratives of the origin of social institutions in the mid-seventeenth century. It permeates both texts which we locate as political theory and texts of conjectural history which, as the discipline of political science has created its canon have been remade as marginal to political science and understood as, at best, proto-anthropological, such as Bulwer's *Anthropometamorphosis*.

Hobbes and Bulwer are both, in different contexts, using a language in which what we would think of as the 'biological' and the 'social' are interrelated, with a vocabulary which moves fluidly between ideas of body and commonwealth as artificed. In each case the suggestion is that the body might be adapted and transformed. In such a discourse the ape acts as a figure not for a fixed animal-human border, nor for the stability of social institutions, but for the simultaneous transformability of body and commonwealth – figured in Bulwer's use of Hobbes's self-improving ape.

Discursive fluidity and the tendency of 'art' (associated with time and narrative) to usurp the realm of the natural in the writing of Hobbes and Bulwer provides one context for the way in which Tyson's anatomy, claiming to define the ape as animal, retains social and mythic aspects of the ape.[35] It also suggests that, besides the use of Tyson's anatomy as a foundation for empirical science, the question of ape-human transformability which lurks in his text might be taken up in Enlightenment social and political theory on the nature of the 'human'. As Thomas Love Peacock had a character put it, satirically, 'As to Buffon, it is astonishing how that great naturalist could have placed him [the ape] among the *singes* when the very words of his description give him all the characteristics of human nature.[36]

IV 'WISE SPECIES': TYSON REMYTHOLOGISED

Mr Forester: He is a specimin of the natural and original man – the wild man of the woods; called, in the language of the more civilised and sophisticated natives of Angola, *Pongo*, and in that of the Indians of South America, *Oran Outang*.[37]

Mythic, social and political conceptions of the human were not on the scrap heap of culture for Tyson; no more were they for those who read him or continued to think about the ape-human border. This is indicated by the way in which the ape continued at the centre of literature on the social institution. Although this writing is seen by some commentators (like Janson) as marginal to the new ape science, or is eliminated from the twentieth-century history of the discipline of comparative anatomy, as I show, these texts were clearly drawing on the whispered potential of 'gradual' transformability hinted at in Tyson's text to discuss the history – and, crucially, the potential – of political institutions.

About fourteen years after Tyson's *Anatomy* was published, the 'Scriblerius' group around Pope produced a mainly satirical essay reading it against the grain to find 'resemblance between the *homo Sylvestris* and our *Humane Body*, in those Organs by which the ratio-nal Soul is exerted'.[38] A version of conjectural history, the essay remythologises the ape using the same material Tyson had used to estrange it. 'Scriblerius' argues that the ape was, though now 'degenerated' from its former status as philosopher politican, yet, with the renewed willingness of 'unprejudiced' women to mate with it, and with encouragement, perfectible once more to the status of full humanity.[39]

The narrator traces the pre-Trojan ape-philosophers from the *Iliad* where, he argues, 'they excell'd as much in the Arts of peaceful Government, tho' there remain no Traces of their Civil Institutions.'[40] Arriving in Europe the ape is certainly politically active: 'in hatred to tyranny, [he] encourag'd the Roman army to proceed against the Hetruscans who would have restored Tarquin.'[41] In his Pan-like appearance the ape resembles Tyson's anthropomorphic illustration: '*shaggy Bearded, Hairy all over, half a Man*, and *half a Beast*, and walking *erect*, with a *Staff*, (the Posture in which his race are to this Day shown among us).'[42] Tyson's 'orang-outang' is represented as the 'last' of the philosophical apes. The essay ends by advocating their rehabilitatition: 'Might not the Talents of each Kind of these be adapted to the Improvement of the several Sciences? The Man-Tegers to instruct Heroes, Statesmen and Scolars? Baboons to teach the Courtiers, Ceremony and Address?'[43]

The question, might ape become man? is mediated by the satirical history, a genre simultaneously a semi-serious essay (combining the findings of natural history and philosphy) and a political satire. The artificiality of the state is acknowledged and the social mores of the court satirised by comparison with apes, even as the text seems fascinated by the possibility that the ape – human divide is mutable. The essay uses the languages Tyson had attempted to de-familiarise – myth – but also the language genres which were coming to compose the discourse of 'natural history' made up from dissective enumeration of epochs of *both* physical and social changes, to reinstate the enigmatic problem of the ape. The connection of the physical and the social enables the ape – human relation to be reconfigured in the terms of art we found in the earlier political and anthropological work of Hobbes and Bulwer. Just as in Hobbes and Bulwer the emphasis on art tended to efface absolute divisions between the human and its others, here the ellision of the social and the physical implies the potential of socialisation to change the meaning of one ape, potentially one individual ape, through an enigmatic quality of improvability, from animal to human. The ape, as border-creature, though it might at this moment be animal, effaces the ape-human split to be figured as having the potential, over even a limited amount of time, to become either human ('whose Kingdom was like the scheme of *Plato*, govern'd by Philosophers)' or ('by their continual commerce with Beasts,') animal.[44]

In using a temporal narrative in which the ape has become human, texts like the Scriblerius essay and Peacock's later *Melincourt* echo the way in which political theorists from Hobbes to Rousseau imagined human government in terms of its institution in time, growing slowly out of an imagined 'state of nature'. Of course, Hobbes's state of nature, the war of all against all, is reversed by Rousseau's view of civilisation as debasing man's natural state.[45] In the *Discourse on Inequality*, narrating a conjectural history of the kind employed by Hobbes and others and investigating the 'physical and moral dimensions of human nature, of which the successive transformations of one into the other' were held to 'mark ... savage mankind's passage from nature to culture' Rousseau returns to the question of the ape. He imagines the possibility of the ape working on itself in such a way as to become human.[46] Buffon's natural history, as Wokler notes, applies the idea of historical epochs to the natural world, fusing ethical-political and physical 'history' in one narrative.[47] As inflected by Rousseau, natural history registered the central role of political environment in determining the individual.[48] The idea that the way in which organs were used – offered by Tyson as a distinguishing feature of the ape-man boundary – might be in part learnt, significantly links natural to political narrative. Rousseau's idea of perfectibility proposed the difference between men and brutes as the presence of 'the faculty of self-improvement which, by the help of circumstances, gradually develops all the rest of our faculties.'

For Rousseau the signs of culture – specifically political institutions – are not natural and he sees no huge chasm between man and ape:

> Precipitous judgements that are not the fruit of an enlightened reason are liable to run to extremes. Our travellers do not hesitate to make beasts by the name of *Pongos, Mandrills, Orang-outangs* of the same beings which the Ancients made into Divinities by the name of *Satyrs, Fauns,* and *Sylvans*. Perhaps after more accurate

investigations it will be found that they are neither beasts nor gods, but men.[49]

Rousseau is sceptical of the divisions travellers – even Buffon – make between men and animals.[50]

For Rousseau it is possible that in the ape lies the source of the distinctively human quality of perfectibility, a quality invisible to the naked eye and still more so to the mind clouded by assumptions concerning the beneficial nature of society. Assuming that the defining quality of the human is invisible, Rousseau attacks observers of the 'natural' world. 'What', he asks would such 'Observers' have made of the feral child found in 1694? The child:

> gave no sign of reason, walked on his hands and feet, had no language and formed sounds in no way resembling those of a man. It took him a long time, continues the same philosopher who provided me with this fact, before he could utter a few words, and then he did so in a barbarous manner. As soon as he could speak, he was questioned about his first state, but he no more remembered it than we remember what happened to us in the Cradle. If, unfortunately for him, this child had fallen into our traveller's hands, there can be no doubt that after taking note of his silence and stupidity, they would have decided to send him back to the woods or to lock him up in a Menagerie; after which they would have spoken of him learnedly in fine reports as a most curious Beast that resembled a man.[51]

Here Rousseau further reinforces the closeness of man and animal, focusing on the human as an *ability* – invisible yet definitional. Where Tyson took the use, rather than form, of organs as definitional to the human, Rousseau rejects the idea that empirical observation can identitify the 'human' with any certainty. The human therefore becomes a quality, the – invisible – quality of perfectibility. Once invisible, perfectibility might rest equally in ape and human, and the very existence of the human might, indeed, be evidence of ape perfectibility in action.

Rousseau's discussion welds together physical and social change rather than holding them apart. Robert Wokler sees the significance of Rousseau's conjectural history and his insistence on the closeness of man and animal as proto-evolutionary. It is also possible to recognise the way in which the discursive elision of physical and social change – the ability of the body and mind to develop in relation to its surroundings – theorises, as it were, already available mythic patterns of thought about the ape in the light of a new assessment of the nature of political institutions. Far from banishing the ape from the realm of politics Rousseau reinstates the ape at the heart of the question of the human, fusing the social and the physical in analysing the place of the ape and of the human in the foundation of political institutions.

The link between natural and social bodies, then, was far from severed by empiricism or Enlightenment philosophy. Rather it was reinforced by the continuing interplay of politico-social theory and natural science, finding expression in *narrative* genres classifiable in Wokler's terms as conjectural history, or natural history. One example is *An Account of a Savage Girl, Caught Wild in the Woods of Champagne* (1768), a case study now thought to be introduced by James Burnett Lord Monboddo, which uses the girl as a contemporary example of the interrelationship of social and natural, foregrounding the changes to the physical body wrought by the girl's residence in France.[52] The pamphlet describes her use of language in terms of bodily adaptations wrought by her experience of the change of cultures:

> it was all spoken from the throat, with very little use of the tongue, and none at all of the lips; and this she represented in a very lively manner ... Her mouth, she says, when she was caught, was much less than it is now, and almost round; and when she laughed, she did not open her mouth as we do, but made a little motion with her upper lip, and a noise in her throat, by drawing her breath inwards.[53]

The pamphlet's interpretation implies a radical alteration of the body by social circumstances and offers evidence of transformability – here implicitly perfectibility. In a welding together of myth and nature, 'historical' narrative and empiricism, the narrator indicates that the account meshes with 'the ancient authors'. His thesis will be rejected only by those who, 'rejecting all testimony, ancient or modern, to the contrary' continue to believe that 'man, the most various of all animals, in the many different states through which he passes, continues still the very same animal ... a proposition which appears to me incredible in itself, though it were not contradicted by the whole history of mankind.'[54] The philosopher, however, will read his example aright and 'observe with amazement the progression of our species from an animal so wild, to men such as we.'[55] Insisting upon both the transformable and the social nature of the body, the narrator seeks to make the distinction between animal and human not in terms of the natural body, but in terms of the different relation to sociality possessed by humans and beasts.[56] In one epitomical life the savage girl shows progression 'from the mere animal to the savage, and from the savage to the civilised man'.[57]

V   THE POLITICS OF APE TRANSFORMATION CONTINUED

What is suggested by this study of a moment when politics and anatomy were mixed, perhaps inseparable, but animal and human were generally desired to be separate? It indicates that the twin foundational discourses of modernity, natural and political science, need to be understood as repeatedly recalled to each other's terrain. The body understood as artificial, social, maybe mythic and ultimately political, finds its way into explanations even at the moment when the anatomical body seems to speak for itself and only of itself. I want to end by returning for a moment to Tyson, in 1699. Tyson's 'pigmie' as I pointed out at the start of the essay, is habitually positioned as a model of forensic and investigative science which nevertheless bears the traces of pre-empiricist myth, of attempts to recuperate classical monsters as monkeys and so on. His discussions of mythical creatures are perceived as lapses into other, archaic, interpretations of the body. As I hope is clear by now, another understanding is possible. On the one hand the 'drive to science' takes as its project the precise location of the border of the human and the other, thing or animal, within the flesh and sinews of the body. But Tyson's account repeatedly voices the difficulty of this; the orang-outang is 'like' a monkey, but also – both in observed viscera and in external appearence – 'like' a person, a human body. Where is difference to be located and where similarity to be located and what, in terms of differentiation, are they to mean?

What happens, in Tyson, is that a relay is produced between the drive to uncover and know this physical body and the need to produce difference which can be yielded only by the different use, not the similar shape, of organs. Tyson's 'orang-outang' or 'pigmie' oscillates textually between the 'natural' body and the social, trans-formable, artificial body of Hobbes and Bulwer. It is not simply that Tyson's text is inhabited by the old science, 'despite' the drive to empiricism, but that the visual evidence before him can make sense only comparatively, narratively and reinscribed in the social – as in the case of 'a sort of Beast, called the Savage Man; whose shape, Stature, Countenance, Arms, Legs and other Members of the Body, are so like us.'[58]

What was taken up from Tyson and similar accounts in the think-ing of Rousseau and Monboddo? One clear link is in an acknowl-edged interplay of the social and the natural world. They also use political discourse – like that of Hobbes – in the representation or dis-cussion of the natural world, and vice versa. More specifically, rather than distinguishing matter and narrative conjectural history in the case of Rousseau and Monboddo the 'human' is produced as invisi-ble perfectibility, and this quality is, against the grain of the official positions (though not the undercurrents) of earlier writing, allowed to the ape. The genealogy I have offered illuminates the transforma-tion of the human *not* into a quality isolable by empirical science, but into an invisible perfectibility whose massive potential is figured by the ever present possibility of ape–human transformation.

As indicated by this genealogical pursuit of the question I opened with – 'What is an ape?' – political and natural history were inter-woven throughout the Enlightenment in ways that were congruent with, and using rather than superseding, ape-myth.[59] 'Scientific' understandings of nature continued to be inhabited by the mythic implications involved in the distinguishing and, ultimately, fusing of animal and human. Moreover, the very languages later taken as constituting the realm of nature were in themselves bound to the social and political world.

Tyson's anatomy is taken as at the inception of a tradition of modernity in treating the human body as material to be dissected. However, although he does at points expel and suppress the social narratives that mark the body whose life is grounded in them, at other points he is capable of treating the body as an almost wholly social text. At stake for Tyson are the fragile borders and temporally alterable, 'gradations' which keep the human from being wholly of the animal. If Tyson's anatomy of the orang-outang is, as it is usually read, a turning point in the anatomical exploration of the human, then it also maintains the possibility that one (the ape) may turn into the other. Or vice versa.

Notes

1. Edward Tyson, *Orang-Outang, sive Homo Sylvestris or the Anatomy of a Pygmie* (London, 1699) p. 1.
2. Donna Haraway, *Primate Visions: Gender, race, and nature in the World of Modern Science* (1989), (Reprinted, London: Verso, 1992), pp. 10, 11.
3. See Steven Shapin, *A Social History of Truth* (Chicago & London: University of Chicago Press, 1994), e.g. p. 42.
4. Exemplary in situating natural history in relation to other histories is N. Jardine, J. A. Secord and E. C. Spary, *Cultures of Natural History* (Cambridge: Cambridge University Press, 1996), pp. 3–12.
5. While the different ways apes were imagined can be put in terms of contrast and development, as Londa Schiebinger succinctly puts it, 'Were these the degenerate sons of Adam and Noah (as Augustine had taught)? Or were they 'natural man', fully human but devoid of civilisation (as Rousseau and Monboddo would conclude years later)?' They can also be considered in terms of overlapping attitudes in which one opinion, rather than being hermetically distinct, is informed by images, implications, and ideas linked to other, apparently opposite, ideas. Londa Schiebinger, *Nature's Body: Sexual Politics and the Making of Modern Science* (London: Pandora, 1993), p. 75.
6. Tyson, *Philological Essay*, p. 1.
7. Edward Topsell, *A Historie of Foure Footed Beastes* (1607), pp. 3, 4. Thanks to Erica Fudge for this reference and for discussion of this section.
8. Thierry Lenain, *Monkey Painting*, First pub. Paris, 1990 trans. Caroline Beamish (London: Reaktion, 1997), p. 31. Lenain's fascinating study of the search for the 'origin' of human art in monkey painting attests to the sustained coexistence of fantasy and scientific speculation on the monkey – human borderline.
9. H. W. Janson, *Apes and Ape Lore in the Middle Ages and the Renaissance* (London: Warburg Institute, 1952), p. 14.
10. *Physiologus* as given by Francis J. Carmody in *University of California Publications in Classical Philology*, 12, no. 7 (Berkeley, California, 1941), p. 121 (Ch 25); quoted by Janson, pp. 16–17.
11. 'The Archangel Michael', reproduced in Bob Claessens and Jeanne Rousseau, *Our Bruegel* (Antwerp: Mercatorfonds, 1969) illustration opp. p. 21.
12. Janson, *Apes and Ape Lore*, e.g. p. 332.
13. Nicolai Tulpi *Observationum Medicarum Libri Tres* (Amsterdam, 1641), pp. 275, 279.
14. *Ephemeri Vita: or the Natural History and Anatomy of the Ephemeron a Fly that Lives but Five Hours* (London, 1681), A2v.
15. When John Strype wrote his continuation of John Stow's *Survey of the cities of London and Westminster* (London, 1720), Tyson provided his own description of Bethlehem. He quotes from a Spital Sermon, p. 197.
16. See, for example, F. J. Cole, *A History of Comparative Anatomy: From Aristotle to the Eighteenth Century* (London: Macmillan, 1949), pp. 198–221.

17. See Robert Wokler, 'Anthropology and Conjectural History,' in Christopher Fox, Roy Porter and Robert Wokler (eds), *Inventing Human Science: Eighteenth-Century Domains* (Berkeley and London: University of California Press, 1995), pp. 31–52.
18. Tyson, *Orang-Outang*, p. ix.
19. Tyson, *Orang-Outang*, p. 56.
20. Robert Wokler, 'Tyson and Buffon on the orang-utan' in *Studies on Voltaire & the Eighteenth Century* (1976) no.v 2301–2319; Robert Wokler, *Rousseau* (Oxford: Oxford University Press, 1995), pp. 41–53.
21. Tyson, *Orang-Outang*, p. 108.
22. Tyson, *Orang-Outang*, A2v.
23. Tyson, *Orang-Outang*, A5r.
24. Tyson, *Orang-Outang*, A6r.
25. Thomas Hobbes, *Leviathan*, ed. C. B. Macpherson (Middlesex: Penguin, 1968, reprint 1986), Introduction, p. 81.
26. Hobbes, *Leviathan*, p. 82.
27. Howard Caygill, *Art of Judgement* (Blackwell, 1989) p. 19; *Leviathan*, p. 82. As Caygill argues, the work of art does not for Hobbes imply a 'unification of diversity' but an illusion of unity (p. 19).
28. John Bulwer, *Chirologia, or the Naturall Language of the Hand* (1644), See e.g. A5r, A6v.
29. John Bulwer, *Anthropometamorphosis*, 'Man Transformed; or, the Artificial Changeling Historically Presented,' (London, 1654). For another recent commentary on Bulwer see *The Body in Parts*, ed. David Hillman and Carla Mazzio (New York and London: Routledge, 1997).
30. Bulwer, *Anthropometamorphosis*, sig.B1v.
31. Bulwer, *Anthropometamorphosis*, sig.B1v.
32. Bulwer, *Anthropometamorphosis*, sig.B1v
33. Patricia Parker, *Literary Fat Ladies* (Routledge: London, 1987), pp. 8–11.
34. Bulwer, *Anthropometamorphosis*, sig.B3r.
35. Hobbes's influence is obvious enough; Bulwer, too was influential and was used by William Hogarth in the rejected passages of his work on beauty. See William Hogarth, *The Analysis of Beauty*, Joseph Burke (ed.), (Clarendon Press: Oxford, 1955), pp. 173–4 'disgustefull and sometimes cruel methods of moulding and forcing the human form out of its natural figure and collour, many of his Instanes remain to this day,' p. 173. See also Plates 1 and 2 which may use Bulwer's frontispiece.
36. Thomas Love Peacock, *Melincourt* (London: 1817), p. 82–3. *Melincourt* uses Sir Oran Outan in political satire; sir Oran Outan 'caught very young in the woods' has been protected by Mr Forester who has bought him a baronetcy, thereby 'ensuring him the respect of society, which always attends on rank and fortune', p. 80.
37. Peacock, *Melincourt*, p. 67.
38. Alexander Pope, *Miscellanies*, vol. 3 (London, 1736), p. 94.
39. As has been noted, the idea of transformation implied here, coming close to that of evolution, also paved the way for apes to be considered

degenerate men. See Robert Wokler, 'Anthropology and Conjectural History,' in Christopher Fox, Roy Porter and Robert Wokler (eds), *Inventing*, p. 36.

40. Pope, *Miscellanies*, pp. 84–5, 92–6.
41. Pope, *Miscellanies*, p. 90
42. Pope, *Miscellanies*, p. 86.
43. Pope, *Miscellanies*, p. 86.
44. Pope, *Miscellanies*, p. 92
45. Wokler, 'The Enlightenment Science of Politics', in Fox, Porter and Wokler (eds), *Inventing*, pp. 323–340, p. 336.
46. Wokler, 'Anthropology and Conjectural History', p. 33.
47. See Count de Buffon, *Natural History*, (Edinburgh: William Creech, 1780), 8 vols, p. 39 et seq. where, as Peacock notes in *Melincourt*, the expulsion of the ape from the category of the human is done in terms which imply readmission; see e.g. pp. 39–76, 40, 41.
48. Wokler, 'Anthropology and Conjectural History', p. 37.
49. Jean Jacques Rousseau, 'Notes' to *Second Discourse in The First and Second Discourses*, edited and translated by Victor Gourevitch (New York and London: Harper & Row, 1986), p. 219, see p. 149, pp. 214–20.
50. *Second Discourse*, translated Gourevitch, 'Notes' p. 220. In arguing, too, that the invention of language, specifically speech, was caused by the passions, Rousseau emphasised the proximity of human and animal. See Jean Jacques Rousseau, *Essay on the Origin of Languages* translated by Gourevitch, p. 245.
51. Rousseau, *Second Discourse*, 'Notes', p. 218.
52. *An Account of a Savage Girl, Caught Wild in the Woods of Champagne* Translated from the French of Mdam H-t with a Preface Containing Several Particulars omitted in the Original Account (London, 1768). An account of the girl's capture had been published in 1731, but the editor of the English version insists on the veracity of the account, and has journeyed to Songi, the place of her capture before she had been placed in a convent at Chalons 'to view the bludgeon used by Le Blanc as her principal weapon, in her wild state' (a3r) – 'before she began to speak French' (a1v).
53. *Savage Girl*, pp. ix–x.
54. *Savage Girl*, pp. xv–xvi.
55. *Savage Girl*, p. xvi.
56. We read: 'He will see evidently, by this example, that though man is by his natural bent and inclination disposed to society, like many other animals, yet he is not by natural *necessity* social, nor obliged to live upon a joint stock, like ants or bees; but is enabled, by his natural powers, to provide for his own subsistence.' Addressing the hot topic of the state of nature, the argument continues that 'those superior faculties of mind, which distinguish our nature from that of any other animal on this earth, are not *congenial* with it, as to the exercise or energy, but *adventitious* and *acquired*' ... 'the *rational man* has grown out of the mere *animal*, and that *reason* and *animal sensation*, however distinct we may imagine them, run into one another by such insensible degrees, that it is ... perhaps more difficult, to draw the line

betwixt these two, than betwixt the *animal* and the *vegetable.*' *Savage Girl*, pp. xvii–xviii.

57. *Savage Girl*, p. xviii.

58. Tyson, *Anatomy*, p. 23. Given his attention to the mythic qualities of the ape it is hardly surprising to find subsequent editors using Tyson's study to discuss not only tribal cultures but native British little people. In 1849 Bertram Windle republished Tyson's 'Philological Essay' recommending a naturalising of myth similar to Tyson's so that fairies might, like animals, be classified 'according to the nature of their habitations'. Thanks to Nicola Bown for discussion of fairies.

59. See Emma Spary, 'Political, natural and bodily economies', in *Cultures of Natural History* N. Jardine, J. A. Secord, and E. C. Spary (eds), pp. 178–196; especially pp. 179, 193.

12

The Economy of Nymphomania: Luxury, Virtue, Sentiment and Desire in Mid-Eighteenth Century Medical Discourse

Mary Peace

In 1775 an English translation of a controversial French medical text was published in London under the title *Nymphomania, or a Dissertation Concerning the* Furor Uterinus. The original text was written by an obscure French doctor, M. D. T. Bienville, and was first published in Amsterdam in 1771. The English translation was the work of Edward Sloane Wilmot, and it is with this edition and the British context into which it appeared that I will principally be concerned in this essay.

Bienville's ostensible argument is that immoderate female desire is not a proper part of women's nature, but the product of an hysterical pathology which he calls alternately nymphomania, the *furor uterinus* or metromania. Bienville describes the factors which he believes precipitate and aggravate the disease, the symptoms by which it can be recognised, and the treatments which he believes to be effective in its cure. The argument seems to anticipate a faith in female passionlessness which we more readily associate with nineteenth century thought; indeed Bienville signals his perception of the novelty of his argument in his concluding paragraph where he claims:

> Mine will be the glory of having placed the first stone of an edifice which, by saving the honour of more families than one, must prove an honour to society! mine will be the honour of

having prevailed on others to extinguish the most tormenting miseries which can debase, afflict, and as it were unhumanize THE FIRST AND LOVELIEST PART OF CREATION.[1]

Embedded, however, in Bienville's argument that female desire is an unnatural, dehumanising pathology is evidence of an entirely contrary one in which women appear as naturally lascivious, and naturally in possession of a bestial sexuality which is liable to prove socially disruptive if not contained. Such an argument is present even in the terms which Bienville chooses to describe this disease – hysteria, or a *furor uterinus* – both of which, as will become evident, have an historical association with theories about the essential bestiality of female sexuality.

This simultaneous representation of women as, at once, the fairest, loveliest and by implication naturally most chaste and humane members of society, and as naturally lascivious and bestial in their sexuality, is a typical feature of mid-eighteenth-century writing. It is evident, for example, in the writings which surround the setting up of the Magdalen Hospital for penitent prostitutes in 1758, where Jonas Hanway, a founder of the institution, vacillates unselfconsciously between descriptions of the 'native ingenuousness' of the minds of prostitutes, and descriptions of prostitutes as an '*abandoned race* ... who infest the most *public streets of London*'.[2] My aim in this essay is to propose a way in which, by situating Bienville's text in its immediate discursive context, we might understand how such apparently contradictory representations can exist quite happily together in the same thesis. My argument will depend to a great extent on the recognition that discussion of the nature of female desire in the mid-century was intimately tied up with concerns about the increasing luxuriousness of society.

I   CLASSICAL REPUBLICANISM, SENTIMENTALITY AND LUXURY

In Book V of *Emile* (1762) Rousseau turns his attention from the education of boys to that of girls, and argues that unlike boys, girls are subject to immoderate desires – desires which are likely to promote social disintegration – and that they ought consequently 'to be vigilant and industrious' and 'constrained very early'.[3] This advice seems to fly in the face of Rousseau's arguments about the education of boys, where he famously advocates a much greater trust in the beneficent attributes of uncultivated nature. Rousseau himself is acutely aware of this contradiction for he remarks somewhat defensively at the end of his section on girls:

> Here someone will stop me and ask whether it is nature which prescribes our expending so much effort for the repression of immoderate desires? My answer is no, but it is not nature which gives us so many immoderate desires. Now, everything that is not nature is against nature. I have proved that countless times.[4]

The implication of this very difficult statement is that girls/women paradoxically have no natural state which is not the product of civilisation; that in some sense, for Rousseau, femininity is naturally synonymous with civilisation.

The association of women with civilisation already has a long history by the middle of the eighteenth century. Such an association can be traced back at least as far as ancient Greece, most famously to Plato's *Republic* – a text with which Rousseau was consciously engaged throughout his writing. In the *Republic* Plato argues that the transition from a primitive to a more civilised society is signalled by the move from an economy in which the inhabitants of a state produce only those things that are necessary to sustain their life at subsistence level, to an economy in which the inhabitants produce luxury items; these include philosophy and literature, but also, significantly, 'everything for women's adornment'.[5] In Plato's *Republic* female desire is cited as one of the principal driving forces of civilisation. Yet the idea that uncurtailed female desire may lead to anarchy can also be traced back to Plato, for, although, in the *Republic*, female desire drives the march of civilisation, it is ultimately responsible for its downfall. Plato argues that when once the population of a state has had its appetite for luxury items stimulated it will become both increasingly warmongering – the desire to satisfy an ever increasing appetite will motivate expansionism – and increasingly unable to defend itself – luxurious indulgence will 'effeminate'; sap the strength of the state. Certainly Plato argues that in the short term the state will be reasonably stable, for the philosophy and arts which he identifies as the likely by-products of a luxurious economy will teach the governors of the state to restrain their appetites. Yet, eventually, even the governors will become 'effeminated' – contaminated and enfeebled by the luxury which surrounds them, and the state will spiral into anarchy.[6]

Rousseau was by no means the only eighteenth-century thinker to be exercised by the arguments of Plato's *Republic*. The classically educated élites of Britain and France, states whose economies were becoming increasingly 'luxurious' in the eighteenth century, were haunted by Plato's pessimistic paradigm, and the traditions of thought which it had inspired. One of the effects of this anxiety was the emergence in the mid-eighteenth century of a cultural obsession with the extent and nature of female desire. In Britain the heated cultural controversy over the 'virtue' of the heroine in Richardson's novel, *Pamela* (1740), and the contemporary prominence of debates about the moral status of prostitutes, must both be read in the light of anxieties about rising luxury.

A controversy, of course, presupposes at least two positions on an issue, and given the huge success of *Pamela* – which depicted the reformation of an aristocrat by an ideally virtuous servant girl – and the eventual establishment in 1758 of the Magdalen Hospital for the rehabilitation of penitent prostitutes, this particular controversy presupposes the existence of an effective argument in support of the benificent attributes of luxury and female nature. This argument, I suggest, is to be found in sentimental discourse. This discourse can be broadly characterised by the idea that human beings are naturally in touch with the ideal through their possession of a moral sense, and that women naturally possess a more acute moral sense – 'sensibility' – than men. In its British context this discourse is clearly tied up with the concern to recuperate effeminacy for a narrative of sustainable social progress. In this light Pamela's 'virtue', and the representation of prostitutes as victims who could be rehabilitated, can be seen as significantly reassuring narratives for a ruling class whose interests were increasingly bound to the success of a burgeoning commerce.

Although I have, so far, identified two opposing voices in the debate about female desire, in this essay I will argue that the opposition is not so clear cut, that sentimental discourse emerges out of a late-seventeenth and early eighteenth-century cultural negotiation with the classical discourse on luxury. Sentimental discourse adopts the terms of the classical discourse but turns them on their head. The discourse accepts that female desire is a central factor in the maintenance of a healthy body politic, but insists that the immoderate desires of women are a fiction; that their desires are somehow 'naturally refined', and contained by their more delicate sensibilities. As David Hume typically argues in 1742, women's passions, though more delicate and acute than those of men, are also less damaging. Unlike those of men, women's passions are considered largely indistinguishable from their naturally refined sensibility, and sensibility is understood to be synonymous with a good taste in both morals and consumables. Men, Hume argues, must harness their passions through the cultivation of their tastes, but, he says, 'we may observe that women, who have more delicate passions than men, have also a more delicate taste of the ornaments of life, of dress, equipage, and the ordinary decencies of behaviour.'[7] Women, in Hume's essay, as elsewhere in sentimental discourse, are constructed as having a naturally-refined taste for virtuous consumption and behaviour which, far from being conducive to social anarchy, is seen to provide a bulwark against the evils of an increasingly appetitive society.

II BIENVILLE, CLASSICAL REPUBLICANISM, SENTIMENTALITY AND LUXURY

Despite Bienville's perception of the novelty of his argument, his ostensible commitment to the essentially passionless nature of women, would seem to indicate that the text might most productively be understood as a product of sentimental discourse. Bienville's text certainly makes itself available to a sentimental reading. Take, for example, the saccharine synonyms which Bienville employs for women. He refers throughout his text to women as the 'fair sex' or as 'THE FIRST AND LOVELIEST PART OF CREATION'; synonyms which seem unmistakably to identify Bienville's writing with the positive reevaluation of femininity which is so central to sentimental writing.[8] Bienville's epistemology also seems decisively sentimental for he asserts in his preface that 'Though all the world were to dissent from what I have advanced, I should still have reason to rely on the evidence of my Senses.'[9] Bienville's anatomical explanations, moreover, seem to owe much to a sentimental understanding of the body. Bienville refers, for example, to the 'exquisite sensibility' of the vagina, and argues, in a manner reminiscent of Hume's essay, that the 'nervous fibres in women are more delicate' than in men.[10]

A closer reading of Bienville's *Nymphomania*, however, throws up all sorts of obstacles to an interpretation of the text as straight-forwardly sentimental in the sense described above. References to women as the 'fair sex' are counterbalanced by references to women as the sex which is 'liable' to a 'prodigious assemblage of imperfections'.[11] Bienville's insistence that he can rely on the evidence of his senses does not necessarily imply his commitment to the idea that our senses provide us with direct knowledge of an ideal as well as a material world, only that he subscribes to the Lockean idea that knowledge derives from a sensual experience of the world rather than from an innate store. Moreover the peculiar 'delicacy' of women's nervous fibres in the Bienville text seems rather to be associated with their propensity to contract the *furor uterinus* – and thus rather to dehumanise the victims, and wreck the honour of their families – than to provide a guarantee of virtuous conduct, as it seems to do in Hume. Bienville explicitly attributes the occurrence of the *furor* in women to:

> a vice in the nervous fibres of the organical parts, which receive more lively impressions, either on account of their delicacy, or of their tension, or on account of their delicacy, and their tension united, which is the reason why they enjoy a much more exquisite sensibility.[12]

Indeed, far from suggesting that the exquisite sensibility of women might contain the excesses of a luxurious economy by guaranteeing a naturally moderate taste for, and consumption of, luxury items, Bienville's central argument is that the consumption of the products of a luxurious economy, from rich food such as chocolate and wine to the reading of novels, is one of the major aggravations of the disease. Bienville states that 'strong wines', 'spiritous liquors' and the 'excessive use of chocolate', are all 'capable of corrupting the animal harmony' and that 'when united, [they] impart additional fury to the flames which burn for ... destruction; all these [he says] throw such sparks amongst the passions, as set fire to the most shameful and unbridled lust.'[13]

Certainly the suggestion that the consumption of luxury products might 'corrupt the animal harmony' can be accommodated within a sentimental reading, for it can be taken to indicate a commitment to a prior state of continent female taste. The conclusion of this passage, however, is clearly more problematic, for it here becomes apparent that the original 'animal harmony' is envisaged by Bienville as one of the highly combustible 'passions', which might flare up into 'unbridled lust' with any passing spark.

The central argument of Bienville's text is clearly that excessive female desire is a pathology and not a natural attribute of femininity, yet the more one scratches at the surface of this text, the less clear cut this interpretation becomes. At some points the *furor uterinus* is 'a serpent which hath insensibly glided into ... [the] heart' of its victim: a metaphor which seems both to locate desire originally outside of the natural constitution of women, and, in allusion to the *Genesis* story, to suggest an original propensity in women for desire.[14] At other points the author unequivocally subscribes to the idea that women's desires are naturally immoderate. The victims of the *furor* are, for example, described as women who feel 'a desperate passion, the gratification of which is opposed by insurmountable obstacles.'[15] In this final statement, passionate desire clearly seems to precede the disease and not to result from it.

An interpretation of the text as a product of sentimental discourse is most directly troubled, however, by Bienville's not infrequent disavowal of sentimental values. Bienville argues at one point, for example, that the innate susceptibility of women to this disease is:

> stimulated, and increased, when they read such luxurious novels as begin by preparing the heart for the impression of every tender sentiment, and end by leading it to the knowledge of all the grosser passions, and causing it to glow with each lascivious sensation.[16]

Here we find Bienville unmistakably rehearsing the classical narrative of the decline and fall attendant upon over-stimulated luxurious desire: tender sentiments will, it seems, as a matter of course, become luxurious desires if luxury is not regulated; they cannot in themselves be trusted to regulate luxury. This statement seems to imply a conscious knowledge of and rejection of sentimental values.

In order to gain some understanding of the apparently irreconcilable contradictions in Bienville's text; to understand the simultaneous adoption and disavowal of sentimental values, we must return to my original proposition that sentimental discourse emerges out of, but never entirely escapes from a late seventeenth- and early eighteenth-century cultural negotiation with the classical discourse on luxury. In terms of Bienville's text this means looking briefly beyond his claim that he is a pioneer in this field of medicine, in order to establish the medical discourses out of which his thesis emerged.

III   A BRIEF HISTORY OF THE *FUROR UTERINUS*

Although the OED cites no use of the term 'nymphomania' before the translation of Bienville into English in 1775, both this term and its synonym the *furor uterinus* had certainly been in circulation before this date. The cultural historian G. S. Rousseau notes that the term 'nymphomania' had appeared in William Cullen's taxonomy of nervous diseases, *Synopsis Methodicae*, in 1769, at least two years before the publication of Bienville's text, and that even in this earlier text the author had seemed confident of assuming a general familiarity with the word, for he provided only the most rudimentary of definitions.[17] Cullen curtly defines the condition as 'Excessive desire of venery in women'.[18] The term *furor uterinus*, moreover, had already been in circulation for well over a century by the time Bienville made use of it. A disease entitled the *furor uterinus*, whose symptoms clearly resemble those described by Bienville, is defined in an Italian medical treatise in 1623, and there are many less explicit references to the disease before this.[19] Bienville makes some concession to this history in his acknowledgement that although most 'ancient and modern authors' have left this subject in the 'obscurity of silence', some have provided an 'imperfect sketch' of the condition.[20] Yet this statement does not do justice to the extent of the existing discussions of the 'illness'; to the fact that such discussions can be found in Italy, France, Spain, Portugal, Germany, and England throughout the sixteenth and seventeenth centuries, and that physicians as eminent as William Jorden and Robert Burton had apparently become 'obsessed' with the condition.[21] Bienville may not, of course, have been familiar with much of this tradition, yet his deployment of the terms nymphomania and *furor uterinus*, and his evident assimilation of many of its medical assumptions, suggest that he was certainly aware of some of it.

A survey of writing on the *furor uterinus* which predates Bienville does not indicate a unanimous body of medical opinion on the subject. Early references to the disease tend, for example, to ascribe its cause to possession by the devil. As religious interpretations of the disease are progressively displaced during the seventeenth century, however, certain constants do emerge.[22] The *furor* is then generally considered to be a type of hysteria, and because of this classification, it tends to be understood in terms of a combination of the classical medical paradigms of Hippocratus, Aristotle, and Galen.[23] In medical writings of the sixteenth and seventeenth century the *furor* is, therefore, most frequently discussed in terms of the one-sex model of the human anatomy. Women are here not considered to be essentially anatomically different from men, rather they are 'Men turn'd Out-side in'; they are incipient men who have never generated enough heat to develop their full manhood.[24] As a by-product of their lack of anatomical heat, women are considered unable to 'concoct blood' into semen and thus are imagined to suffer particular health problems from a superfluity of blood that is usually located in the womb. Overlaid on this model is another tradition of classical thought, attributed to both Plato and Galen, which suggests that women's wombs are like wild animals which, if thwarted in their attempts at sexual union, will travel 'around the body blocking passages, obstructing breathing, and causing diseases'.[25]

The Ladies Dispensatory, an anonymous self-help medical text which was most probably printed in 1739, but which undoubtedly draws on much earlier material, offers a typically bewildering combination and adaptation of classical theories. The text begins by defining the *furor uterinus* as

> such a particular Complication of hysterical Symptoms, from an extraordinary Fulness or Inflammation of the Vessels of the Womb, as forms a sort of Madness, wherein the Patient is preternaturally dispos'd, or involuntarily excited, as it were, to Venereal Embraces.[26]

The disease, the text states, proceeds from one or more of the following causes:

> A vigorous, healthy and sanguine Constitution, high Feeding, Want of Exercise ... a mix'd Conversation ... too large a Dose of Cantharides, and other provocative medicines; or indulging vehement Desires, and too great Familiarity, but short of Enjoyment, with the other Sex.[27]

Later in the chapter the possibility of an 'Obstruction or Suppression of the Monthly Courses, from too great a Quantity of Blood, or from too indulgent Life' is added to the list of causes.[28] In the chapter on hysteria the author comments that the creation of an overly large clitoris through the frequent practice of masturbation may also occasion the *furor*.[29] The list seems to indicate a commitment both to the idea that the womb is a desirous animal which if thwarted will produce disease, and to a one-sex model of human anatomy in which the overly cool anatomies of women produce a superfluity of blood which, in turn, leads to illness. The effect of this conflation of classical medical models is to suggest at once that the *furor* produces immoderate desires in women, and that immoderate desire is what renders women susceptible to the disease. Women are not considered to be self-regulating in their desires, and are certainly not imagined to regulate luxurious expansion through native good taste. The recommended treatment in *The Ladies Dispensatory*, as elsewhere in this medical tradition, is the avoidance of all immoderate stimulation and luxury, except where it can be safely contained within a sanctioned social practice. The text recommends for the patient that:

> Her Diet should be thin and cooling, and not taken in large Quantities; her Exercize, between the Fits, moderate. Let her be kept, as much as possible, from the Company of Men; and especially if Love be the suspected Cause, from that Man whom she is known to affect, unless it be to bring them entirely together, and cure the Disease by removing its Origin.[30]

The text, in other words, appears to operate more as a secular conduct book for women, than as a medical text book.

The appearance of *The Ladies Dispensatory* in 1739[?] seems to have been an anachronism. For in discussing the *furor* it subscribes to theories which, according to medical historians, had been largely discredited by contemporary doctors. G. S. Rousseau asserts, for example, that 'Virtually no important doctor in the first half of the eighteenth century placed the root of hysteria in the uterus.'[31] Since the work of Sydenham (1624–1689) in the mid-seventeenth century, Rousseau argues, there had been a 'paradigmatic shift from a uterine to a nervous model for hysteria'.[32] Indeed there is evidence to suggest that as a result of this shift in paradigm no important doctor was talking seriously about the *furor uterinus* either. The 'raging womb' had no obvious place in a discussion of hysteria which increasingly attributed the disease to a derangement of the nervous system.[33] The shift from a uterine to a nervous model of hysteria even to some extent removed the gender implications of the disease, for although women in the early eighteenth century were still considered to be more susceptible to nervous derangement because of their more fragile nervous apparatus, men were also now believed to suffer from the condition.[34] It is accordingly with some bewilderment that the recent historian of hysteria Mark Micale notes that the late eighteenth century witnessed what he describes as a regenderisation or re-eroticisation of the disease in the work of Cullen and Sauvages quoted above, and also, I would add, in the work of Bienville.[35]

Why then did the shift from a uterine to a nervous model of hysteria lead paradoxically to a re-eroticisation of the disease in the mid-eighteenth century? Why did a text such as Bienville's *Nymphomania* appear in the 1770s? It seems to me that in order to have any understanding of this we must abandon the idea that this re-eroticisation was paradoxical, indeed we must abandon the idea that there was a re-eroticisation, and work rather with the idea that hysteria never had truly been de-eroticised.

The move from a uterine to a nervous model of hysteria must be interpreted as early evidence of the emergence of a sentimental discourse. Sentimental medical discourse adopted the terms of the classical medical discourse but increasingly recuperated them for an economy of virtue. In the terms of the debate about hysteria, the disruptive desires of the rampant uterus of classical writing are redesignated as the tastes of a refined and delicate nervous system. Such refined tastes, and even hysteria itself, are identified as the product and therefore also the mark of a civilised society, and yet such refined tastes never entirely escape from the stigma of immoderate female desire. A sentimental medic such as George Cheyne (1671–1743) goes so far as to argue that those who are suffering from weak nerves 'have a great Degree of Sensibility; are quick Thinkers, feel Pleasure or Pain the most readily, and are of the most lively Imagination.'[36] Thus, he argues, 'Persons of slender and weak Nerves are generally of the first Class: the Activity, Mobility and Delicacy of their Intellectual Organs make them so.'[37] Yet even in Cheyne's work there is no real faith that the nice tastes and delicate nerves of this first-class, civilised world, will not ultimately lead to decline. The following passage from *The English Malady* (1733) suggests that refined tastes can never be sufficiently distanced from dangerous desires:

The *Egyptians* as they seem to have been the first who cultivated the Arts of Ingenuity and Politeness, so they seem likewise to have been the first who brought *Physick* to any tolerable Degree of Perfection. The Ancient *Greeks*, while they lived in their Simplicity and Virtue were Healthy, Strong and Valiant: But afterwards, in Proportion as they advanced in Learning, and the Knowledge of the Sciences, and distinguished themselves from other Nations by their Politeness and Refinement they sunk into *Effeminacy, Luxury,* and *Diseases,* and began to study *Physick,* to remedy those Evils which their Luxury and Laziness had brought upon them.[38]

Desire is redesignated as refined taste in the work of Cheyne, and is governed by the nervous system and not the uterus, both men and women are considered liable to suffer from the nervous diseases of civilisation. Yet the continued presence in such writing of the narrative of a decline into a dangerous effeminacy suggests that the link between the uterus and hysteria had never entirely been severed, at least at a figurative level. A re-eroticisation was, in other words, always likely to emerge from this discourse.

IV   BIENVILLE AND THE HISTORY OF THE *FUROR UTERINUS*

As suggested above, Bienville has to a large extent adopted the medical discourse of sentiment. Bienville seems to locate the origin of the disease in the nervous system and not the uterus, so that in his analysis it is precisely the 'exquisite sensibility' of the female parts which renders women so susceptible to this disease.[39] Femininity is, consequently, to some extent redeemed in this model: rampant desire is identified as a product of an illness facilitated by the delicacy of the female nervous system, the same delicacy which in Hume is responsible for providing women with a natural taste for modesty and virtue, and which elsewhere in sentimental discourse is a mark of a highly civilised individual.

Yet Bienville's text is also very much still committed to the peculiar medley of classical ideas which characterised sixteenth and seventeenth-century writings on the *furor uterinus*: much more glaringly so than Cheyne's *English Malady*. Like *The Ladies Dispensatory,* there is in Bienville, no resolute rejection of the one-sex model of anatomy. Bienville not only frequently describes the female anatomy in terms of the male – when, for example, he refers to the *'ovaria'* as the 'testicles of woman', and the *'ova'* as the 'spermatic liquor', he also seems quite convinced by the idea that one of the symptoms of the *furor* is an over-elongated, penis-like clitoris.[40] He is, moreover, quite clear that the *furor uterinus* might proceed from a superabundance of blood, which he states:

> generally happens when the woman is accustomed to pleasure, and high living, but particularly to rich sauces, and spiced meats; for we may take it for granted, that a thousand little indulgences which she allows herself, added to a table luxuriously set out, and at which a delicate appetite may be gratified in every taste, must excite the most voluptuous desires.[41]

Most significantly, despite G. S. Rousseau's argument to the contrary, there has, in Bienville, been no wholesale abandonment of uterine explanations of hysteria in favour of nervous explanations. Bienville's text discovers a more than figurative association between the two.[42] Bienville asserts in his preface, for example, that 'The first chapter will contain proofs of the weakness of the sex, drawn from their organical construction, in order to give the reader a clear idea of the nature of the fibres, and muscles, which perform a principle part in the accidents of the matrix.'[43] And he later states that 'we may absolutely conclude that the [sexual] organs of women receive much more lively impressions, and are, of course, more liable to inflammations than the organs of men.'[44] The nervous system is certainly present in Bienville's explanation, but it is here explicitly identified as more delicate in the area of the womb.

The effect of this more than figurative connection is a much more evident proximity in Bienville than in Cheyne between 'THE FIRST AND LOVELIEST PART OF THE CREATION' and the 'monsters in human shape' – his description of women suffering from the *furor* – and consequently, a much more evident pessimism about the value of civilisation.[45] There is very little sense here that either civilisation or women can be trusted to be self-regulating, as Bienville says 'luxurious novels … [which] begin by preparing the heart for the impression of every tender sentiment … end by leading it to the knowledge of all the grosser passions, and causing it to glow with each lascivious sensation.'[46] The civilisation which is fuelled by luxurious desire is always in danger of falling into anarchy.

Far from arguing, however, that Bienville's text should not be understood as sentimental because of the force of the countervailing arguments in his text, these countervailing arguments, I suggest, are a typical feature of sentimental writing. Indeed, the disavowal of sentimental discourse which is apparently contained in the above statement should be understood as a characteristic of sentimental writing, whether the text in question be a novel, a conduct book, a sermon, or a charity tract. Much as many eighteenth-century writers of fiction are at pains to distinguish their works from the debased genres of romance, whilst evidently heavily indebted to its traditions and values, writers of sentimental literature seem acutely aware that the authority of their work depends upon their ability to distance themselves from sentimental excesses whilst manifesting an evident investment in sentimental values.[47] Bienville's disavowal should not, then, in any simple way be understood as evidence of anti-sentimentality, indeed, it arguably places him in the company of such arch sentimentalists such as William Dodd, the first chaplain of the Magdalen Hospital for Penitent Prostitutes: Dodd's pathetic sermons notoriously appealed to the sensibility: they aspired to wring a tear of sympathy from the congregation for the plight of women who had fallen as a result of having their own sensibilities over stimulated.[48] To be a sentimentalist in the mid-eighteenth century is always, on some level, to disavow sentimentality, to signal one's awareness that an excessively delicate sensibility may ultimately lead to a fall.

Bienville's recognition of the dangers of sentimental excess in no way, then, disqualifies his text from being read as a product of mid-eighteenth-century sentimentality. Certainly there are sentimental optimists such as David Hume, who seem convinced that sensibility need not degenerate into desire, that the civilised countries of modern Europe need not re-enact the fall of Rome, yet even his writings are haunted by the classical narrative of decline. At the end of the essay 'On the Refinement of the Arts', in which Hume argues that the progress of civilisation and luxury need not lead to decline, he goes on to supplement his discussion with what appears to be a mere after-thought. He states that 'if libertine love, or even infidelity to the marriage-bed, be more frequent in polite ages, when it is often regarded only as a piece of gallantry; drunkenness, on the other hand, is much less common.'[49] Given that the fall of civilisation is attributed to licentious desire in the classical discourse on luxury, and not to drunkenness, this supplementary and apparently baseless consolation can only be interpreted as anxiety.

V THE NECESSARY CONTRADICTIONS OF SENTIMENTALITY

Very little, if any, sentimental writing from the mid-eighteenth century escapes entirely from the clutches of the classical paradigm, for to effect such an escape would be to place absolute faith in the virtue and continence of an uncultivated female nature which paradoxically, as Rousseau suggests, figures civilisation. Such faith would make little sense in terms of the characteristically didactic purpose of sentimental discourse. One need only think of Richardson's much imitated sentimental novel, *Pamela*, to become aware of quite how much the desire to reform female manners is the occasion for such literature. David Hume perhaps comes closest to placing his faith in uncultivated female nature in his assertion that there is a natural connection between the 'delicate passions of women' and a 'delicate taste of the ornaments of life, of dress, equipage, and the ordinary decencies of behavior'. Yet even this assertion is hedged around with ambiguity, for it appears only in a footnote to the essay, and then only in a late edition of the essay.[50]

Hume's assertion of the natural connection between the female constitution and a taste for virtue, is in itself a typical feature of sentimental literature. John Gregory, for example, in his sentimental conduct book *A Father's Legacy to His Daughters* (1774) characteristically argues that 'the natural softness and sensibility of your dispositions particularly fit you for the practice of those duties where the heart is chiefly concerned', and goes on to state that 'Every man who knows human nature, connects a religious taste in your sex with softness and sensibility of heart.'[51] What is striking about Hume's text, however, is that it does not supplement this statement with an assertion of the importance of a strict education in policing such an ostensibly natural connection. Hume, unlike Gregory, does not state that the 'superior delicacy' and 'modesty' of women must be supplemented by a 'severity of ... education'.[52]

Sentimental literature typically subscribes to a notion of natural refinement: a phrase whose oxymoronic properties point to precisely the paradox which is central to the sentimental construction of femininity. Women's nature can be trusted to police the morals of an increasingly luxurious society, just as luxurious desire can be trusted, but only if this nature or desire is refined, processed by education. Most sentimental texts do not make this paradox explicit, for in doing so the legitimacy of 'nature' is severely undermined. But one has only to look to such a self-reflectively sentimental text as Goldsmith's *Vicar of Wakefield* to bring us face to face with this paradox. This is particularly evident where the Vicar says:

> I wrote a[n] ... epitaph for ... my wife, though still living, in which ... I extolled her prudence, oeconomy, and obedience till death; and having got it copied fair, with an elegant frame, it was placed over the chimney-piece, where it answered several very useful purposes. It admonished my wife of her duty to me, and my fidelity to her; it inspired her with a passion for fame, and constantly put her in mind of her end.[53]

Goldsmith's Vicar, it seems, has got the measure of sentimentality: his description of the great virtues of his wife turn out to be very much a prescription for how she might attain such virtue.

Similarly, it is clear in Bienville that the description of women as 'THE FIRST AND LOVELIEST OF THE CREATION' is in fact a prescription. Women, Bienville suggests in a moment of reverie, are in fact only the first and loveliest, the preservers of the social good, if they submit themselves to the laws of society, and such submission is precisely what is liable to make them ill, as their true nature is one of immoderate desire. Bienville states:

> The laws of society are public wants, to which it was necessary to sacrifice several particular wants; they establish remedies, and preservatives, which it was requisite to devise, in order to repair the real evils which might destroy, or trouble the advantageous, and even necessary order which exists. It is thus, that the privileges and limits suitable to each sex were established. The present mode of polite education proceed from this principle, and are submitted to these remedies. Hence it happens that our young ladies are brought up in restraint, and decency, which frequently are capable of irritating their passions, of causing a revolution, and disorder in the physical system of their nature, and of rendering them victims of the public good, whensoever a constitution inflamed by nature, or by the imagination, occasion these accidents.[54]

It is in this context that I would like to return to Rousseau's discussion of female education in *Emile*, and to discuss how Rousseau's writing itself fits into the sentimental tradition as described above, and how this relates to Bienville's text.

VI BIENVILLE AND ROUSSEAUVIAN SENTIMENTALITY

Rousseau's writing, as I have argued, is very much exercised by the Platonic paradigm of luxurious decline. In his 'Discourse on the Sciences and the Arts' (1750) he describes in a way that must now be familiar to us how luxurious desire initially produces the virtues of civilisation, but ultimately leads to destruction. Luxury, he argues, produces 'that delicate and refined taste on which ... [we pride ourselves]; that softness of character and urbanity of customs which make relations among ... [us] so amiable and easy.'[55] Yet, he says, these virtues are not real virtues, he refers to these apparently positive productions of economic progress as having 'the semblance of all the virtues without the possession of any'.[56] The virtues of civilisation are, of course, the virtues of femininity as Rousseau makes very clear in his discussion about women in *Emile*. Rousseau's ideal woman, Sophie, looks very like the heroines of sentimental fiction. Sophie has a sensitive heart; though well-born she dresses in a modest fashion, and she has 'devoted herself to all the details of the household.'[57] Yet Rousseau makes no attempt to suggest that she is the product of nature. He says, for example of her modest attire, that,

> There is no girl who appears to be dressed with less study and whose outfit is more studied; not a single piece of her clothing is chosen at random, and yet art is apparent nowhere. Her adornment is very modest in appearance and very coquettish in fact. She does not display her charms; she covers them, but, in covering them, she knows how to make them imagined.[58]

Sophie has the 'semblance of all the virtues without the possession of any', her politeness and refinement might at any point give way to her naturally immoderate desires. Women are, Rousseau states, 'Extreme in everything'.[59]

Rousseau is a sentimentalist, but a frankly pessimistic one, both in respect of women and of civilisation. One can allow the nature of boys to remain uncultivated, he argues, because it really is natural and thus positive, whereas the nature of women is culture and that involves the possession of delicate tastes which might at any point descend into immoderate desires.

Rousseau represents the pessimistic end of the spectrum of sentimental writing, where commercial society and women are deemed inherently corrupt and their virtues only another element of the masquerades of a vicious civilisation. Hume stands at the more optimistic end, where both women and luxury can almost be trusted to regulate themselves for the general good of society. Between these poles one can situate the whole range of mid-eighteenth century sentimental writing. I would want to situate Bienville somewhere very close to Rousseau, and this is perhaps an indication of the generally more problematic engagement of the French upper classes with the growth of commerce. It is, I think, significant in this light that Bienville's translator, Edward Sloane Wilmot, felt the need to temper some of Bienville's more pessimistic statements for the English market. Of Bienville's wholesale condemnation of the eating of chocolate, an obvious luxury item, on the grounds that it irritates the blood, Wilmot adds the following footnote:

> The *Spanish* chocolate is more compound than any other ... [and as such] is doubly inflammatory. The *Paris* chocolate is somewhat less pernicious. The makers generally use the *Caracca*, which is the best nut, together with a little cinnamon, the freshest vanilla, and the finest sugar. The *English* chocolate, to which only the last articles are, sometimes, added, is the most plain and innocent ...[60]

Wilmot seems very evidently here to be reassuring the English consumer that a luxurious society need not be an entirely immoral society. However, his footnote still concludes with the characteristically sentimental disclaimer that it must be acknowledged that even such plain and innocent chocolate as England produces has 'noxious qualities' which will rather 'kindle than extinguish the flame' of the 'voluptuous passions'. In this discourse, I suggest, the representation of the natural humanity of women on the grounds of their heightened sensibility is never far from the representation of the essential bestiality of women on the grounds of their more extreme desires.

Notes

1.   M. D. T. Bienville, *Nymphomania, or, a Dissertation Concerning the Furor Uterinus*, translated by Edward Sloane Wilmot (London: J. Bew, 1775), p. 186.
2.   [Jonas Hanway], *Thoughts on the Plan for a Magdalen-House for Repentant Prostitutes* (London: J. Waugh, 1758), p. 42.

3. Jean-Jacques Rousseau, *Emile, or On Education*, introduced and translated by Allan Bloom (1979) (Reprinted, London: Penguin, 1991), p. 369.
4. Rousseau, *Emile*, p. 405.
5. Plato, *The Republic of Plato*, translated by Francis Macdonald Cornford (Oxford: Clarendon Press, 1941), p. 60.
6. Plato, *The Republic*, pp. 59–61, 109, 274–91.
7. David Hume, 'Of the Delicacy of Taste and Passion', in *Essays Moral, Political and Literary*, ed. Eugene F. Miller, (Indiana: Liberty Classics, 1987), p. 603. Note added to the text of the essay in 1758.
8. Bienville, *Nymphomania*, pp. iv, xi, 186.
9. Bienville, *Nymphomania*, p. xi.
10. Bienville, *Nymphomania*, pp. 19, 60.
11. Bienville, *Nymphomania*, p. vii.
12. Bienville, *Nymphomania*, p. 72.
13. Bienville, *Nymphomania*, pp. 32–3.
14. Bienville, *Nymphomania*, p. 29.
15. Bienville, *Nymphomania*, p. 29.
16. Bienville, *Nymphomania*, p. 30.
17. G. S. Rousseau, 'Nymphomania, Bienville and the Rise of Erotic Sensibility' in Paul-Gabriel Boucé (ed.), *Sexuality in Eighteenth-Century Britain* (Manchester: Manchester University Press, 1982), p. 96.
18. William Cullen, *Synopsis Nosologiae Methodicae* (Edinburgh: n.p., 1818), n.p., 'entry 103'.
19. Carol Groneman, 'Nymphomania: The Historical Construction of Female Sexuality', in *Signs: Journal of Women in Culture and Society* 1994, vol. 19, no. 2, 343.
20. Bienville, *Nymphomania*, p. ii.
21. Groneman, 'Nymphomania', 343; G. S. Rousseau, '"A Strange Pathology": Hysteria in the Early Modern World, 1500–1800', in Sander Gilman *et al.* (eds), *Hysteria Beyond Freud* (Berkeley, California: University of California Press, 1993), p. 112.
22. G. S. Rousseau, 'Nymphomania', p. 99.
23. See G. S. Rousseau, '"A Strange Pathology"', and Helen King, 'Once Upon a Text: Hysteria from Hippocrates', in Gilman *et al.* (eds), *Hysteria*; also Mark Micale, *Approaching Hysteria: Disease and Its Interpretations* (Princeton, New Jersey: Princeton University Press, 1995).
24. *Aristotle's Compleat Master-Piece*, 23rd ed. (1749), p. 23. For further discussion of the one-sex model of anatomy see King, 'Once Upon a Text', and Thomas Laqueur, *Making Sex: Body and Gender from the Greeks to Freud* (Cambridge, Mass.: Harvard University Press, 1990).
25. King, 'Once Upon a Text', p. 25.
26. *The Ladies Dispensatory: Or, Every Woman Her Own Physician* (London: John Hodges and John James, [1739?]), p. 107.
27. *The Ladies Dispensatory*, p. 107.
28. *The Ladies Dispensatory*, p. 108.
29. *The Ladies Dispensatory*, p. 10.
30. *The Ladies Dispensatory*, p. 109.
31. G. S. Rousseau, '"A Strange Pathology"', p. 157.

32. G. S. Rousseau, '"A Strange Pathology"', p. 148. Although Ilza Veith, in her highly influential study of hysteria, argues that 'The eventual permanent abandonment of the belief that hysteria had a uterine origin and that it occurred only in females came about quite independently and with no direct reference to the writings of Sydenham.' Veith, *Hysteria: the History of a Disease* (Chicago: University of Chicago Press, 1965), p. 145.

33. G. S. Rousseau, '"A Strange Pathology"', p. 140.

34. Micale, *Approaching Hysteria*, p. 22; G. S. Rousseau, '"A Strange Pathology"', p. 140.

35. Micale, *Approaching Hysteria*, p. 23.

36. George Cheyne, *The English Malady*, ed. Roy Porter (London: Routledge, 1991), p. xxii.

37. Cheyne, *The English Malady*, p. xxv.

38. Cheyne, *The English Malady*, p. xxviii.

39. Bienville, *Nymphomania*, p. 19.

40. Bienville, *Nymphomania*, pp. 21, 24, 74.

41. Bienville, *Nymphomania*, p. 56.

42. G. S. Rousseau asserts of Bienville that 'there is no sense that the irritation or excitation of the genital area specifically is the cause of his new nymphomania'. G. S. Rousseau, '"A Strange Pathology"', p. 172.

43. Bienville, *Nymphomania*, p. xiv.

44. Bienville, *Nymphomania*, pp. 53–4.

45. Bienville, *Nymphomania*, pp. 187, 37.

46. Bienville, *Nymphomania*, p. 30.

47. See Laurie Langbauer's argument in Langbauer, *Women and Romance: The Consolations of Gender in the English Novel* (Ithaca, New York: Cornell University Press, 1990).

48. See, for example, William Dodd, *A Sermon on St. Matthew, Chap, IX, Ver. 12, 13. Preach'd at the Parish Church of St. Laurence, near Guild-Hall, April the 26th, 1759, before the President, Vice-Presidents, Treasurer and Governors of the Magdalen House for the Reception of Penitent Prostitutes* (London: L. Davis and C. Reymers, [1759?]).

49. Hume, 'Of Refinement in the Arts', in *Essays*, p. 272.

50. See endnote 5.

51. John Gregory, *A Father's Legacy to His Daughters* (London: W. Strahan et al., 1774), pp. 10, 23.

52. Gregory, *A Father's Legacy*, pp. 9–10.

53. Oliver Goldsmith, *The Vicar of Wakefield*, Stephen Coote ed., (London: Penguin, 1982), p. 41.

54. Bienville, *Nymphomania*, pp. 160–1.

55. Jean-Jacques Rousseau, 'Discourse on the Sciences and Arts', *The First and Second Discourses* (ed. Roger D. Masters, trans. Roger D. and Judith R. Masters), (New York: St Martin's Press, 1964), p. 36.

56. Jean-Jacques Rousseau, 'Discourse', p. 52.

57. Jean Jacques Rousseau, *Emile*, p. 394.

58. Jean-Jacques Rousseau, *Emile*, p. 394.

59. Jean-Jacques Rousseau, *Emile*, p. 370.

60. Bienville, *Nymphomania*, pp. 52–3, note (e).

Index